Dreaming of Gold,
Dreaming of Home

ASIAN AMERICA
A series edited by Gordon H. Chang

The increasing size and diversity of the Asian American population, its grow-ing significance in American society and culture, and the expanded appreci-ation, both popular and scholarly, of the importance of Asian Americans in the country's present and past—all these developments have converged to stimulate wide interest in scholarly work on topics related to the Asian American experience. The general recognition of the pivotal role that race and ethnicity have played in American life, and in relations between the United States and other countries, has also fostered this heightened attention.

Although Asian Americans were a subject of serious inquiry in the late nineteenth and early twentieth centuries, they were subsequently ignored by the mainstream scholarly community for several decades. In recent years, however, this neglect has ended, with an increasing number of writers examining a good many aspects of Asian American life and culture. More-over, many students of American society are recognizing that the study of issues related to Asian America speak to, and may be essential for, many cur-rent discussions on the part of the informed public and various scholarly communities.

The Stanford series on Asian America seeks to address these interests. The series will include work from the humanities and social sciences, including history, anthropology, political science, American studies, law, literary criti-cism, sociology, and interdisciplinary and policy studies.

Dreaming of Gold, Dreaming of Home

TRANSNATIONALISM
AND MIGRATION BETWEEN
THE UNITED STATES AND
SOUTH CHINA, 1882–1943

Madeline Yuan-yin Hsu

STANFORD UNIVERSITY PRESS

STANFORD, CALIFORNIA

Stanford University Press
Stanford, California
© 2000 by the Board of Trustees of the
Leland Stanford Junior University

Printed in the United States of America

Library of Congress Cataloging-in-Publication Data

Hsu, Madeline Yuan-yin.
    Dreaming of gold, dreaming of home : transnationalism and
migration between the United States and South China,
1882–1943 / Madeline Yuan-yin Hsu.
        p.   cm. — (Asian America)
    Includes bibliographical references and index.
    ISBN 0-8047-3814-9 (cloth: alk. paper) : ISBN 0-8047-4687-7 (pbk.: alk. paper)
        1. Chinese Americans—History   2. Chinese Migrations—
History.   3. Chinese Americans—Ethnic identity.   4. Chinese
Americans—Social conditions.   5. United States—Emigration
and immigration—History.   6. California—Emigration and
immigration—History.   7. China—Emigration and immigration—
History.   8. Ta'i-shan hsien (Guangdong Sheng, China)—
Emigration and immigration—History.   9. Nationalism—Social
aspects—China—History.   10. Nationalism—Social Aspects—
United States—History.   I. Title.   II. Series.

E184.06 H78 2000
973'04951—dc21   00-056355

Original printing 2000

Last figure below indicates the year of this printing:

09   08   07   06   05   04   03   02

Typeset in Adobe Garamond by BookMatters

In loving memory of my grandfathers,
Xu Fuguan (1903–1982) and Wai G. Chun (1910–2000).
The ideas of one and the life of the other inspired much
of this book.

Acknowledgments

Without assistance and good wishes from many quarters, this exploration of migration and transnationality would have taken much longer to reach fruition.

My experiences as a graduate student at Yale University nurtured the questions and methodological training that produced this book. The seeds grew from a seminar paper written for Deborah Davis's class on Chinese families in the twentieth century. Helen Siu's workshop on globalization and localization conducted in the summer of 1993 in Hong Kong introduced me to the distinctive sociocultural dynamics of the history of Guangdong and the Pearl River Delta. Each of my dissertation committee members, in their own ways, contributed to this monograph. At a time when it was not yet fashionable, Beatrice Bartlett encouraged my interest in the history of Chinese overseas and gave me the opportunity to help teach her class, "Chinese Pioneers." Jonathan Spence taught me much about the art of writing and producing the strongest narrative by making the most of telling details. All but sight unseen, David Montgomery valiantly agreed to introduce a novice student to past and future approaches to the field of American immigration history. I have benefited immeasurably from their ideas about what a study of Chinese history and American migration should be. Funding for my dissertation research and writing came from several sources: the Council on East Asian Studies, a Henry Hart Rice Advanced Research fellowship, the Bradley Foundation, and the I.S.P. / Smith Richardson Foundation.

Completing the research for this study of migration required that I travel to many places. It was my good fortune to encounter generous scholars, librarians, archivists, and local hosts willing to provide advice, access to materials, personal connections, or simply a place to live and work. The list that follows is long but could be even longer: Chen Wenjun of *Xinning Magazine*; Suellen Cheng of the Chinese Historical Society of Southern California; Kay Chu and Sangem Hsu of Hong Kong; Dorothy Fujita Rony of U.C. Irvine; Professor Hu Shouwei of Zhongshan University; Kong Wing Hong of Hong Kong and Taishan City; Erika Lee of the University of Minnesota; Li Suimei of the Guangzhou Museum; Liu Mei-lin, formerly of the Museum of Chinese in the Americas; Kay and Earl Ness of El Cerrito, California; Ni Junming of the Guangzhou Provincial Library; Wei Chi Poon of the Ethnic Studies Library at U.C. Berkeley; Neil Thompsen of the San Bruno, California, branch of the National Archives; Y. C. Wan of Special Collections at the University of Hong Kong library; Laiming Wong and Steve Tom of Self-Help for the Elderly; Wu Xingci of the Overseas Chinese Affairs Office of Guangdong Province; Wu Yanna of the Taishan County Archives; and Professor Zhang Yingqiu of the Institute of Southeast Asian Studies of Zhongshan University. In particular, I would like to thank Him Mark Lai for laying the foundations of Chinese American historical research for younger generations of scholars. Andrea Louie and Benito M. Vergara Jr. enriched my thinking about migration by introducing me to anthropological literature on culture, identity, and transnationalism.

Colleagues and administrators at San Francisco State University greatly facilitated the transformation of my Ph.D. dissertation into a book. In Asian American Studies, Marlon Hom and Lorraine Dong were conscientious and generous mentors who helped me to balance teaching and university service responsibilities with continued writing and research. In the form of sabbatical leave, funding for travel and research, and release time, the offices of Robert Corrigan, university president; Thomas La Belle, provost and vice-president; Gerald West, dean of faculty affairs and professional development; and Paul Fonteyn, associate vice president for research and sponsored programs, provided crucial support.

At every stage of the writing process, my thinking and ability to articulate ideas grew with the feedback of many readers. I am especially grateful to those who read and commented on the manuscript or dissertation in full: Mark Halperin, Valerie Hansen, Marlon Hom, Him Mark Lai, Sucheta Mazumdar, K. Scott Wong, Benito M. Vergara Jr., and Judy Yung. Others who read chapters include Carlton Benson, Ryan Dunch, Dorothy Fujita Rony, Susan Glosser, Joshua Howard, Shirley Hune, Keith Knapp, Erika Lee, Karin Myrhe, Christopher Reed, Brett Sheehan, Benito Vergara Sr., Tim Weston, and Marcia Yonemoto. At Stanford University Press, Gordon Chang, Muriel Bell, Janet Mowery, and Elizabeth Berg led me through the final, complicated stages of transforming my hodge-podge of text, notes, tables, and illustrations into this book. I am grateful for the clarity and directness of their guidance as well as their support of this project.

Mom and Dad had enough faith to let me choose my own path when law school seemed by far the most practical option for a child with a liberal arts degree. My grandparents in Arkansas, Wai G. and Wai Ying Chun, shared with me their stories of both China and America. My husband, Benito M. Vergara, eased the worst pain of the writing process by sharing with humor and grace his ideas and observations as well as an equal burden of the day-to-day tasks of cooking, washing dishes, fielding telemarketers, and walking the dog. This book is dedicated, with my love, to him.

M.Y.H.

Contents

Illustrations

Tables, Figure, and Maps

Tables

Figure

Maps

A Note on Translations and Conversions

I have used *putonghua* pronunciations in pinyin romanization for most of the Chinese names and terms in this book. According to this system, Canton is written as Guangzhou, Amoy is Xiamen, Swatou is Shantou, and the Kuomintang is the Guomindang. For a handful of names, most notably Sun Yatsen and Chiang Kaishek, I have departed from this practice for people, places, and businesses that are better known by the Anglicized versions of their names in dialect.

The reader should also note that in some instances it was not possible to provide the *putonghua* and pinyin for names and places recorded in pre–World War II English-language sources such as government documents and oral histories. These materials usually referred to the Cantonese or Four County dialect pronunciations for Chinese names and places without using a consistent system of romanization. For these reasons, when sources do not include the corresponding Chinese characters, it is difficult to determine the correct *putonghua* pronunciations.

As a transnational community characterized by frequent migration and remitted incomes, Taishan used a variety of currencies, including U.S., Hong Kong, and Chinese dollars. According to C. F. Remer, the average value of a Chinese dollar between 1894 and 1901 was 0.5 U.S. dollars. This value dropped to 0.46 between 1902 and 1913 and rose to 0.52 between 1913 and 1930. During the late 1920s, Hong Kong dollars were roughly equivalent in value to Chinese dollars. In the 1930s, the value of the Chinese dollar fell to US$0.29.

A Chinese *mu* of land is equivalent to 0.165 acres. Each *li* of distance is about one-half kilometer.

Dreaming of Gold,
Dreaming of Home

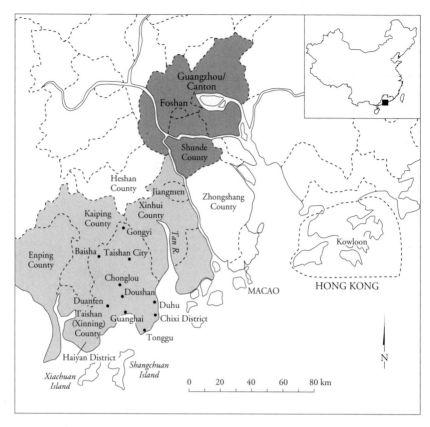

Taishan County, Guangdong, and the Pearl River Delta

SOURCE: Graham Johnson and Glen Petersen, eds., *Historical Dictionary of Guangzhou (Canton) and Guangdong*. Lanham, Md.: Scarecrow Press, 1999.

ONE

Introduction: An Elastic Community

In the spring of 1984, Taishan County officials erected a statue to commemorate the man whose life represented the highest attainment of ambition, idealism, and patriotism in recent local history.[1] The man so honored was neither a conquering general nor a communist zealot. Taishan's chosen hero was Chen Yixi, a master of commerce and industry, who overcame the early disadvantages of birth to an impoverished family to become a wealthy and successful businessman, a powerful labor contractor, a railroad engineer, and owner of a thriving import-export business based in the American city of Seattle. Chen Yixi (1844–1928) was not distinguished by his financial success alone, for many other Taishanese men went to America and by dint of hard work, determination, and luck also became rich.[2] Chen Yixi became a local champion because he brought his fortune and technical expertise back to Taishan in an effort to benefit other Taishanese. Loyalty to native place led him to undertake the ambitious project of building a railroad that he hoped would hurtle Taishan's moribund agricultural economy into a state of industrialized prosperity and thereby render future migrations unnecessary for other Taishanese.

The life of Chen Yixi represents the expanding sweep of Taishanese aspirations and economic horizons as well as the patterns of Taishan's incorporation into the world economy. The statue of Chen Yixi in a dusty downtown square evokes the juxtaposition of the local and the global in Taishan.

Rendered in bronze, his likeness wears the humble Chinese suit deemed appropriate by his Communist-era admirers. This latter-day simplicity contrasts with the grandeur of the photograph on which his features and bearing were based, a photograph in which Chen wears the embroidered silks and peacock-feathered cap of a Qing mandarin. He had purchased these symbols of official authority so that he could better use his American fortune to build a railroad in Taishan and thereby plant the Western seed of modernization that would produce industrial and commercial prosperity in one small corner of China's southern coast.

The migration overseas of hundreds of thousands of men like Chen Yixi transformed the social and economic dynamics of Taishan County in the last half of the nineteenth century and the first half of the twentieth. Taishanese actively pursued the opportunities offered by the ever-quickening spread of capitalism in the form of thickening webs of international trade, steadily improving transportation and communications technology, and the dramatic surge of job opportunities in colonial economies throughout the world. Taishan County evolved into a community that survived the physical dispersion of its members by strategically adapting traditional practices based on loyalty to family, clan, and native place. By embracing and even celebrating the achievements and contributions of those who left, Taishanese forged a new sense of identity and local belonging in which, at least for a period of time, globalization did not subsume the interests of local society.

Taishanese migration to and from the United States provides insights into how individuals from a rural Asian community negotiated their encounters with an industrializing, Western-dominated world. The mobility and adaptability of Taishanese is all the more illuminating because it occurred in an era of heightened nationalism and ethnic conflict.[3] Well before either the U.S. government or the ruling Qing dynasty recognized or was prepared to accept the human mobility that accompanied their incorporation into an intersecting, capitalist system, Taishanese had successfully used developing networks of transport, communications, and trade to make working on the other edge of the Pacific an employment option regularly chosen, and even highly preferred, by Taishanese young men.

Taishanese migration overseas started becoming significant in the late eighteenth century when a combination of overpopulation in China and the colonial expansion of Europe into Asia began to lure men abroad in search of their fortunes. The North American continent loomed particularly large in their dreams of fast and easy overseas fortunes because, during the 1850s, California had entered the consciousness of Taishanese as the fabled Gold Mountain, a place where gold could be found on the streets for the taking. Although in reality it was never so easy to become wealthy by traveling to America, enough men returned bearing gold during the 1850s and 1860s to make the dream of winning a fortune on Gold Mountain one that endured long after the gold ran out and the hostility of white settlers had reduced the great American frontier to a few dank and crowded urban Chinatown streets for most Taishanese. Dreams of gold and blighted conditions at home continued to draw them to North America and remain potent motivators to migrate to the present day. Up to 1960, well over half of all Chinese in the United States came from this single county.[4]

The attraction of Taishanese to Gold Mountain indicates the limited ability of nation-states to control migration. Taishanese entered and worked in the United States in stubborn defiance of Anglo-American conceptions of national identity that explicitly rejected Chinese as inferior, unassimilable, and even dangerous to democratic forms of government. Between 1882 and 1943 most Chinese could gain access to America's opportunities only by circumventing U.S. federal laws and bureaucracies that forbade the entry of all but a few strictly defined and carefully scrutinized categories. Despite these attempts to deny access to Chinese, generation after generation of Taishanese men pursued their Gold Mountain dream at the cost of enduring precarious lives, physically and conceptually confined to the margins of American society. They existed as unrooted denizens of a predominantly male bachelor community, seeming to shuttle between long hours in the menial trades of laundering, restaurant work, domestic service, and Chinatown storekeeping and the recreational vices of prostitution, gambling, and opium smoking. They sent money from their meager earnings to China to support rarely seen families and dependents, all the while attempting to save enough to finance their own glorious, but often unattainable, retirement in Taishan. Continually in transit, they belonged neither here nor there; they were not really American and not really Chinese. Because of their doubly marginal status, the history of Taishanese American migration bears considerable significance for understanding both the homeland they departed and the host nation in which they transgressed.

When asserting the importance of migratory peoples, a key difficulty has been that "people are often thought of, and think of themselves, as being rooted in place and as deriving their identity from that rootedness."[5] According to such territorialized definitions of identity and culture, Chinese in America became lesser Chinese through the act of traveling overseas, even as they seemed incapable of becoming real Americans. These traditional conceptions of space and identity privilege the territorial boundaries imposed by nation-states while falling far short of describing the complex realities and potential significance of people who move from place to place. Their migration constituted a violation of the national prerogatives of both the United States, and, for a period of time, China as well. While hundreds of thousands of Chinese entered the United States illegally during the years of Exclusion, the Qing did not legalize the return of Chinese émigrés until 1893.

The ability of Taishanese to claim an economic niche in the United States even as they remained valued and active members of family and village units in China intertwines with key issues defining the twentieth century for both China and the United States. I argue that Taishanese American experiences and patterns of mobility shed new light on China's quest for modernity, the limitations of nationalism, and the authority of nation-states, as well as the flexibility and heterogeneity attending the lives of people uncontrollably on the move. In emphasizing the fluid realities of communities and identities composed of geographically diverse elements, I construct bridges between the historically related but as yet critically unlinked fields of Asian American and Asian studies. Despite their excluded status, Taishanese managed to forge an enduring claim on the United States and thereby expand the geographic scope of their cooperative quest for better economic opportunities to evolve into a community that was somehow Chinese *and* American, with an internal logic and set of priorities that drew upon conditions and possibilities in both China and the United States. The stubborn existence of this dispersed community provides historical context and fuel for rethinking the discourse on ethnicity and immigration in the United States as well as contributing new perspectives on the cultural resources and potential for success that Chinese bring to their negotiations with a Western-defined modernity.

The history of Taishan during the late nineteenth and early twentieth centuries cannot be told as the story of one place. Even as they became immersed in work overseas and were able to return to Taishan only infrequently, if at all, many Taishanese men remained bound to life in Taishan, primarily by commitments to close relatives such as wives, parents, children, and siblings. Their main priorities were very much local in scope: establishing and maintaining a family, improving that family's standard of living, and ascending in the social and economic hierarchy of village, district, and county life. This remained true even as their pursuit of an international field of economic endeavor subjected them to the business cycles, public opinion, and immigration policies of the United States. In these encounters with international commerce and labor markets, Taishanese employed a cultural repertoire of organizational practices and affiliations adapted from traditional structures of society and politics in China. During the years covered by this study, they participated in global structures of power, competition, and economic expansion in which they exerted little influence and yet managed to maintain coherent identities and community sensibilities in ways that accommodated the dramatically different conditions of survival and success in all the physical sites that Taishanese America grew to encompass. Taishanese weighed the relative opportunities and costs in both countries to carve out a community and society with its own priorities and rationales for existence and development that survived in spite of the nationalist imperatives of both China and the United States.

In this book I describe the evolution of this in-between and yet all-encompassing community. Doing justice to all of the fluid realities of Taishanese Americans requires that we examine some traditional conceptions of migration and identity.

'Tis Better to Give Than to Receive: Attitudes Toward Migration

For those on the receiving end, migration is a messy business. Their almost instinctive assumption that "primordial ties" bind a particular people to a specific location and national polity is challenged by people who move from place to place. Their need to defend the purity of national cultures and identities from infection by mobile peoples was apparent in the rise of Australia's One Nation Party founded under the nativist leadership of Pauline Hanson in 1997, in California's 1998 vote to dismantle bilingual education, as well as in the extreme difficulty, even today, of gaining citizenship by naturalization in Japan. Migration's most disturbing manifestations commonly assume the form of recent arrivals who look wrong, speak wrong, and eat wrong, and who can conveniently be blamed for the most recent downturns in the local economy.

Migration also has an unsettling influence on traditional academic categories of classification and analysis, which have largely been based on the division of physical space. In an essay titled "Migration and Its Enemies," historian Wang Gungwu describes a few of the problems: "People were identified by the territory, whether large or small, to which they belonged. . . . Migration studies were generally placed in the context of local, national, and regional history."[6] When people are identified chiefly by specific sites on a map, as are French, Japanese, and Paraguayans, who and what do they become when they leave that place? Is it possible to belong to more than one place at the same time?

Such questions have been of central importance to conceptions of national identity and boundaries in the United States, long self-proclaimed to be a "nation of immigrants." For many years, the idea of the great American melting pot provided the most alluring paradigm for understanding migration and ethnicity. As defined by scholars like University of Chicago sociologist Robert Park and Harvard historian Oscar Handlin, uprooted immigrants fled poverty and tragedy in their homelands to come to the land of opportunity where, through hard work, sacrifice, and eventual success, they emerged as wholly new, ruggedly individual Americans. As long as this model prevailed, academics and the common masses agreed about the invisibility that all immigrants should eventually attain.[7]

Although conceived in a liberal spirit, Park's theories regarding cycles of assimilation have only exacerbated the seemingly indelible outsider status of Chinese immigrants to the United States. The assumptions that immigrants are unformed lumps of clay, that they do not and should not retain loyalties and cultural sensibilities linking them to their homelands, that they are erased only to be reinscribed as Americans, grossly oversimplifies the ways in which human beings interact with their environments, their families and friends, and their conceptions of self. For these reasons, as well as legal definitions of Chinese as un-American, it was virtually impossible for Chinese to lose their ethnic distinctiveness.[8] This failure to "become" American overshadowed almost all scholarly examinations of the Chinese

American community well into the 1960s and 1970s. Rather than challenging the basic premises of the melting pot paradigm, both white and Chinese American academics focused on either explicating passage of the Exclusion laws against what was then a minuscule minority in the United States or struggling to explain the unassimilability of Chinese. In a related approach, some Chinese American scholars emphasized the extent to which they had indeed assimilated and contributed to American life.[9] Since the 1970s, this need to either apologize or celebrate has dissipated, resulting in many revealing studies of Chinese Americans.[10] However, to this day, many scholars lack the Chinese-language skills needed to understand the global nature of migrants' experiences.[11] This incomplete understanding of the realities of immigrants in America produces an unfinished picture of the border-spanning loyalties, standards of living, senses of achievement, long-term goals, cultural repertoires, and personal relationships, to recite but a partial list, that structured the lives of most immigrants to this country.

With the surge of community-based activism of the late 1960s and the validation of ethnic identities that followed, more pluralistic understandings of American society gained acceptance and made possible new research agendas for scholars of immigration. Scholars of American immigration explored alternatives to the American melting pot by emphasizing that conditions in sending countries significantly influenced the choices and behavior of migrants in their places of settlement.[12] Although popular sentiment may still cling to the ideal of the melting pot, many scholars no longer regard migration as a "unidirectional shift" or believe migrants "to move between distinct, spatially demarcated communities and, in the long run, to be capable of maintaining an involvement in only one of them."[13] Indeed, these changing perceptions of mobility and culture have become a booming academic trend encapsulated in the idea of transnationalism.

The anthropologists Nina Glick Schiller, Linda Basch, and Cristina Blanc-Szanton provide a useful working definition of transnationalism:

> [It is] the emergence of a social process in which migrants establish social fields that cross geographic, cultural, and political borders. Immigrants are understood to be transmigrants when they develop and maintain multiple relations—familial, economic, social, organizational, religious, and political—that span borders. . . . The multiplicity of migrants' involvements in both the home and host societies is a central element of transnationalism.[14]

In this fluid new world of seemingly inconsequential national boundaries, some scholars of migration have discarded the once dominant models of uprooting and assimilation in favor of concepts like "the deterritorialized nation-state," "borderlands," "transnational migrant circuit," and "diaspora."[15] The conceptual construct that seems most applicable in the case of Taishan is the transnational migrant circuit, which is described by Roger Rouse as forming across a variety of geographic sites "through the continuous circulation of people, money, goods, and information, [so that] the various settlements . . . become so closely woven together that, in an important sense, they have come to constitute a single community."[16] The transnational migrant circuit of Taishan in the nineteenth and twentieth centuries included people and the flow of money, ideas, and relationships between "sites" in Taishan, Shanghai, Guangzhou, Hong Kong, Singapore, Kuala Lumpur, Burma, Penang, Sydney, Melbourne, New Zealand, Mexico, Los Angeles, Vancouver, San Francisco, New York, Chicago, Baltimore, and St. Louis.[17]

Despite the apparent relevance of transnationalism to the experiences of Taishanese, I must at this point add an important caveat. The most prominent theorists of transnationalism, primarily anthropologists, conceptualize it as a postmodern phenomenon, highly dependent upon technologies that allow for almost instantaneous global communication such as that provided by fax machines, jet airplanes, telephones, e-mail, the Internet, and mass-media artifacts like movies, books, magazines, newspapers, and pop music. Aihwa Ong's formidable monograph *Flexible Citizenship* offers a wide-ranging analysis of the extreme mobility of wealthy and professional classes of ethnic Chinese overseas in the 1990s but does not historicize their experiences. An emphasis on recent revolutions in communications and marketing technology ignores the long and varied practices of migration.[18]

Because China has primarily "given" migrants to others, scholars of China and overseas Chinese do not think of immigration and transnationalism in the same way that American specialists do. From China's point of view, emigration does not threaten ethnic homogeneity; the assumption of continuing loyalty on the part of Chinese overseas as well as the remittances they send back enrich, rather than threaten, national identity. In the late nineteenth century, even the Chinese government came to accept the practical realities of human mobility. Although for much of the Ming (1368–

1644) and Qing dynasties (1644–1911) imperial authorities viewed those who left China as traitors, during the 1880s they came to realize the potential benefits of maintaining amicable relationships with Chinese overseas. Qing emissaries began traveling the world and noticed that although Chinese émigrés had become impressively rich, they also remained concerned about the dependents and native places they had left behind, as expressed by their sending back significant sums of money. To a nearly bankrupt regime, the possibilities seemed promising. From that time forward, from the highest reaches of government to the most local of village heads, China-bound Chinese courted those who left by treating them as honored members of the same family, community, and organizational groups. At certain historical junctures, Chinese overseas have rewarded this inclusiveness with considerable generosity.

The willingness of overseas Chinese to return the gaze of their immobile compatriots was rooted in religious beliefs that bound Chinese to return to their native place in order to worship and be buried among their ancestors. Dialect and locally differentiated cultural practices reinforced this spiritual tie. Chinese attachments to their native place, or *guxiang*, is a key marker of identity and belonging in China, along with kinship, surname, and profession. Because Chinese believe that people are characterized by and should remain loyal to their native place, even after generations of separation, host communities within China were accepting of sojourning and the maintenance of native-place loyalties among migrants. These were practices replicated in manifold variety throughout the length and breadth of Chinese history and society.[19] Very often, people used these bonds as the basis for cooperative action when living among strangers.[20]

The assumptions underlying studies of Chinese migration differ markedly from those on American immigration. Since the mid-1980s, many reputable scholars have published monographs that demonstrate the richly varied patterns of mobility that existed within China. Whether from countryside to city or from overpopulated macroregional core to uncultivated frontier, in a plethora of economic niches, "in traditional China large numbers of persons pursued their occupational calling away from home."[21] These experiences of sojourning within China provided the foundations for the expectations and goals of Chinese who traveled abroad as well as their strategies for economic and social adaptation overseas.

Chinese migration abroad skyrocketed in the late eighteenth century when demographic crisis in China combined with the development of colonial empires by Western industrializing nations and rapid improvements in long-distance shipping technology to make the prospects and costs of working overseas an extremely attractive option. Between 1840 and 1900 alone, 2,355,000 Chinese lived and worked in Indonesia, Thailand, Malaysia, Myanmar, the West Indies, North and South America, Australia, New Zealand, Hong Kong, Vietnam, Russia, the Philippines, Japan, and Korea.[22] In many of those places, a handful of extremely successful ethnic Chinese entrepreneurs demonstrated the adaptability and cohesiveness of the networking of Chinese overseas.

This highly visible dispersion has received considerable scholarly attention, much of it still focused on determining to which place Chinese overseas belong. Approaches include institutional studies of Chinese government policies, celebrations of the loyalty, achievements, and contributions of Chinese overseas to China, and multifaceted analyses of how ethnic Chinese fit into the political, economic, and social structures of their countries of settlement.[23] Beginning in the 1990s, ethnic Chinese entrepreneurial successes overseas have attracted occasionally reductionist analysis that nonetheless suggests how migratory people can offer glimpses of a Chinese path to modernity.[24]

The scholarship that has resonated most closely with the goals of this project emphasize how readily localities and kinship organizations in China have adapted to migration overseas. The anthropologists Chen T'a and James Watson, as well as sociologist Yuen-fong Woon and historian Zheng Dehua, examine the impact of migration on the home communities of merchants and laborers from Guangdong and the New Territories and find that continuities far outweighed changes in local society. Watson, in particular, describes the continued immersion of émigrés in clan and family relationships that bound them to their native-place communities. He and Woon conclude that migration perhaps even strengthened lineage cohesion by replacing corporate land holdings with preferential access to employment opportunities overseas. Their findings suggest the extent to which people adapted their family and community practices to accommodate the long-term absences of money-earning men.[25] Absent from the work of Chen, Woon, and to a lesser degree Watson, however, is a more holistic explanation of how Chinese communities with members in multiple sites overseas maintained coherence and common interests in the face of extended separations and diverse living environments. To understand the inner workings of transnationality and community, we must examine how Taishanese at home and abroad pursued mutual goals to build linkages and fill in the cracks between the often conflicting agendas and political realities of both China and the United States.

To do this, we must conceptualize how the physically separated components of Taishanese America nonetheless functioned as a cohesive whole. Without greater understanding of how commitments to families and socioeconomic achievements back in Taishan influenced perceptions of life in the United States, the eagerness of Taishanese men to live as despised "bachelors" in American Chinatowns remains inexplicable.

Significance and Summary

When delving into the world-view of migratory peoples, Wang Gungwu's reconsideration of the meaning of sojourning provides helpful guidance. Wang asserts that sojourning should become part of the lexicon of migration studies and draws our attention to its varied patterns: brief visits circumscribed by definite plans to return home, extended periods of stay by "venturesome and entrepreneurial individuals and trading communities," as well as "experimental migration over long periods of time or migration with extended options." He stresses that the decision whether to resettle permanently or continue sojourning depended very much on "the treatment received in the host country, their prospects there, and conditions in their place of origin."[26]

True to Wang's analysis, Taishanese Americans adapted and made choices as they journeyed from place to place. They compared the merits and possibilities across a geographically dispersed field of action when deciding where to work, where to locate their families, and whether to consign their loyalties more permanently to one place.

In order to capture this kind of kaleidoscopic reality, I portray migration as a fluid process of mobility and diversification rather than as an invasion or uprooting. Migration transformed Taishan into a community unbounded by physical space. Despite strong, locally focused sensibilities marked by a distinctive dialect, cuisine, and sense of native place, Taishanese experienced life as active participants in global systems of trade, labor, and colonization. Taishanese applied traditional practices and expectations of family life, loyalty to native place, kinship organization, and sojourning to the project of carving out their share of a globalizing economy. They demonstrate the ability of people from a rural Asian society to successfully negotiate their encounters with a Western-dominated, industrializing world in pursuit of its own goals.

Taishanese American patterns of migration emphasize that it is necessary to move beyond the borders of nation-states in order to understand migration as a global phenomenon played out on a global field of opportunities. Otherwise it would be impossible to account for the transnational social and economic networks, loyalties, aspirations, and standards of living that structure the lives of migrants throughout the world. Perhaps more strongly than in most other cases, Taishanese migration to America illustrates that in the continuing struggle of nation-states to maintain an idealized state of ethnic purity by controlling the movements of migrants, the latter bring tremendous determination and creativity to their efforts to cross borders in search of better lives.

The ability of Taishanese Americans to defy the U.S. immigration bureaucracy also demonstrates the viability and adaptability of traditional structures of family, clan, and native-place networks in an industrializing, often hostile, modern world.[27] Their social practices evolved to provide invaluable resources for the survival and hard-won success of their economic endeavors overseas. That rural, working-class Taishanese continued to enter a country secured by the Exclusion laws suggests that we should reconsider the manner and chances for success of Chinese encounters with Western-defined modernity. Their incorporation into nineteenth- and twentieth-century structures of imperialism and capitalism differs significantly in manner and results from the more heavily researched efforts of elite scholar officials, intellectuals, generals, and diplomats to reconcile China's long history of cultural and regional preeminence with the spread of Western-dominated industrial capitalism. Exclusion-era Taishanese Americans are kin to the tremendously successful overseas Chinese family conglomerates so prominent in the economy of the Pacific Rim. The utility of Taishanese commercial expertise, long traditions of sojourning, and the adaptability of social and economic networks suggest that Chinese in general are well equipped to cope with modern life without shedding everything that makes them Chinese.

The complexities of Taishanese Americans' mobile community require an equally ambulatory course of research. This history springs from explorations carried out in several key sites of Taishanese migration and draws upon a variety of historical materials: late Qing and Republican-era documents stored in the Taishan County Archives; the Guangzhou Provincial Library; the Institute of Southeast Asian Studies of Zhongshan University; Special Collections and the Fung Ping Shan Library at the University of Hong Kong; the Hoover Institution; U.C. Berkeley's East Asian and Ethnic Studies libraries; letter collections preserved at New York's Museum of Chinese in the Americas; the University of Washington's Special Collections; the Guangzhou Museum; collections of oral interviews of Chinese Americans conducted in Los Angeles and San Francisco; and immigration files from the San Bruno, California, branch of the National Archives. I also interviewed Taishanese in Taishan, Guangzhou, Hong Kong, and San Francisco.

I set the stage for this book by describing the evolution of Taishanese fascination with Gold Mountain. "California Dreaming" traces the history of migration to and from Taishan and then recounts the many material benefits, in the form of new houses, land, schools and railroads, that Taishanese gained from the income of men working abroad. In their eager pursuit of these opportunities overseas, however, many Taishanese lost sight of the real hardships that accompanied sojourns in the United States.

American attempts to exclude Chinese are the focus of "Slipping Through the Golden Gate." I discuss the ideological, economic, and legal discriminations faced by Taishanese, as well as their determination to continue to gain access to the narrow economic niches available here. On the basis of kinship and native-place bonds, Taishanese developed informal systems for information transmission and witness preparation in order to match and usually best the concerted exclusionary efforts of a developing immigration bureaucracy.

"Surviving the Gold Mountain Dream" explores the ways in which migration threatened the very institution that it was intended to protect: the family. The long-term absence of men financed the socioeconomic ascent of families in Taishan but made procreation difficult and alienated friends and relatives. Legal restrictions, cultural mores, international politics, and economic realities delayed family reunification for decades and sometimes forever. The families of Gold Mountain men managed to survive these extended separations either by adhering steadfastly to the permanent responsibilities associated with marital bonds, or, when reunification seemed impossible, by resorting to the adaptive strategies of remarriage and adoption.

Beyond the relationships secured by ties of blood, connections to clan and native place also compelled the loyalty and support of overseas Taishanese. The responsibilities associated with these bonds were, however, less clearly defined and in need of reinforcement and organization in order to be of systematic benefit for native place and clan. "Magazines as Marketplaces" describes the efforts of several scores of organizations to write and publish magazines in Taishan for distribution and consumption internationally. In form and content, the magazines' articles and advertisements reveal how communities defined by kinship and native place maintained themselves in spite of physical dispersion. During the era of Exclusion, these magazines successfully courted émigrés and their descendants by propagating a vision of Taishanese society in which the most talented, most fortunate, and most accountable Taishanese had in fact left Taishan to work overseas and thereby bore the greatest burden for improving life in their native place.

Taishanese at home and abroad believed that the latter would bring modernity to Taishan through investments of capital and technological expertise. In "Heroic Returns," I examine the attempts of the most ambitious and visionary of Taishan's overseas sons to fulfill this expectation by building a railroad in Taishan. Chen Yixi, the man whose description begins this book, would fall short in his attempt to transform Taishan into a center of industry and commerce. The extent of his success, and the reasons for his failure, however, reveal the limits of the benefits that Taishanese could hope to attain through transnationality.

I conclude with a discussion of the fragility of Taishan's transnational balancing act in the face of rapidly changing conditions of global war and peace as well as growing American acceptance of immigrants. "Unraveling the Bonds of Native Place" describes the steady shift of Taishanese American inclinations to abandon Taishan and settle in the United States. Beginning with the repeal of the Exclusion laws in 1943, social attitudes and legal restrictions toward Chinese immigrants softened, culminating in the U.S. civil rights movement and the 1965 Immigration Act. Even as it became possible to leave Chinatown and escape economic niches in the United States, the Cold War further attenuated the bonds between Taishanese Americans and Taishanese at home. With legal rights of immigration and the prospect of better lives for future generations, Taishanese American families have migrated en masse to the United States, abruptly abandoning their native place and the tall houses that once so proudly symbolized their long-distance access to the Gold Mountain dream.

TWO

California Dreaming:
Migration and Dependency

Until 1994 a large sign in front of Taishan City's main bus station greeted arrivals with the following words in both Chinese and English, "You Are Welcome to Tai Shan—The Home of Oversea [sic] Chinese."[1] This sign conveys an unusual message, for it implies that the people of Taishan identify their county not by those who live there, but by those who have gone away. It seems that Taishanese identity is predicated on absence, that Taishanese consider their most distinguishing characteristic to be the large number of people who have left Taishan. However, the sign is not intended to be self-deprecating. Most of the visitors who actually see it are Taishanese returned from overseas. It has been erected to remind absentee sons and daughters of Taishan that their presence in that town square is much appreciated and that they can always consider Taishan their home, regardless of how long ago either they or their ancestors departed the place. In other words, the sign does not denigrate Taishan as a place worth leaving but emphasizes that it is a place worth "returning to," even for those with attenuated claims to being Taishanese.

This inclusive definition of Taishanese permeates even census-taking activities. In the count completed by the Taishan County Statistical Bureau in 1988, the county government found that Taishanese living in Taishan numbered 963,314, but Taishanese living abroad numbered more than 1.1 million.[2] This figure included people living in 78 countries around the globe,

16

including sizable communities in the United States, Canada, Cuba, Mexico, Singapore, Malaysia, and Hong Kong.[3] The Statistical Bureau did not offer an official definition of overseas Taishanese, but this widely published and commonly quoted estimate almost certainly includes thousands of assimilated Chinese separated from Taishan by one, two, three, and even four generations of life abroad.

This habit of clinging to Taishanese who live overseas developed from a century of believing that Taishan's best hopes for progress and economic security lay with those who managed to escape bleak economic prospects within Taishan to live and work abroad. People "trapped" behind believed that without those overseas workers and the money they managed to send back those in Taishan might very well starve. Taishanese also believed that their overseas countymen could acquire enough capital and technology to transform Taishan's moribund agrarian economy into a far more lucrative industrial and commercial one. For all these reasons, Taishanese encouraged those overseas to think of Taishan as their home and to continue contributing. In this chapter, I describe how Taishan acquired this taste for dependency and became, by self-proclamation, the premier home community to overseas Chinese.

Three circumstances led to Taishan's transformation into an emigrant community that relied heavily on out-migration as a survival strategy. The first was the high level of overseas migration. In Taishan, population pressures on insufficient land combined with bloody local conflicts to give many men reason to leave just as industrialization abroad increased the demand for cheap labor. The second circumstance was the development of regular and reliable trade and communications networks that allowed Taishanese to travel overseas safely yet remain in touch with life in Taishan through letters, remittances, return visits, migration chains, the consumption of Chinese groceries, books and magazines, and participation in local charitable projects and war relief drives. The third circumstance was a mutual desire for keeping the home community intact. In order for Taishan to survive as an emigrant community that included people living in Taishan as well as scattered throughout Southeast Asia, North and South America, and Australia, Taishanese overseas and at home had to share some commitment to remaining within the same family groups, clan organizations, and economic partnerships. Although this commitment did not always survive in the hearts of

Taishanese overseas, Taishanese at home have yet to lose sight of those who went away.

These three circumstances combined in Taishan to produce a community and society that functioned in two parts, physically dispersed yet bound together by an uneven distribution of emotional and economic capital. Taishanese abroad made money so that their dependents in Taishan could enjoy comfortable lives, become educated, and hope for better futures. The overseas breadwinners worked hard because they had families whose lives depended on the fruits of their toil. If they did not work hard, their families would suffer. And as long as exclusionary immigration policies and economic realities made it difficult for Chinese to bring their families to America or start new ones abroad, overseas Taishanese continued to look back to Taishan for the emotional satisfaction of marrying and having children. Until wives, children, and normal family life became possibilities for more men living in America, it would be difficult for them to uproot from Taishan. And until they felt less compelled to send support to Taishan, their relatives at home would continue gazing across the Pacific, hoping for a letter containing yet more money or a summons to go abroad themselves.

Leaving Taishan

Most of the people who left Taishan did so for economic reasons that played out in complicated ways during the eighteenth and nineteenth centuries. The primary reason, however, which has been a problem for hundreds of years and is still one today, is land.

Descriptions of Taishan's terrain have two main themes. The first theme focuses upon the beauties of Taishan. *Scenery of the Four Counties*, written during the 1970s, provides an example: "Taishan is a beautiful, abundant place at the edge of the Southern Sea; inland there are flat plains, hills, and high mountains."[4] The second theme is more common and much grimmer:

> Xinning is an out-of-the-way place. Although the land is broad, rural areas are narrow, probably 60 or 70 percent mountains and seas. An examination of production [reveals that] it is certainly not enough to satisfy necessity. The people of this place consider this a matter of life and death. The

insufficiencies [suffered by] the people [are why] they hire themselves out overseas.[5]

Both descriptions contain some measure of truth, for Taishan is a pretty place with blue skies, white clouds, and fields laid out in a patchwork of varying shades and textures of green tucked between tree-covered hills. These hills, which are so picturesque, pose the greatest obstacle to economic development in Taishan because they are difficult to cultivate, and they make the cost of building roads, railroads, or canals, which might improve commerce, prohibitively expensive. In a county that by 1893 produced only enough grain to feed its inhabitants for half a year, such limits to economic growth posed serious problems.[6]

Although its own geography limits its ability to produce wealth, Taishan closely borders neighboring counties and towns better endowed by nature. It is close to three international ports—130 kilometers south of Guangzhou, 170 kilometers west of Hong Kong, and 119 kilometers northwest of Macao—and sits on the southwest corner of the Pearl River Delta's cornucopia of commercial farms.[7] Since 1573, Guangzhou and its environs had also been part of a profitable trading network in silk, silver, porcelain, peppers, and cloves with the Americas, the Philippines, Japan, and Southeast Asia.[8] Unfortunately, Taishan has neither the natural waterways nor the acres of rich alluvial soil needed to duplicate the successes of these nearby regions.

Taishan lies on the southern coast of Guangdong, wedged in the middle of three other counties that together with Taishan are known as the Four Counties, whose residents speak the dialect most commonly found in Chinatowns in the United States and Canada.[9] Taishan itself forms a triangle between the counties of Xinhui to the northeast and Kaiping and Enping to the northwest. In this north-pointing wedge are the county seat, Taishan City, as well as the districts of Duhu, Sijiu, Shuibu, Dajiang, Gongyi, Sanhe, Duanfen, Sanba, Baisha, Chonglou, and Doushan.[10] This is the hilliest portion of the county and the most heavily populated. The southern portion of the county has more arable land and access to fishing but fewer people. These southern districts border the ocean and include Tiantou and Guanghai as well as a spur jutting southwest from the main wedge consisting of the districts of Longwen, Shalan, Haiyan, Wencun, Shenjing, Beidou, and Nafu. This southwestern arm is known collectively as

Haiyan. Seventy-seven islands sit off the coast of Taishan, the largest of which are Shangchuan and Xiachuan Islands.

With 587.7 kilometers of shoreline, Taishan seems advantageously situated for travel across the ocean. Recorded contact with Southeast Asia occurred as early as 1373, when one Ruan Dixian of Doushan took to the seas and fled to Vietnam to escape punishment for a crime he did not commit.[11] Direct contact with Europeans also occurred fairly early, with the Portuguese establishing a trading center on Shangchuan Island in 1516. By the next year, Taishanese were trading copper coins, silver, silk, porcelain, and tea for rhinoceros horns, ivory, crystal, and rattan. Missionaries followed on the heels of merchants, and in 1523 a Jesuit monk, Francis Xavier, came to proselytize in Guanghai and Shangchuan.[12]

Despite this proximity to the ocean and early foreign contacts, Taishan never became a center even for local trade, much less coastal or international commerce, as did the nearby cities of Guangzhou, Macao, Jiangmen, and later Hong Kong. The hilly terrain prevented the ready transport of goods by land. Water transport was also inconvenient, for none of the many rivers that flow through Taishan can carry a boat directly from the ocean port of Guanghai north to Taishan City and on to Guangzhou or Jiangmen. The three largest rivers in the north, the Taicheng, the Baisha, and the Dajiang, flow north into the Tan River away from rivers that flow into the ocean. Rivers in the eastern part of the county initially flow west toward Xinhui and then turn south to empty into the ocean. In the south, the Sanjia and Duhu Rivers run south from the Haiyan plain into the ocean.

Expensive schemes to improve communications between Taishan and its more prosperous neighboring areas either failed or never materialized. During the reign of the Ming emperor Chenghua (1465–68), an official in Xinhui County, Tao Lu, proposed building a canal that would link Xinhui to the ocean at Guanghai by connecting the Sanhe River in Xinhui to the Gan Village River in Taishan. This plan was never carried out.[13] In the last years of the Qing, a successful Taishanese American merchant, Chen Yixi, began an ambitious communications project that would consume the last two decades of his life as well as much of his personal fortune. Chen Yixi hoped to build a railroad that would connect Taishan with Guangzhou, then Hong Kong, then the rest of China, Vietnam, and Southeast Asia, and finally to Europe and the rest of the world. After many delays and much expense, the Xinning Railroad started operation in 1914 and eventually linked the Taishanese market towns of Baisha and Doushan to Jiangmen. Never, however, did it connect Taishan to enough places to transform the county from a rural backwater to a commercial metropolis.[14]

Thus the cornerstone of Taishan's economy was and still is agriculture. In a study conducted in the 1890s, Zhao Tianxi found that 400,000 out of 600,000 Taishanese earned at least part of their living from agriculture.[15] Twentieth-century statistics reveal an even greater preponderance of farmers: 83.7 percent in 1952, 89.4 percent in 1956, and 90 percent in 1964.[16] Although Taishanese also fished and produced goods such as cotton cloth, salt, sugar, tea, and noodles in the nineteenth century, most relied on farming.[17]

In poorly endowed Taishan, depending on the land and weather conditions was particularly risky. Fifty-six percent of the county's surface area is taken up by hills and mountains, and only 1,659,100 *mu*, or 34.9 percent of the total land area of 4,748,000 *mu*, is cultivable.[18] Frederic Wakeman estimates that in 1812, there was only 1.67 *mu* of land for each person in Guangdong Province, or one-quarter of an acre.[19] This figure contrasts sadly with the 4.0 *mu* needed for "bare subsistence."[20] In Taishan the situation was even more dire, for the soil is of poor quality, being red or yellow in color and often mixed with stones, sand, or salt.[21] Good land produced two crops of rice per year and poor land only one. The demands of planting and harvesting rice structured the year for farmers, requiring them to plant in the third lunar month of each year, harvest and then replant in the sixth month, and then harvest again in the tenth. But despite the poor quality of soil and limited land, farming provided a varied diet; in addition to starches such as rice, taro, and sweet potatoes, crops included 24 types of vegetables, 12 kinds of melons, and 24 different fruits, as well as chicken, ducks, geese, and pigs.[22]

With its less-than-ideal natural endowment, Taishan was poorly equipped to absorb a population that grew throughout the Qing dynasty. Before the Qing dynasty, Taishan had never faced the problem of overcrowding. The first Han Chinese settlers moved south during the seventh century. The next big wave of migration occurred in 1263 during the southern Song. The 33 clans that moved to Taishan from Nanxiong Prefecture in northern Guangdong settled in an area then renowned for having "plentiful land, few people, and an abundance of products, and for being untouched by war."[23] Many local genealogies date the founding of their lineages to this time.

Another group of Han settlers arrived in 1531, attracted by tax breaks offered by the Ming government.[24] A century later the Qing conquered China, and during the course of the war Taishan's population dropped from more than 20,000 to only 13,653 inhabitants. The population was further depleted by Qing attempts to eradicate the pirate Koxinga (also known as Zheng Chenggong), by forcing all Chinese living on the coasts of Guangdong and Fujian to move 25 kilometers inland. Enacted in 1661, this drastic policy forced many Taishanese to leave Taishan altogether. Many never returned. Haiyan, for example, regained only 10 to 20 percent of its populace.[25] After the rescinding of this order, Taishan's population began to grow again, by natural increase and through official edicts. In 1683, government attempts to resettle vacated coastal areas attracted groups of Hakka settlers (*kejia*). Known tellingly as "guest people," they were by custom and dialect different from the Cantonese-speaking Chinese who had arrived earlier and called themselves "natives" or *bendi*. When competition for land became fiercer in the mid-nineteenth century, these differences ignited a major conflict between the Cantonese and their "guests." But during the eighteenth century, tensions had yet to arise, and as late as 1732 a government official, Tao Zhengzhong, inspected barren lands in Taishan and assigned Hakka to come and till them. During the course of the Qianlong (1736–95) and Jiaqing (1796–1820) reigns, 30,000 Hakka came from Huiyang, Chaozhou, and Jiaying prefecture and settled in southeastern Taishan. Around the same time, salt processing began on Xiachuan Island and attracted five large clans, the Chens, the Fangs, the Luos, the Dengs, and the Zhus, from Hunan, Guangxi, Zhejiang, Fujian, and Jiangxi.

Despite these influxes of settlers, sometime during the eighteenth century the balance tipped, and Taishanese began to feel insecure on the amount of land they had to farm. Population had increased dramatically over the course of the seventeenth and eighteenth centuries, and in 1838 the county's population was 196,972, an increase of 1,440 percent since 1657. Less than 100 years later, in 1920, the local population had quadrupled to approximately 800,000.[26] If increasing emigration is any indication of when the tide of population turned, Taishan became too crowded sometime in the 1870s, when Taishanese men started going overseas in greater numbers.

The links between high rates of migration, population density, and agricultural productivity are supported by a comparison of the situations of northern and southern Taishan. Emigration is highest from the northern Tanjiang plain, which has the highest population density, an average of 600 people per square kilometer.[27] The regions in the northern half of Taishan— Taishan City and the surrounding towns of Dajiang, Shuibu, Sanba, Sijiu, Baisha, Doushan, and Duanfen—are the most dependent on overseas Chinese.[28] In contrast, Haiyan and the southern plain enjoy higher agricultural productivity and lower population density. In these areas, emigration rates are lower.

In the middle of the eighteenth century, Taishanese farmers began looking for work in nearby cities during the slack winter months to supplement their earnings.[29] By working around the demands of the growing season, they could both farm and earn a little extra money along the docks and in the factories of the closest urban centers. This incremental migration led to more extensive travels after 1760, when Guangzhou became the only place in China where foreign merchants could trade. The city's growth attracted thousands seeking employment as porters, coolies, compradors, and boatmen and other forms of labor related to the trade in tea and textiles. Although no figures are available for the eighteenth century, a study conducted in the 1890s suggests that at least half of Taishan's population made its living by combining farming with other pursuits. At that time, Zhao Tianxi found that only 100,000 Taishanese made a living by farming alone, 300,000 through a combination of industry, commerce, and farming, and 200,000 in industry and commerce jobs.[30] The necessity of going to port cities such as Guangzhou and Macao to find work brought these part-time or full-time laborers into regular contact with foreign-bound ships and persons presenting opportunities to go abroad.

One person who went overseas in this two-step process was Cao Yazhi (1782–1830). Having been born into a poor family, Cao left the farm, started peddling, and ended up wandering into Macao while still a youth. Through a friend's connections, he boarded an English ship as a hired laborer and in 1819 followed the troops of Stamford Raffles into Singapore. Cao remained in Singapore for the rest of his life and helped to found the Singapore Ningyang Benevolent Association on May 26, 1822.[31]

Another early way that Taishanese went overseas is illustrated by the example of Mei Yaoxuan (dates unknown). Mei was among the first consignment of laborers "recruited" by British shippers to go to Penang in 1786.

He managed to survive his stint as a coolie laborer and in 1831 helped to found the Penang Ningyang Benevolent Association.[32]

Both Cao and Mei went abroad despite Qing strictures against leaving China. Because the statutes promised to punish only those who tried to come back, not those trying to leave, neither Cao nor Mei ever faced the wrath of government authorities. Chinese could leave the country as long as they did not try to return. However, in the nineteenth century even this measure of migration control fell by the wayside when beleaguered Qing officials became fully occupied with defending the dynasty from attacks by foreigners armed with cannons and warships and bands of millenarian rebels. In 1868, the Qing legalized the emigration of Chinese laborers by signing the Burlingame Treaty with the United States. In 1893, in recognition of the financial possibilities of overseas remittances, the Qing officially lifted the already defunct ban against those wishing to return.

Despite Qing laws, sizable numbers of Taishanese went to Southeast Asia to live and work, and by the 1820s and 1830s Taishanese benevolent associations existed in Singapore and Penang. Other parts of Malaysia, Vietnam, Burma, and Thailand were also common destinations during this time. They were relatively easy for Chinese to get to, and they needed workers. The development of plantations, mines, new cities, and ports by colonizing powers required enormous amounts of cheap labor. Chinese went abroad in large numbers to answer this demand. In turn, these communities of overseas Chinese attracted merchants who sold them Chinese foods and products. To this day, excluding Taiwan, Southeast Asia remains home to the largest communities of ethnic Chinese. Most emigrants from Taishan, however, chose the more distant destinations of North America and Australia.

The tide of overseas migration from Taishan changed direction after the first Opium War (1839–42) for several reasons. Most directly, the Treaty of Nanjing legalized the coolie trade and the forced migration of thousands of Chinese. More indirectly, but importantly, the Treaty established Shanghai and Ningbo as major treaty ports that usurped the centrality of Guangzhou's position in the export of tea and textiles. Thousands of coolies, porters, warehousemen, shroff merchants, and compradors in Guangdong lost their jobs as a result. The economic distress that ensued led many under- or unemployed to join the Red Turban and Taiping rebellions, and they later fled China to escape Qing wrath. The Treaty of Nanjing also gave Britain control of Hong Kong, whose development into an international entrepot would offer Taishanese reliable overseas transportation. Taishan itself sustained a long sequence of local disruptions and violence: an ethnic war between the *bendi* and the Hakka (1856–68), as well as fourteen serious floods, seven typhoons, four earthquakes, two severe droughts, four epidemics, and five great famines between 1851 and 1908.[33]

The first decisive push to go overseas occurred in 1847, when a credit crisis extending from British banks to warehouses along the Pearl River shut down trade in Guangzhou almost completely for that year and the next. Although business recovered for a few years, Guangzhou's temporary tailspin hastened the inevitable rise of Shanghai as the new center for China's export of tea and silk. The tea trade split between the two cities, with northern teas going to Shanghai and southern teas to Guangzhou, and 100,000 porters and boatmen in Guangdong lost their jobs. Many of these men joined other unemployed weavers, handicraftsmen, iron workers, junk crews, and dislocated peasants in roving bandit gangs known as triads.[34]

Conditions only worsened with poor agricultural harvests in 1852 and dismal trade in Guangzhou in 1853. More porters, coolies, and compradors lost their jobs while marginal peasants became even less able to pay their rising taxes. As economic decline rolled through Guangdong, triad numbers swelled with the addition of yet more urban unemployed and poor rural tenants.[35]

Triads, also known as secret societies, are usually associated with movements to topple the Qing and return the Ming to power. In truth, their robbing and terrorizing of local villages had more to do with the economic needs of each member than with broader-ranging political goals. Triads functioned more as mutual aid societies than as dynasty-threatening rebel uprisings. Members became bandits because they had no other way of supporting themselves and their families. Triad activity began to increase after 1755, fed by the growing number of men forced by financial hardship to leave their native places and seek employment elsewhere.[36] As economic conditions worsened over the course of the nineteenth century, triads became bolder. In Guangdong by 1838, the Triple Dot Society had openly recruited members in the Pearl River Delta "in every market town of Southeast China." In the winter of 1843, bandits from Xinhui and Taishan held meetings in broad daylight to solicit new members: "Several hundred would gather at a crossroad, post guards with guns, and encourage local peasants to join." During the 1840s and 1850s, triad bandits were able to frighten entire villages into joining for self-protection. In 1843 farmers left responsible for their own protection joined the Three Unities Society for 300 copper coins to avoid "onerous extractions." During these times, even subclerks, yamen runners, and district magistrates in local government became triad members.[37]

In the two years following the first Opium War, the Three Unities Society, later to become better known as the Red Turbans, ran rampant through Guangdong. They were finally brought to heel by local militia and driven into neighboring Guangxi in 1843. After the economic setbacks of 1852 and 1853, however, the numbers of men in triads swelled, and in June 1853 the Red Turban Uprising began in earnest. After raging through the province for two years, occupying the city of Foshan and threatening Guangzhou, the rebellion was finally crushed by Governor Ye Mingchen in early 1855, and the rebel forces in Taishan and Xinhui were dispersed by December 1854.[38]

The terror did not end with the defeat of the Red Turbans, for Governor Ye was determined to wipe out the Red Turban threat completely by rounding up all known members and punishing those who had collaborated, however unwillingly, with the bandits. This last group included poor lineages and villages that had paid taxes under duress. Mass executions soon ensued. In the summer of 1855, as many as 70,000 beheadings occurred. Estimates of the death toll from government reprisals alone reached 1 million.[39]

The Taiping Rebellion (1851–64) added to the toll of death and departure suffered by Taishan during the 1850s and 1860s. Much larger in number and ambition than the Red Turbans, the Taipings cut a broad and bloody swath through southern China that stopped only with their conquest of Nanjing in March 1854. They threatened to end Qing rule. Government reprisals were commensurate with the threat survived. As with the Red Turban uprisings, Taishanese participants like Zhao Yu (dates unknown) of Longxi village in Doushan were forced to flee Taishan or face execution. Zhao, reputed to be a general for the Taipings, was forced to flee to Kuala Lumpur after power struggles between the Taiping leaders led to the persecution of the followers of Hong Xiuquan and Yang Xiuching. He mined tin with a fellow Taiping, Ye Delai. The two defended Kuala Lumpur during the 1865 civil war in Sri

Lanka, and for their services to the state were appointed *kapitans* of the local Chinese community. Zhao later would donate more than 9,000 dollars to build the Guangzhao Benevolent Association.[40]

As destructive as the Taiping and Red Turban rebellions were, their repercussions affected mostly those Taishanese who actually participated, leaving relatively untouched those Taishanese who remained at home. Red Turbans did enter Taishan three times during 1854, and the Taipings attacked Danjia Mountain once on July 14, 1854.[41] Despite the broad reach of both these uprisings, however, Taishan suffered the most destruction during a highly localized conflict over land rights between two competing ethnic groups, the Hakka and the *bendi*.

Fleeing Times of Trouble

Taishanese preferences for migrating to North America stem in part from the severe impact of the Hakka-*bendi* war on local life. The conflict raged throughout the time that the North American continent held out the greatest promise of prosperity for Chinese in the form of the Gold Rush, the building of the transcontinental railroad, and the first flush of industrial development in California. Between 1854 and 1867, 200,000 died in the fighting.[42] Although the conflict also affected the neighboring counties of Enping, Kaiping, Xinhui, and Heshan, Taishan alone suffered the deaths or departures of 100,000. Taishanese suffered more during the war, and thus were more motivated to depart, because of Taishan's terrain and the patterns of Hakka settlement in Guangdong.

The Hakka-*bendi* war was caused by ethnic tensions and competition over resources and land. Many of the Cantonese-speaking *bendi* traced their presence in the southern part of Guangdong to a thirteenth-century southern Song wave of migration from Nanxiong in northern Guangdong. They staked their claim to the more prosperous lowland farming areas, so when the ethnically distinct Hakka arrived later they were left with more marginal, hilly land. By the mid-eighteenth century, however, populations had grown and there was less room for two groups whose distinctive dialects and customs only heightened competition for economic resources. Each side thought the other was encroaching on its land, and clan leaders on both sides grew increasingly jumpy and mistrustful of the other. By the mid-nineteenth century, decades of ethnic tension provided the fuel for any sudden spark. Village communities that had armed themselves against the roaming Red Turbans already had militias and weapons at hand when in March 1855 clan leaders called on their followers to assert their competing interests in the land. The war between the Hakka and *bendi* peoples lasted thirteen years and raged so fiercely that despite repeated government attempts to mediate, peace was achieved only by physically separating the two groups and giving the Hakka a district carved from one corner of Taishan.

As suggested earlier, Taishan's geography affected local patterns of Hakka settlement and even intensified the conflict between "native" and "guest" peoples. Taishan gained a substantial population of Hakka, up to one-third in all, because as a coastal area the county had been subject to Qing attempts to wipe out the pirate-warlord Koxinga, by ordering all Chinese to move 25 kilometers inland in 1661. Because of the loss of population after the order was rescinded in 1683, government officials invited new settlers, the Hakka, to make use of the land.

Taishan contains a high proportion of the hilly terrain that tended to be left fallow by *bendi* farmers. It was this marginal land that government edicts encouraged Hakka to cultivate.[43] Even though Taishan did not support the highest density of Hakka, as populations increased and competition for resources became fiercer the conflicts between Hakka and *bendi* were more intense because they lived nearer together.

There are other indications that ethnic strife in Taishan was greater than in other areas affected by the Hakka-*bendi* war. Competition between Hakka and *bendi* also showed itself in the official examinations required for government positions. As Hakka candidates did well on these tests and came to disproportionately claim government offices, ethnic conflict grew, leading the imperial government to set subquotas for the Hakka in localities most affected by the fighting. According to Sow-theng Leong, Taishan had such a quota by 1788, 20 years before its neighbors in Kaiping and Dongguan.[44]

When the competition and conflict came to a head in 1855, it was extremely destructive because it was fought on home ground. Over the next twelve years, 100,000 Taishanese alone either died or fled.[45] Sickness took a heavy toll, many fled to the nearby area of Yangjiang or to Hong Kong. Those captured by the enemy were sold as coolies and usually ended up in the guano pits and sugar fields of Peru and Cuba. Some even sold themselves in order to get away. Estimates of those going overseas to escape the war range from 20,000 to 30,000.[46]

Chen Huangyang (dates unknown) was one of those who left Taishan in order to escape the devastation. Born into a middle-class doctor's family, he was more able than others to afford to go overseas. He chose to travel to the United States and ended up in Savannah, Georgia, where he set up shop as an herbalist in the 1870s. Chen spent most of his life in the American South and died in Mississippi.[47]

In Search of Opportunity

Those fleeing war and government persecution in Taishan were joined by others leaving simply to seek out new and better opportunities. Economic hardship led men not only to become bandits but also to go overseas to avoid vengeful Qing troops. In 1852, a year marked by serious crop failures in southern China, 20,026 Chinese entered the United States through the San Francisco Customs House. The previous year, only 2,716 had done so. In 1853 the number dropped to 4,270 but rose again to 16,084 in 1854. These men journeyed in search of gold in the California hills, word of which was sent back by merchants who had gone to the United States in 1849 and 1850, seeking to reestablish themselves after Guangdong's credit crash of 1847.[48] These transplanted merchants reported fortunes easy in the making, thereby inspiring other Chinese to follow them overseas. Louis Ahmouy (1826–?) illustrates the growth potential of a well-placed informant. He had been a carpenter in Singapore and Malaysia before going to Australia in 1851 as a coolie. While building houses in Melbourne, he learned of gold strikes in Victoria and described the find in letters to Taishan. He is credited with inspiring more than 1,000 men from the Four Counties to go to Australia.[49]

Thus North America and to a lesser extent Australia became the destinations of choice for Taishanese by the 1850s. Many captives from the Hakka-*bendi* war were sold as coolies to Peru or Cuba, but Taishanese who had some say in the matter went to the United States or Canada.[50] At first they went to find gold, but after gold became harder to find they went to build railroads. By the 1870s, Chinese in the United States had moved into such disparate areas as truck gardening, shoe and cigar manufacturing, cooking, fish and shellfish harvesting and processing, domestic service, importing and selling Chinese goods, and of course restaurant and laundry work. After the gold ran out in the late 1850s and 1860s, Taishanese men and their neighbors from the other Four Counties found these kinds of contract labor and small business opportunities reason enough to continue dreaming of going to the United States. Unlike their counterparts in the prosperous Pearl River Delta, they had few local opportunities that could compete with the possibilities of sojourning on Gold Mountain.[51] This imbalance between local hardship and well-advertised, well-paying work abroad eventually led to Taishanese dominance of American Chinatown communities.

Although many of the jobs available to Chinese before World War II were menial, they enabled men to elevate their families in China to a middle class symbolized by land ownership, new houses, and education for the young. George F. Woo claims that in his home village about 30 families had had connections to railroad workers in the nineteenth century: "To their standards, these families in China were well-off."[52] By 1900 most of these avenues of employment were closed to Chinese, but by working as laundrymen, cooks and waiters, and domestic servants, and by selling groceries to fellow Chinese, men in America could still provide their families with good lives.[53]

It is difficult to find accurate figures for nineteenth-century Chinese migration to the United States, much less any for Taishanese. Customs and census records tend to undercount because many Chinese entered the United States illegally and avoided contact with official agencies. Approximations of the Taishanese presence in the United States are even harder to find because government representatives did not distinguish Chinese by province or by county. The statistics that are available are scanty. Of the three Chinese recorded as being in the United States between 1820 and 1830, one was Taishanese.[54] By 1851, Chinese from the Four Counties had come to California in sufficient numbers to form the Szeyup Benevolent Association (Siyi huiguan).[55] In 1853, this company had more than 10,000 members. In 1852, however, 3,000 Taishanese had formed a company of their own, the more exclusive Ning Yung Benevolent Association (Ningyang huiguan) for Taishanese alone.[56] In 1876, two years after the Philadelphia Exposition, the first Chinese minister to visit San Francisco recorded that 70,000, or approximately 45 percent of 155,000 Chinese in the United States, were members of the Ning Yung Benevolent Association.[57] In 1876 another visitor to the United States estimated that the Ning Yung Benevolent Association had 75,000 members.[58] In 1931 government representative Chen Jitang claimed that by 1900 the number of Taishanese in North America had reached 120,000.[59] The *Chixi Gazetteer* estimated that by 1901 more than 200,000 Taishanese had gone overseas. Together, these two estimates suggest that the great majority of Taishanese went to the United States or Canada. If the estimate of 200,000 is combined with the 1921 population estimate of 800,000 (the year closest to 1900 for which there are population estimates), and assuming population was lower in 1900 than it was in 1921, then well over one-fourth of Taishan's population in 1900 had been overseas.[60]

As noted more succinctly by the *Taishan Gazetteer* of 1893: "Ever since the destructions of the Red Turban uprising and the Cantonese-Hakka war, the numbers of people going abroad have increased dramatically. The strong and healthy regularly go to the four corners of the earth."[61] But because it was North America that loomed largest in the imagination and economy of Taishanese, in the pages that follow I focus on their pursuit of the American dream.[62]

Staying in Touch

Overseas migration in the hundreds of thousands was not accomplished by crossing the Pacific on fishing boats, wooden junks, or even clipper ships. Migration in such numbers demanded equipment and global networks of trade more sophisticated and reliable than had existed in China before the nineteenth century. Such facilities developed in Hong Kong after it came under British rule. Southern Chinese had only to go to this nearby port city in order to find shipping companies, labor recruiters, friends, and businessmen who could tell them about opportunities abroad and give them credit to buy the tickets to get there. Hong Kong supplied other links in the chain between Chinese in China and Chinese overseas by providing a secure and reliable channel for the back-and-forth flow of people, remittances, information, capital, political ideals, Chinese groceries, and technology. As

Taishan became increasingly dependent on foreign sources of money, the evolution of Hong Kong into an entrepot was essential to enabling Taishanese to go overseas and yet stay in touch with people, places, events, and way of life left behind in China.

In 1860 the average cost of passage from Hong Kong to San Francisco was US$50. By 1860, 73,890 Chinese had entered the United States through the San Francisco Customs House.[63] Between 1860 and 1874, 112,362 Chinese left Hong Kong bound for the United States, paying some HK$5,618,100 in travel fare.[64] This was big business. Monthly trans-Pacific steamship services began when the Pacific Mail Steamship Company launched the *Colorado* from Hong Kong to San Francisco on January 1, 1867. Demand was such that these trans-Pacific passages increased to twice a month in 1872.[65] Shipping companies and labor brokers contributed their share to the number of Chinese going overseas by spreading word of the economic opportunities available abroad. In the early 1850s, Hong Kong newspapers reported that gold could be found on the streets in the United States, and in 1867 similar advertisements announced the availability of jobs in agriculture and on the railroads.[66]

Labor brokers played their part by recruiting friends and relatives as well as strangers from Hong Kong, Guangzhou, and their home villages to work for foreign railroad companies, light manufacturers, and commercial farmers. These brokers made money on both ends by collecting fees from employers seeking cheap labor and by charging interest on the boat tickets they sold to their labor recruits on credit. In 1877, Li Chudu of Shalan returned to Taishan and persuaded more than 200 people to go to the United States and work on the railroad. In 1891, Wei Laoying of Duhu recruited 1,800 workers from Hong Kong, Macao, and the Four Counties to build railroads for English and American companies in Mexico. Over half of these men died. In 1898, Ma Zhuo of Baisha represented a British firm in locating more than 1,000 laborers to go to the United States. In 1884, 1,158 out of 5,056 Cantonese recruited in Hong Kong to go to British Columbia in Canada were Taishanese.[67] Although they faced high interest rates and lengthy periods of indentured labor, most men in Taishan could not have borne the expense of going to the United States during the nineteenth century without the help of credit tickets and labor recruiters.

The expense of traveling began to decline during the 1890s when overseas migrants began to have some choice in shipping companies. In 1891 the Canadian Pacific Railway Company joined the Pacific Mail Steamship Company in the trans-Pacific passenger trade by assigning three steamers to sail between Hong Kong, Japan, Victoria, and Vancouver. In the 1890s the Japanese firm Nippon Yusen Kaisha started a regular line linking Hong Kong to Hawaii, Australia, and Seattle. This company assigned the *Minnesota*, a twin-screw steamship with the latest technology and largest capacity of its time, to the route between Seattle, Japan, and Hong Kong. The Toyo Kisen Kaisha's service between Hong Kong and North America was even more popular, and the first three ships assigned this route, each 6,200 tons gross, could not keep up with the demand. In 1908 the company scheduled them for replacement by three much larger, 14,000-ton ships.[68]

In 1916 the Pacific Mail Steamship Company offered four classes of travel to San Francisco: supreme class for 36 pounds, first class for 17 pounds, second class for 79 yuan, third class for 51 yuan. In addition, each passenger had to pay 4 yuan in tax and get an eye examination with the ship's doctor; those with a history of hookworm had to obtain a certificate of health from a Western doctor. Tickets were available through the company's agent, the Hongfa Company.[69]

By the 1930s there were still four classes, but Chinese generally traveled as cheaply as possible, as described by one emigrant who left China in the 1930s:

> The richer ones spend more money on a better seat, which would cost about, I would say, three hundred dollars American money. This is first class. First class is about $350, $400. Then the second class runs about $250. Then there's semi . . . between second and third. The third one is way down in the bottom. You sleeping like dogs more or less. In big rooms, you know, not much privacy. I was fortunate to get into what they called between second and third. That means you stay with about four or six people in one compartment, in double bunks.[70]

By the 1920s and 30s, 95 percent of those traveling "down in the bottom" on the trans-Pacific route were Chinese.[71] By this time, those going overseas included people from all walks of life: village boys, village storekeepers, Hong Kong small merchants and clerks, politicians, schoolteachers, students, seamen, playboys, and loafers.[72]

The Chinese who traveled overseas benefited shipping firms by more than buying tickets. Their demand for food and things Chinese produced a thriving export trade throughout Southeast Asia and the Americas:

> The Chinese communities abroad clung to the Chinese way of life, and Hong Kong became the center of an international trade catering to their needs. The arrival of large numbers of Chinese immigrants to the United States in the latter half of the nineteenth century created a demand for rice, tea, foodstuffs, drugs, and sundries from China. Hong Kong developed a flourishing trade with the United States, where a Chinese merchant class prospered by selling Chinese imports.[73]

The businesses that handled this new demand for Chinese groceries in foreign places were called *jinshanzhuang*, or Gold Mountain firms.[74] *Jinshanzhuang* began operating sometime during the 1850s and had close links to Chinese businesses abroad, which were often run by kinsmen or people from the same village.[75] On behalf of overseas merchants, *jinshanzhuang* managers took orders for Chinese goods and arranged for their shipment. By 1922 there were 116 *jinshanzhuang* based in Hong Kong doing business with North American firms. By 1930 business was so good that their number had more than doubled, to 290.[76]

Jinshanzhuang made it possible for overseas Chinese to buy a tremendous variety of Chinese goods, including Chinese books and magazines, herbal medicines, fruits such as lychees, pineapples, ginger, water chestnuts, water lily roots, yuengans, pears, manis preserved in sugar syrup, seafood in the form of flower fish, blackfish, eels, and oysters, as well as Chinese ducks, fried rice birds, and quail.[77] They also supplied "dried oysters, shrimps, cuttlefish, mushrooms, dried bean curd, bamboo shoots, sweetmeats, duck liver and kidneys, [and] water chestnut flour" to Chinese in the United States. Preserved ginger was another popular item, and in 1908 alone about 450,000 pounds were exported, mostly to San Francisco. Rice imports from China, Hong Kong and Hawaii to the United States rose from 18.7 million pounds in 1867 to 59.6 million pounds in 1876 and 61.1 million pounds in 1878.[78] Gilbert Leong recalls that during the 1920s his father did not need to go to China to get supplies for his Chinese restaurant in Los Angeles because everything he needed was available locally.[79]

Chinese-run businesses scattered throughout North America had connections with *jinshanzhuang*, thereby ensuring that in a large number of cities local Chinese could buy Chinese items. The distribution network of magazines published in Taishan gives us some sense of the dispersion of Chinese grocery stores in North America. In 1927, Chinese could pick up their copy of *Xinning Magazine* and buy items like dried shrimps and canned water chestnuts from stores in Pittsburgh, Los Angeles, Newark, San Diego, Portland, Washington, D.C., Chicago, Philadelphia, New York City, Boston, Baltimore, Seattle, Vancouver, Toronto, Victoria, Calgary, Winnipeg, Montreal, Houston, Hawaii, Hobart, and Detroit.[80]

The networks of trade that linked *jinshanzhuang* in Hong Kong to points all over the world did more than bring salted fish and rice to Chinese overseas. They also made it possible for Chinese living in urban centers like San Francisco, Chicago, Havana, Melbourne, and Singapore to send letters, money, and information to villages in the backwaters of rural Guangdong. To the reader accustomed to the conveniences of late-twentieth-century life, the problem perhaps seems simpler than it was. In the reality of nineteenth- and early-twentieth-century China, there were no government postal agencies whose reach extended from a big city like New York to a village like Sanba tucked in the hills of Taishan. After 1876, when Hong Kong joined the Postal Union, it was possible to send and receive mail in most cities in the world from the British colony.[81] However, after arriving in Hong Kong, letters had to get to Taishan. And if a letter contained money, recipients in Taishan had to find a way to change foreign dollars into currency that they could spend at the local marketplace.[82]

During the nineteenth century, it *was* possible to get money to China from parts overseas. However, the three main methods were unreliable.[83] Overseas Chinese could ask returning relatives or friends to bring small amounts of cash back to their dependents free of charge, but such opportunities occurred irregularly. With payment of a 5 percent commission, they could hire a courier, also known as a "water guest" (*shuike*) or "city-circuit horse" (*xunchengma*), to take back money and letters along with goods for import or export. Water guests made deliveries in person and would wait to take back letters written by recipients in reply. However, the overseas Taishanese had to trust that the courier would not run away with their money. The third method, in which people brought back money themselves, was less risky but required that while overseas they exchange their foreign currency for Chinese currency.[84]

Jinshanzhuang managed to resolve this multitude of problems. From their base in Hong Kong, they had well-established connections to businesses in Chinatowns around the world. Their transactions with others were guaranteed, not by contracts but by relationships based on kinship or native-place ties.[85] As such, *jinshanzhuang* were the best-qualified and most accountable agents for ensuring that money sent to Hong Kong would be forwarded to its designated recipients in their home villages. In addition, by sending letters through the closest Chinese store, Chinese overseas did not have to deal with the unfamiliar language and rules of banks and post offices in foreign places.

To reach all the places not served by banks and post offices of the time, *jinshanzhuang* had to have a network of partners in Taishan as well as around the world.[86] Huaying Chang (Wah Ying Cheong), located at 290 Des Voeux Road in the Central District of Hong Kong, is an example of a *jinshanzhuang* that handled large amounts of remittances with the help of widely dispersed business connections. The firm was founded in the late nineteenth century and run by members of the Chen clan from Doushan District in Taishan. Most of its customers were either of the Chen surname or from Doushan.[87] Its overseas business partners included several firms located in San Francisco, Los Angeles, New York, Seattle, and Portland.[88] Huaying Chang also handled money sent in from San Diego, Boston, Victoria, Chicago, Montreal, Singapore, Rangoon, New Zealand, Vancouver, Osaka, and the Philippines.

Within Taishan, Huaying Chang's partners were based in market towns in or around Doushan. The main Taishan contact was the firm of Yichang in Doushan. Almost twenty other partners were located in Doushan and the five districts of Nafu, Duhu, Guanghai, Xialang, and Chonglou.[89]

Some, like the Baochang Money Shop located on Duhu Street in Taishan City, were known as money shops and specialized in the receipt of letters and remittances as well as money exchange.[90] Other businesses, for example, the firm of Wansheng Hao, acted as a postal drop as a sideline to other commercial activities. When not handling remittances, Wansheng Hao sold food items such as oil, rice, and sugar.[91] A wide range of businesses accepted letters and remittances for other people: gold stores, medicine firms, and even china shops, such as Yu Lianhe's Zhenji Porcelain Store.[92] Some businesses gave up their original function altogether in favor of handling overseas

Chinese money alone. In 1919 the Yongtai Firm of West Kuo Hill announced plans to sell off its stocks of oil, sugar, and white rice in order to concentrate solely on the business of exchanging money and receiving remittances and letters. Interested customers were advised to contact the store's Hong Kong partner, Yongdecheng Hao, at 280 Des Voeux Road.[93] Before 1937 there were at least 100 banks and stores in Taishan that directly communicated with *jinshanzhuang* in Hong Kong for the transfer of funds.[94]

Sending money and letters to Taishan through a *jinshanzhuang* required the following steps. In the United States, the frugal Gold Mountain guest bought a cashier's check for the required amount, wrote a letter with instructions as to destination and recipient, and sent both via registered mail to the *jinshanzhuang* of choice in Hong Kong. Or, if the Gold Mountain guest did not wish to deal with American banks, he could go to the nearest store run by a trusted connection and ask the proprietor to send the money and instructions. The store's owner waited until a pile of such remittances had accumulated before purchasing a single cashier's check for the total to be sent with a bundle of individual instructions.[95] Once the money arrived in Hong Kong, the accountant at the *jinshanzhuang* cashed the check at a bank, exchanged it for silver or Hong Kong dollars, deducted service fees, calculated the amounts to send to business partners in Taishan, then figured out how to get everything to the right place, usually by courier.[96] All *jinshanzhuang* charged the same nominal service fee of 2 percent to carry out these transactions. *Jinshanzhuang* owners liked to advertise this fact as a symbol of their devotion and generosity to overseas Chinese. However, they did manage to profit from the remittance business through their manipulation of exchange rates.

After the money arrived at the branch store in Taishan, the proprietor contacted the designated recipients, usually by word of mouth, to come to town and fetch their mail. For example, one woman living in Tangmei village in Zhudong walked down the road to the nearby market of Hua'nanchang to pick up her money.[97] Sending letters overseas followed much the same process, in reverse.

Besides helping to send money, *jinshanzhuang* began providing their customers with services normally associated with banks. Some rented out safety deposit boxes and administered savings plans that paid interest. The Bai'anlong Yinhao at 41 Bonham Strand in Hong Kong was a fairly typical *jinshanzhuang* of the 1930s. It was backed by capital of 200,000 yuan and helped customers with remittances, currency exchange, savings accounts, and the storage of valuables in U.S. metal security boxes. The interest rate on savings accounts was four *li* for six months, five for one year, six for two years, and variable for deposits of unfixed duration (*huoqi*).[98]

If they were successful, overseas Taishanese eventually had recourse to the full range of a *jinshanzhuang*'s financial services, as did Chen Kongzhao of New York. Chen appears in the Huaying Chang books over the course of 30 years, during which his position changed from that of a laborer sending back remittances in small amounts, to a businessman with large sums to invest, and finally to a retiree living comfortably in Hong Kong on a sizable income from dividends and interest on savings.[99] In 1905 Chen could only afford to send $90 to his mother, Woman Wu, and $42 to a cousin. Ten years later, he was doing well enough to put $1,000 in his savings account, send $60 to yet another cousin, and donate money to build a school in the Six Villages. In 1920 he sent $350 to one Chen Qinqing, $2 per person to two cousins, and added another $1,000 to his savings account. In 1929 he put $34.50 into the Qinji Company, $2,500 into his account, and collected $25.75 in interest from the Qinji Company. By 1935 he had returned to live in Hong Kong and personally dropped by Huaying Chang to collect $470.80 in dividends from the Qinji Company, as well as a total of $1,818.88 in income from his savings account and relatives overseas.[100]

For trusted customers, *jinshanzhuang* offered a special line of services. When short on cash and faced with a family crisis at home, these special customers could ask the *jinshanzhuang* to forward money to Taishan with the understanding that the full amount would be repaid at the U.S. branch when the customer was able.[101] *Jinshanzhuang* also acted as trustees for their overseas customers. Those with sizable savings (several thousand up to US$10,000) and unreliable sons, wives, or younger brothers could send a lump sum of money to the *jinshanzhuang*, which would then use the interest to make a regular payment to the family in China.[102] Thus merchants and restaurateurs who could not leave their businesses to personally supervise the upbringing of their heirs could delegate the responsibility.

Jinshanzhuang also offered assistance to all classes of Taishanese negotiating the complicated process of immigrating overseas. *Jinshanzhuang* personnel helped the sons, nephews, cousins, wives, and daughters of their overseas customers by buying tickets, arranging health exams, preparing evidence of identity, and filling out forms at the U.S. consulate.[103] Liu Zanchen at 234 Des Veoux Road in Hong Kong specialized in such services and claimed twenty years of experience bringing people from their villages in Taishan to the United States.[104] *Jinshanzhuang* provided these prospective emigrants with a place to stay for the two or three weeks they had to spend in Hong Kong waiting for paperwork to be processed and boats to arrive. Larger *jinshanzhuang*, such as the Huaxin Ginseng Company, had offices complete with living rooms and bedrooms for their clients.[105] They also sold emigrants the necessities that would be needed at their destinations, such as bedding, food, leather trunks, soap, and a mat.[106] The Huaxin Ginseng Company became known as the Chonglou Courier Station (Chonglou shizhan) because everybody from the district who went overseas stayed there.[107]

With the intimacy and completeness of services offered by *jinshanzhuang* to their customers, it is no wonder that until World War II *jinshanzhuang* were well able to withstand the attempts of government banks and postal services to take control of overseas Chinese remittances during the 1930s.

In an attempt to displace *jinshanzhuang*, the Bank of China opened branches in New York and London as well as Jiangmen and Taishan. The Bank of Canton also opened offices in San Francisco and New York as well as in each county seat in the Guangzhou and Pearl River Delta region.[108] Billy W. Lew recalls that his grandfather's business, Sun Wing Wo in Los Angeles, had connections to the Bank of Canton's San Francisco branch. As the bank's representative in Los Angeles, Sun Wing Wo collected money, wrote drafts in Hong Kong or Chinese silver dollars, deducted a commission of around 10 percent, and forwarded the money to San Francisco. The Bank of Canton then took care of transferring the funds to Hong Kong and China.[109] The Linghai Bank Ltd., which had branches on Bonham Strand, Hong Kong, Ximen Xu in Taicheng, Guangzhou, Jiangmen, and Xinchang, was another modern institution that attempted to enter the remittance trade.[110] Despite these challenges, *jinshanzhuang* continued to thrive. Liu Zuoren, head of the Bank of Guangdong Research Office during the 1930s, estimated that 70 percent of remittances entered China via *jinshanzhuang*.[111] One recent estimate was that in 1937, 35.1 percent (Ch.$24,275,000) of remittances entered China through banks, 1.1 percent (Ch.$777,700) through post offices, and 63.8 percent (Ch.$44,220,000) through *jinshan-zhuang*.[112]

It is difficult to calculate the amount of remittances that went to Taishan because the money usually remained in private hands. There are no comprehensive government statistics for the Republican period, and most of the records that do exist belong to family businesses that avoid public scrutiny. Wing Fong Lau offers the estimate that at the beginning of the twentieth century remittances to Taishan reached several million Chinese dollars per year.[113] In 1937, Ch.$59,187,750 was remitted to Taishan, and more than twice that, Ch.$128,396,625, in 1939.[114] Estimates for all of China are presented in Table 1.

In the 1920s and early 1930s, remittances to Taishan from the United States alone constituted one-eighth of all money transmitted to China from abroad.[115] Thus we have an idea of the crude impact of overseas Chinese money on the Chinese economy but no details about how foreign incomes affected the day-to-day lives of ordinary Taishanese. Historical records do reveal, however, that the considerable amount of overseas money sent back allowed many of the dependents of Gold Mountain guests to adopt a life of leisure that did not require them to work.

Gazing Across the Pacific

By the 1890s, Taishanese were firmly embedded in a life of dependence on Taishanese overseas. Contemporary local scholars and officials noted the trend with disapproval:

> In Taishan County, the quality of earth is bitter and barren, its customs simple, reverential, and thrifty. Ever since the beginning of the Tongzhi reign (1862–1874), more and more people have been going overseas, making money, returning to China, and building houses. In a flash, clothing and food tend toward Chinese American (*huamei*), the business of marriage becomes especially contentious, wasteful, and excessively extravagant. The tremendous change in environment, the price rise of food and implements, as well as the multitude of bandits also arise from this [emigration].[116]

TABLE 1

Estimated Remittances to China, 1903–1937

Source	Year	Amount (million Ch.$)
H. B. Morse	1903	110.0
	1906	150.0
C. F. Remer[a]	1928	228.2
	1929	253.6
	1930	286.3
Wu Ch'eng-hsi	1931	421.1
	1932	325.4
	1933	305.7
	1934	316.0
Chang Kia-ngau[b]	1937	455.8
Far Eastern Economic Review[b]	1937	517.2

SOURCE: Chun-hsi Wu, *Dollars, Dependents and Dogma: Overseas Chinese Remittances to Communist China* (Palo Alto, Calif.: Hoover Institution, 1966), pp. 78–79.
a. For money sent via Hong Kong.
b. Original figures from Chang and the *Far Eastern Economic Review* were cited in U.S. dollars ($131.9 million and $150.0 million respectively).

Taishanese working overseas made it possible for their friends and families in Taishan to build new houses and lead better lives. It also encouraged waste and ostentation where previously there had been thrift and modesty. Luxurious life styles caused prices to go up and attracted roving bandits. But these were not the only problems stemming from an abundance of overseas funds. According to the *Taishan Gazetteer* of 1893, money imported from overseas had brought many improvements to life in Taishan, but that ready access to foreign incomes had developed into a disturbing imbalance between the ability of Taishan residents to spend and their willingness to work:

In recent years, considerable amounts of money from overseas [have been used to pay for] lecture halls, orphanages, charitable hospitals, lavatories, and clan lands [for the needy]. These various charities are everywhere. But the customs of the people are gradually becoming wasteful. Capping ceremonies and wedding banquets require the expenditure of several hundred gold pieces. Fields lie barren and infertile and cannot be restored to their original state [of productivity].[117]

Zheng Dehua, who has extensively researched the roots of the Hakka-*bendi* war, claims that Taishan was actually self-supporting in the mid-1800s but that by 1900 it was not. Agricultural production fell and consumption increased. Output from light manufacturing and food processing also decreased. The number of families involved in sugar production dropped from more than ten to only three over this time period, and the number of peanut oil processors fell from ten to none. Zheng suggests three reasons for this decline: those most able to work went overseas; hired laborers were more careless in farming and so irrigation systems broke down; and, with newly found affluence, women left the fields and handicraft industries to stay at home.[118]

Dependence upon remittances and declining productivity produced a society that could not do without foreign money. According to the following statement from the 1893 gazetteer, Taishan did not produce enough rice to feed its own and had to buy rice from elsewhere: "Annual harvests provide food enough for only half the year; the rest of the time foreign rice must be bought. It is lamentable that when the ships occasionally cannot [sail] fires in kitchens immediately stop burning."[119] The rice deficit was so severe that when imports were temporarily held up there was no food to eat. Even money to pay for this basic staple had to come from overseas.

This dependence on foreign rice and foreign incomes disturbed the authors of the *Taishan Gazetteer* but did not seem to bother the rest of Taishan's populace, most of whom seemed content to sit back and enjoy the fruits of overseas Taishanese labor. Swan Yee recalls that when his grandfather went to work on the railroads in the United States he left behind his wife and a cow-herding business that nobody took over. The relatives in China simply relied on him to send back money.[120]

As explained earlier, there are few statistics on how much money was actually sent back. From the turn of the century until 1937, yearly remittances to Taishan exceeded agricultural output.[121] But there are no exact figures available for this time period. However, the anthropologist Chen T'a surveyed the families of Southeast Asian Chinese living in eastern Guang-

TABLE 2

Sources of Income of 100 Emigrant Families in Guangdong, 1935

Monthly income per family (Ch.$)	Number of families	Average monthly remittance per family (Ch.$)	Average total monthly income per family (Ch.$)	Percentage of total
Less than 20	17	11.40	15.10	75.5
21–49	49	25.70	31.90	80.6
50–124	21	68.10	86.60	78.6
125–250	13	192.60	228.90	84.1
	100	53.90	66.20	81.4

SOURCE: Chen T'a, *Emigrant Communities in South China* (Shanghai: Kelly and Walsh, 1939), p. 83.

dong in 1935 and found that they received most of their income from abroad (see Table 2).

In 1917, the *Shafu Monthly* estimated that overseas Taishanese sent back 20,000–30,000 yuan each year.[122] Other evidence is more anecdotal. During the 1920s, hired laundrymen could earn US$50 in a good week.[123] In the first decade of the twentieth century, they could support a family in China on $100–150 per year. However, it was not uncommon for the families of overseas Chinese to have considerably more money lying around the house.[124] Returned Gold Mountain guest Mei Rongmou and his wife were sleeping in their home when a robber entered and stole more than 300,000 yuan worth of valuables, including U.S. dollars, cashier's checks, silver, and gold. Despite these losses, Mei could still afford to offer a 500 yuan reward for the capture of the thief.[125]

This influx of foreign currency generated a hunger for consumption that could not be satisfied by local goods. During the 1920s, Taishan had a balance of trade that ran at a surplus of about 30 to one.[126] The money enabled some families to move up the hierarchy of urbanization and become city folk.[127] Others, however, chose to remain in their home villages and buy land and houses in the best manner of traditional wealthy Chinese families.[128]

Overseas money produced a new class of upwardly mobile actors in Taishan's social scene. A new vocabulary and set of stereotypes developed to describe the people who entered Taishan's upper or middle classes on the strength of remitted incomes. Gold assumed a prominent place in the new language. Gold Mountain guests, or *jinshanke*, were the men with enough wealth or family connections to find work in North America or Australia. Rarely did villagers in Taishan consider the hard labor, long hours, and daily discrimination faced by these men. As ruefully noted by one former wastrel who ended up going to Gold Mountain:

> Now I begin to see what sort of life you fellows have had here. I thought it was easy to make money in America. That was why I spent so freely when I was in China. I thought I could spend it all and make it back when I came over myself. If I had only realized the real conditions, I wouldn't have come, and I wouldn't have spent so freely.[129]

Men who returned to Taishan were eager to maintain the illusion of their good fortune and rarely told the truth about the hardship they had endured. In this way, the legend of fortunes to be made as easily as picking gold off the streets survived.[130] The women lucky enough to marry such men were called Gold Mountain wives, or *jinshanpo*, and their sons were called Gold Mountain youths, or *jinshanshao*. Gold Mountain wives were subject to both local envy and gossip as the recipients of large remittances from overseas and as young women living without a husband in the house. Gold Mountain youths enjoyed the enviable future of following in their fathers' footsteps overseas as well as childhoods cushioned by the benefits of overseas money. Robert F. Lee, who was born in 1918 in the village of Tung Wo, Taishan, recalls that his family's home had two bedrooms, a large living room with a fifteen-foot ceiling, and two cooking areas. His mother did the cooking, raised animals in the house, and farmed her own two acres of rice fields while his father sent back money.[131] Compared to that of their neighbors, it was a good life.

Gold Mountain guests who managed to save money above and beyond providing for their families' daily needs usually tried to build a new house. During the 1920s and 1930s, "new villages" (*xincun*) sprouted up beside the old ones. These new villages consisted of clusters of fifteen to 30 "foreign" houses (*yanglou*), built of oven-fired gray brick and concrete and decorated with Western motifs: stained-glass windows, Greek columns, and porches, as well as bas-relief moldings in plaster and tile. The new houses, built for both comfort and show, sometimes rose to three or four stories, towering over the older houses in the village. Keong Lee lived in just such a brick house in the village of Lone Gwall. Lee's father worked as a hotel cook and later opened a produce market in Los Angeles. Before his retirement in 1933, this man managed to elevate his family into the land-owning middle class. Lee himself went to the United States to continue supporting the family in his father's place while his younger brother prepared to become a scholar, as befitted a family aspiring to the leisure class.[132]

The successes of families like those of Robert Lee and Keong Lee affected entire villages and districts in Taishan. For example, in 1934 in the administrative unit of Zhudong, which included ten villages, 600 of the male population of 1,000 worked abroad. Most of the families in this region were well-to-do, and the region had turned the clan temple into a private school for 200 male and female students.[133]

Schools were another manifestation of the benefits of overseas money. After providing for their families, overseas Taishanese proved most committed to the cause of bringing education to Taishan. Wing Fong Lau argues that in Taishan there was a direct link between high levels of education and the large numbers who went overseas: "At the end of the Qing, education in Taishan flourished in the footsteps of those who went overseas who caused the economy to prosper. Those who went abroad to work told those at home that they had to learn the rudiments of reading and writing, for the sake of earning a living and keeping in touch with relatives."[134] The roots of this boom in education go back to the 1860s. During the last 100 years of the Qing dynasty, twenty new schools were built in Taishan, sixteen of them after 1860. Of these, fourteen were private or clan schools.[135]

Taishanese refer to the first decade of the twentieth century as the beginning of the import of overseas Chinese knowledge and resources for the betterment of Taishan. More than ten schools were built during this time. In 1900, Wu Limen of Meiwan Village and Wu Hui of Xize Village collected money from approximately 500 clan members in the United States to build a clan school of 872 square meters. In 1905, Wu Huci solicited 200,000 yuan

TABLE 3
Number of Middle Schools and Teachers in
Selected Districts of Guangdong, 1934

District	Number of middle schools	Number of teachers
Taishan	9	232
Guangzhou City	65	2,075
Shantou City	9	238
Panyu	2	139
Nanhai	8	133
Mei County	12	221

SOURCE: Wing Fong Lau, "Educational Development in Taishan County,"
pp. 207–8, citing the 1934 *Guangdongsheng ershisannianduo jiaoyu gaikuang* [General
situation of education in Guangdong Province, 1934], published by the Guangdong
Provincial Educational Bureau.

from U.S. compatriots to build the Chengwu Elementary School in
Duanfen. Over the next few decades, overseas capital and the initial prod-
ding of education-minded county magistrate Tan Shoufang produced at
least 86 elementary schools and nine middle schools before 1949.[136] In 1909
remittances made possible the construction of the Libian elementary school
in Sanba. The next year, Taishan's first and foremost middle school, the
Taishan Public Middle School, opened its doors to more than 100 students,
courtesy of funds from overseas. Other major projects completed with overseas Taishanese backing included the County Teachers' College in 1928,[137]
the Taishan County Library in 1922, the Women's Teachers' College in 1930,
and the first clan middle school built with overseas capital in 1932. Overseas
Taishanese also made improvements to these schools possible. In 1926,
Canadian Taishanese donated Can.$249,596 to add new classrooms and the
No. 3 dormitory to the Taishan Middle School. Not to be outdone, U.S.
Taishanese donated US$240,000 to build a library, high-school classrooms,
and dorms in 1929. In addition, some of these funds were used to buy rental
properties in Guangzhou and Hong Kong to add to the school's revenues.

TABLE 4

School Attendance in Selected Guangdong Counties, 1935

County	Number of school-age children	Number of school-age children in school	Percentage in school
Taishan	89,136	66,645	75
Zhongshan	147,870	52,815	36
Shantou	20,515	15,959	78
Shunde	56,740	31,873	56
Enping	24,360	16,664	68
Kaiping	71,078	71,078	36
Chixi	2,851	1,033	36
Xinhui	180,000	61,875	34

SOURCE: Wing Fong Lau, "Educational Development in Taishan County," pp. 204–6, citing statistics from the 1935 edition of *Guangdongsheng ershisinnianduo jiaoyu gaikuang* [General situation of education in Guangdong Province, 1935], published by the Guangdong Provincial Educational Bureau.

According to provincial statistics, by 1932, Taishan had 268 elementary schools and 1,010 lower-level elementary schools.[138] Excepting Guangzhou, Taishan was among the most well endowed with middle schools and middle-school teachers (see Table 3).

In 1934, Taishan's education budget of 1,181,307 yuan exceeded that of all other areas, including the wealthier counties of the Pearl River Delta, Zhongshan, Panyu, Nanhai, Shunde, and Dongguan, and outpaced by five times the budget of neighboring Xinhui.[139]

This expenditure resulted in high rates of school attendance as well as a greater number of children being educated. In 1932, Taishan had a 75 percent school attendance rate, male and female children included (see Table 4). And the number of children taught to read in Taishan far exceeded the number in even the better-endowed neighboring counties.

Prosperity and progress in Taishan manifested themselves in other ways as well. In 1909, through the vigorous efforts of Chen Yixi, Taishan became only the second place in China to boast a wholly Chinese-financed, wholly Chinese-built, functioning railroad. In 1904 and 1905, Chen Yixi and his partner, Yu Shi, raised money by touring Chinese communities in North America, Southeast Asia, and Hong Kong calling for the support of their compatriots. The recovery of railroad rights in China was the hot issue of the time, and many overseas Chinese were willing to contribute to the cause. Chen and Yu managed to collect Ch.$2.7 million. The first stage of the railroad was completed in March 1909 and linked Doushan to Taishan City and Gongyi. It took eleven more years and 3.4 million more dollars to lay a total of 137 kilometers of track centering on Taishan City and extending from the county seat of Xinhui to North Street in Jiangmen and on to Baisha.[140]

Although the railroad never reached Guangzhou and thus never connected to Hong Kong via the all-important Guangzhou-Kowloon line, it did bring many changes to Taishan. Merchants and laborers began going to Taishan City in increasing numbers. The town increased in size and population from 0.5 square kilometers and several thousand people to one square kilometer and more than 20,000 in population. In 1923 the ancient city walls were torn down and Taishan City expanded to include the neighboring areas of Xi'ning City and Ximen. Families of Gold Mountain guests began moving in and building homes and shops. There were several hundred businesses: banks; receiving agencies; doctors and herbalists; stores selling cloth, sundries, and building materials; old-fashioned Chinese banks; restaurants; and hotels.[141] With paved roads, electric streetlights, and Western storefronts, the town came to be known as "Little Guangzhou." Along with these highly visible signs of commercial growth, the railroad also brought the Gongyi machine factory and the Ningcheng Printing Shop, the first of nine print shops to start up in Taishan.[142]

Under the instigation of provincial leader Chen Jiongming, the Taishan Public Road Bureau came into being in 1921. During the 1920s and 1930s, 31 roads were built, with Taishan City at their center. In 1924 the first was completed linking Taishan City to Guangzhou via Sanbu. Another road finished that year connected Guanghai to the ports of Jiangmen and Macao. In 1926, Haiyan was connected to Taishan City as part of this network, and in 1928 Dajiang and Doushan became part of the web as well.[143]

To take advantage of these convenient new roads, Li Jinzhao requested permission to start the Jinshu Bus Company.[144] Additional bus services became available in 1926 when Huang Zaihua founded the privately run

Public Road Bus Company (Gonglu xingche gongsi).[145] That year, with the railroad, new roads, and two companies offering bus services, travel within Taishan became dramatically more convenient than it had been twenty years earlier, when walking was still the main form of local transport.

Gold Mountain guests imported other technological marvels to Taishan. In 1911 one businessman used machinery purchased in the United States to start a textile factory producing knit socks and knit shirts. In 1919 overseas capital brought light to the public streets of Taishan City with the Ever Bright Electric Company (Yongming dianli gongsi).[146] In 1926, in addition to starting a bus company, Huang Zaihua, a graduate of Columbia University's radio department, started the Zaihua Vocational School and began setting up a telephone system for Taishan, which went into operation in 1928 under the name Same-Sound Telephone Company (Tongsheng dianhua gongsi).[147] That was also the first year that Taishanese could enjoy moving pictures at the Guangsheng Movie Theater.

The influence of overseas Taishanese showed up in ways that were not as concrete but were equally tangible. Gold Mountain guests returned to Taishan dressed in Western suits and hats. They spoke a Taishanese infected with English terms. In 1900 one Guo Qizhao, who spent his youth overseas, produced a Taishanese-English dictionary.[148] To this day, Taishanese still use phrases such as *fan* rather than *wan* to mean "fun," *fan lian* rather than *xiaotiqing* for "violin," *lo mien* rather than *laoren* for "old man," and *pok sen* rather than *daquan* for "boxing."[149] In ways that required contact more personal than money, trickles of life in the United States seeped into Taishan, emphasizing the special characteristics and attributes acquired by Taishanese remaining at home because they had connections to people living abroad.

It is no wonder that by the 1930s, Taishanese attributed the best and most modern facets of life in their home county to the contributions of overseas Chinese. As one reporter wrote: "In the days when overseas Taishanese capital held its head high, the glory of Taishan permeated the entire world. Everyone cannot help but see the tremendous advances in the construction of roads, the remodeling of towns and cities, the making of houses, and the building of schools."[150]

Other aspects of life made possible by Chinese overseas generated less-beneficial results. The shimmering prosperity that came with Gold

Mountain remittances attracted bandits and thieves to Taishan. After houses and schools, the most commonly constructed buildings were guard towers, designed to help village militia keep watch for incoming raids and to house people and their valuables during actual attacks. Between 1912 and 1926, 5,000 such fortifications were built.[151] According to a 1949 survey, there were over 48,000 guns in Taishan's private sector.[152]

Banditry was a problem throughout the nineteenth century but seemed to worsen after the fall of the Qing. For example, between 1917 and 1926, Guanghai endured 73 bandit raids affecting 3,214 households.[153] Gold Mountain guests and their families were favored targets. In the first six months of 1922, *Xinning Magazine* reported 32 bandit attacks in which ten were wounded, twelve killed, and more than 100 kidnapped. Chonglou, Doushan, and Duhu, all regions with high concentrations of overseas Taishanese, suffered the greatest losses.[154] Assaults ranged from kidnapping and murder to ordinary mugging, breaking and entering during the night, petty theft, and pickpocketing.

Bessie Jeong recalls that her father and two brothers were kidnapped when they returned to visit China in 1918. The bandits demanded a ransom of US$10,000 and released one brother to go to Hong Kong to borrow the money. Her father managed to survive the ordeal, although her other brother was killed.[155] Often the demands of the kidnappers could be met only at the cost of bankrupting the Gold Mountain guest's family. In 1921, You Zuoheng of Shanju New Village in Haiyan was kidnapped. A village elder went to the bandits' base of Fucao to bargain for his safe return. Simply negotiating You's survival cost US$250. The ransom itself was US$3,800. You Zuoheng emerged from the experience unscathed but had to return to the United States, his once middle-class family now impoverished by the bandits' demands.[156]

Gold Mountain guests had to be careful in their day-to-day activities. One returnee, known only as Mr. Li of Tongan Village, lost Ch.$600 dollars to a pickpocket while boarding a crowded train at Ximen Station.[157] And the wives of Gold Mountain guests could not be too ostentatious. In December 1934 a woman recently married to a man returned from abroad, Huang Wenzong of Chengdong Cangan Village, went to visit her mother "dressed in fashionable clothes, wearing jewelry of gold that dazzled the eye." On her way home, she encountered a man with a knife who made off with valuables worth more than 200 yuan.[158] Overseas Chinese were not even safe in their graves. Yuan Yiyan of Cow Road Village near Taishan City had supported his family from overseas for twenty years and had accumulated lots of savings. He retired to Hong Kong in 1931 but died of illness the next year. His body was shipped back to Taishan to be buried. However, thieves heard that the coffin contained 300 ounces of silver and went to dig it up. Because the coffin had been most strongly made in Hong Kong, they managed to pry open only one corner and when dawn broke were caught by Yuan's relatives.[159]

A more bizarre attack involved Woman Tan, the wife of an overseas Taishanese surnamed Zhang, as well as her six-year-old son and mother-in-law. Woman Tan took her son to visit her mother in Taishan City. In their absence, a bandit entered the house and took everything, but stayed long enough to cook enough rice to mold into the likeness of a six-year-old boy. He put clothes on the figure, stuck two chopsticks in its head, emptied the night-soil bucket over Woman Tan's bed, and left without attracting the notice of the elderly mother-in-law. When the old woman entered the kitchen and saw what appeared to be the corpse of her grandson sitting with two chopsticks stuck in his head, she nearly died of fright. After this incident, Woman Tan persuaded one of her sisters-in-law to stay with them.[160]

Most people had to provide for their own protection from such incidents because both provincial and county authorities proved unable to restore safe conditions.[161] When Howard Louis and his 92-year-old father, Ah Louis, returned to Lung On Village in Oak Gong, they decided to throw a huge banquet. In addition to buying gifts for the village, building a two-story building especially for the feast, inviting 1,200 people from the surrounding area, hiring a Chinese orchestra, locating enough bowls and chopsticks to feed all the guests at the same time, and purchasing numerous chickens, ducks, twelve pigs, and six goats, Louis and his father had to hire road guards to protect against bandits. The guards remained on alert for the several days that the festivities continued. As the banquet ended, the guards warned that bandits were moving in but that people still had enough time to escape to Guangzhou. Louis and his father managed to do so, and the guards caught the bandits. The two returned once to the village to make their farewells but were careful to leave most of their belongings in Guangzhou. Louis's father, who had intended to retire to Taishan, found himself tremendously disappointed by the lack of local safety and the presence of only one person from his childhood still surviving in the village, and so he determined to return to San Luis Obispo in California to die.[162]

But for better or worse, by the 1930s the economy and society of Taishan were inextricably yoked to the lives of overseas workers. When the Great Depression took its toll on Chinese working in the United States, people in Taishan also suffered. *Xinning Magazine* described the crisis: "Before our Taishan was prosperous, and now it is suddenly embroiled in great financial difficulties. Why? When we investigate and consider the reasons, we find they can be divided into two kinds: the internal and the external. As for the external reasons, the world economy is in crisis and overseas Taishanese [*hai-wai yiqiao*] are out of work and have no means of helping with expenses in the home villages."[163] For those who still had jobs, wages fell dramatically. During the 1920s, $50 per week for a laundryman had been considered a good income. During the Depression, people settled for $20 to $25.[164] Sam K. W. Yee remembers of the Great Depression: "There were no jobs, everyone with money went back to China and killed time there, but they went home. For example they finished their work and went back home to kill time, that's better than killing time here." Added Yee's wife, "Back home there was land to farm!"[165] But many who returned to China had no savings and no land. They returned bearing neither gifts nor gold. Those at home did not blame them for losing their jobs or for failing to honor the ancestors by returning without fanfare and stories of their grand success. Rather they sympathized with their plight, complained loudly about discrimination against Chinese overseas, and coined a new term to describe unemployed Gold Mountain guests, *nanqiao*, or down-on-their-luck overseas Chinese. Quietly these men reentered life in Taishan. The county government took steps to register them and allocate relief and, in a reversal of the accustomed flow of aid, raised money to establish a relief center (*jiujiyuan*) for unemployed overseas Taishanese.[166]

Some Gold Mountain guests managed to hang on in the United States, and a few were able to keep sending money. Taishan itself survived the Depression, although many businesses had failed by the time the Chinese economy recovered in 1936.[167] Throughout the bad times, despite the droves of dejected *nanqiao* returning to Taishan and Guangzhou, Taishanese retained their belief that it was better to go abroad than to stay at home.

Educating the young and importing manufacturing and communications technology did not fundamentally change job opportunities in Taishan, and young men, no matter how good their training, still ended up working overseas, as did Ray Lue, who went to school for five years, and Eddie E. Lee's older brothers, who attended school for nine.[168] In 1934, Robert Lee, a well-educated graduate of the county teachers' college, came to the United States at his father's insistence "for the sake of survival."[169] Other parents and Gold Mountain guests shared the same insecurities about remaining in Taishan:

> Well, I tell you one thing. In those days, in China, or Hong Kong, you get out of school, means you don't get a job, period. That means life is probably pretty tough for you. It's almost impossible to find a job. So coming to America is one of the better ways perhaps to have a better future. So everybody told you it's good here. They don't tell you the laundrymen, people work eighteen hours a day, they don't tell you this. They only tell you, it's a lot of gold, go and dig.[170]

A laundryman interviewed by Paul Siu in Chicago remembers his state of mind before going to Gold Mountain: "Oh! I don't know. When I heard about a chance to go to America, the hardship just didn't occur to me. All I got excited about was to take the chance—going to America! . . . Now I am here, I begin to feel America is work, work, work. It is nothing to get excited about."[171] Another Chicago laundryman interviewed by Paul Siu recalls arguing with his mother over the fate of his younger brother. The Gold Mountain guest believed that since the brother was trained as a tailor he should be able to make a decent living in China. However, their mother wanted to have yet another son in the United States.[172] Their differences of opinion stemmed from the mother's ignorance of the difficult working conditions in the United States and the unwillingness of overseas Taishanese to tell people in Taishan that Gold Mountain guests were, in reality, nothing more than clothes washers, waiters, and cooks. They used the euphemism clothing store (*yishangguan*) instead of laundry (*xiyiguan*) to disguise that they worked as much as seventeen hours each day standing in the damp heat generated by steaming irons and boiling machines. They pretended to be men of business so that they might preserve the honor and envy that accrued to those lucky enough to go to Gold Mountain.[173]

Conclusion

After arriving in their new homes, most immigrants think in terms of expectations for a better future or compare their lives with the lower standards of the place they have just left. This displacement from immediate realities makes bearable the extreme hardships endured for the sake of future rewards or undertaken for the welfare of well-loved dependents left behind. Taishanese Americans were no different. Many of them went about their daily lives commuting between the two extremes of exaggerated expectations for America and the enhanced satisfaction and comfort they would enjoy once they managed to return home. Faith in a better future, someplace else, made bearable the loneliness, the long hours of toil, the arduous trans-Pacific crossings, and the fears that one might never see loved ones again. Taishanese wanted to believe, despite evidence to the contrary, that by going to Gold Mountain men could make fast and easy fortunes, then retire to Taishan and enjoy life with wives and sons. This dream persisted in spite of the thousands of men who sacrificed their youth and their health in decades of hard labor and, in the end, never went back to Taishan. Some did manage to establish new lives and families for themselves abroad; others clung to the hope of returning but never made enough money to realize their dream. Despite the considerable odds, Taishanese continued to chase the rainbow on both sides of the Pacific, believing that a pot of gold was waiting in America at one end and family and a life of leisure at the other.

Slipping Through the Golden Gate: Immigration Under Chinese Exclusion

There are doubtless now in this country at least as many Chinese not entitled to residence here as of the lawfully resident class, and they have entered in every way that can be imagined, from the apparently regular method of deceiving the officers to being packed in refrigerator freight cars or in the refrigerators of dining cars crossing the land boundaries, or in the coal bunkers, chain lockers, or forepeaks of vessels sailing from the Orient, or the West Indies. A Chinaman apparently will undergo any hardship or torture, take any risk, or pay any sum of money up to $1,000 to enjoy the forbidden but much coveted privilege of living and working in the United States.

—*U.S. Commissioner of Immigration, 1909*

Pursuit of opportunities on Gold Mountain led Taishanese to defy U.S. immigration laws designed to secure national borders against the presence of unwanted Chinese. The dependence of Taishanese on out-migration as an economic strategy brought them into direct opposition with the racially defined protectionist agendas of both the U.S. government and a majority of white Americans. Believing Chinese to be un-American, unassimilable, and unworthy of participation in a democratic society, the U.S. government attempted to exclude Chinese from the American economy, polity, and geographic territory.

In 1882, Congress passed the first of many anti-Chinese Exclusion acts that would prohibit all but a few carefully specified classes of Chinese from entering the United States. These laws barred Chinese from acquiring U.S. citizenship by naturalization and required each Chinese resident in the country to carry on his or her person at all times a certificate verifying legal entry into the country; anyone who failed to do so risked deportation.[1] Exclusion also took the form of economic boycotts, social ostracism, physical attacks, and statutes that penalized Chinese business practices. It was, however, the immigration laws that provided the most vivid symbol of the status of Chinese living in America before World War II. These laws cemented the outsider status of Chinese Americans: although they failed to prevent Chinese from migrating to the United States, they ensured that most who did come after 1882 could only do so illegally. The widely practiced crime of immigration fraud prevented Chinese Americans from joining mainstream society while embedding them even more firmly into the networks of kinship and native place that bound their lives to Guangdong.

The bulk of this chapter describes the terms of Exclusion and the attempts of the U.S. government to protect its national territory against the continuing incursions of Taishanese. I begin by briefly describing the economic activities of Chinese during the nineteenth century and the racist backlash that ensued. White, working-class fears of unfair competition from slave-like "coolies" eventually led to the confining of Chinese into the narrow economic niches with which they are still commonly identified: laundries, restaurants, domestic service, and curio stores in downtown Chinatown tourist strips. I then briefly explore anti-Chinese sentiments during the 1870s and 1880s that fed into racialized constructions of a national identity threatened by hordes of ungodly Mongolian masses. Widespread fears of conquest by "Orientals" made the anti-Chinese movement a potent political platform and Exclusion an all but undeniable necessity. In 1882, Congress took its first steps toward excluding Chinese by strictly limiting and defining the categories of Chinese who could enter the United States. Chinese laborers and Chinese women were the primary targets of Exclusion. Broadly interpreted in law and practice, the term "laborer" made most Chinese men ineligible to enter the United States, and the widespread assumption that most Chinese women were members of the legally restricted category of prostitutes reduced the number of women who came to a trickle. A developing immigration bureaucracy enforced these laws by claiming increasing powers to demand and evaluate evidence in hopes of preventing ineligible Chinese, especially the dangerous Chinese laborer, from coming under false pretenses. Despite all the measures taken by both Congress and the immigration bureau, however, the U.S. government failed to secure its borders against Chinese.

The main problem encountered by the immigration service was that Chinese, and Taishanese in particular, refused to accept the terms of the Exclusion laws and persisted in coming to the United States.[2] Economic and legal discrimination did not discourage Chinese from coming; it only made those who managed to immigrate less inclined to settle permanently and much more dependent on other Chinese. The Exclusion laws and zealous immigration bureaucracy required Chinese to have extensive and reliable networks of friends, kinsmen, or fellow villagers already in the country. To survive the scrutiny of immigration authorities, Chinese had to systematically produce paper identities, or slots, of people eligible to enter the United States, as well as supporting evidence for each paper identity. Chinese relied a great deal upon other Chinese in networks secured by ties of kinship and native-place to help them document their status.

Because Taishanese had immigrated in relatively greater numbers during the 1860s and 1870s, they had the most connections to help them continue coming after immigration conditions became more restrictive. Thus, Exclusion extended the preponderance of Taishanese in Chinese American society. In 1876, two different Chinese visitors to the United States estimated that Taishanese numbered 70,000 to 75,000, or 45 to 48 percent of the total estimated population of 155,000 Chinese.[3] In addition, perhaps half of the 40,000 members of the Hehe Association were also Taishanese. In the mid-1930s, the number of Taishanese in the United States was approximately 13,500 out of a total population of 27,500 Chinese, or around 49 percent of the total.[4] In effect, Exclusion reinforced the relationships binding Taishanese in America to each other and to Taishan. Circumventing discriminatory immigration laws required high levels of organization and coordination. That Taishanese managed to continue immigrating to the United States for decades after the law was passed is testament to the effectiveness of their network and their ability to adjust to complex changes in immigration policy and enforcement. However, their success at outwitting immigration authorities did not bode well for their future in America. Most Taishanese could enter America only by breaking its laws, an act that distanced them even further from mainstream white society and magnified the importance of networking and secrecy within the Taishanese American community.

Economic Exclusion

Chinese did not begin their American lives in such isolation. In the nineteenth century they worked in a score of different arenas, making invaluable contributions to the development of the California economy.[5] By the second decade of the twentieth century, however, discrimination reduced the choice of economic endeavors available to Chinese to a mere handful.

Chinese first started leaving China for the United States in significant numbers during the 1850s in search of gold. In 1860 over 70 percent of Chinese men older than fifteen in California were miners. When the gold ran out or the opposition of white miners made mining too risky, they turned to other tasks. During the 1860s and 1870s, Chinese built intercontinental railroads around and through high mountain ranges and across wide expanses of inhospitable desert. They grew vegetables and peddled them from the back of carts. They helped to establish the foundations of California's agricultural fortunes by teaching other farmers how to grow fruit. It was Chinese who performed the backbreaking labor of draining swampy marshes and building levees needed to transform the Sacramento delta into valuable farmland.[6] In 1870, Chinese constituted about one-twelfth of the population of the state but contributed one-quarter of its hired labor.[7]

Chinese turned to a variety of other enterprises, some entrepreneurial, some not. Between 1870 and 1880, increasing numbers of Chinese began working in factories that produced goods as varied as brooms and women's underwear. Chinese opened their own cigar factories, and independently ventured into manufacturing shoes, slippers, boots, candles, and matches as well.[8] As independents, they fished for shrimp in camps throughout the Bay Area and caught abalone around San Diego, Los Angeles, and Santa Barbara. In 1859, Chinese began working in the cigar industry in San Francisco before leaving to produce and market their own lower-priced goods during the 1860s using Spanish-sounding labels such as Cabanes and Co. and Ramirez and Co.[9] And of course they opened their own restaurants, grocery stores, and laundries.

As early as July 1849, a California newspaper, the *Alta California*, made the first mention of a Chinese restaurant, the Canton Restaurant on Jackson Street in San Francisco. In 1851, in response to a local need for laundry washers so desperate that men sent their shirts to China to be washed, one Wah Lee started the first laundry in San Francisco: "By 1870, the majority of more than 2,000 laundry men in San Francisco were Chinese." Six years later, San Francisco boasted some 300 Chinese laundries manned by an average of five workers each.[10] Because whites disdained the odor and backbreaking work, Chinese were able to develop a niche in the American economy, and Chinese-run laundries soon appeared in Chicago, St. Louis, Baltimore, New York, Montreal, and Quebec during the 1870s. By the turn of the century, such small enterprises were about the only businesses available for ownership or employment to Chinese.

Economic discrimination assumed various guises. The city of San Francisco and the state of California passed laws that targeted Chinese for harassment. A sampling includes the Foreign Miners' Tax (1853), which was collected only from Chinese; the "Queue" Ordinance (1873), which mandated that the hair of imprisoned Chinese be cut off in violation of Qing laws;[11] the Laundry Ordinance (1873), which imposed a tax on laundries that did *not* use horses and vehicles for delivery—that is, the businesses of Chinese; and a law prohibiting pedestrians from carrying poles on their shoulders while walking on sidewalks (1873).[12]

Some anti-Chinese activity was also violent. Attacks against Chinese began as early as May 1852, when white miners held meetings in both Yuba County in northern California and the Columbia Mining District in southern California resolving to expel Chinese from the mines. Chinese as far north as Shasta County were forced to leave their claims. On October 24, 1871, in Los Angeles, nineteen Chinese out of the city's total population of 172 were killed in the Chinese quarter. Six years later, several Chinese buildings in the area were burned and razed. On October 13, 1880, several thousand white men attacked 400 Chinese in downtown Denver, killing one, and burning and looting property worth $53,655 for several days thereafter. Perhaps the most infamous incident was the massacre at Rock Springs in Montana. Angered that the Union Pacific had hired more Chinese than whites to work on the Rock Springs mines, about 150 armed white men attacked their Chinese coworkers, killing 28, wounding fifteen, and driving the rest out of town on September 2, 1885. This period of violence resulted in the physical condensation of the Chinese American community as small groups of Chinese scattered across the American West working mines and building railroads retreated to the relative safety of urban Chinatowns.

Unions and business leaders headed more organized efforts that struck at Chinese economically. Through a series of laws and boycotts, Chinese were forced to leave all forms of manufacturing and food-processing work. In the mid-1880s, the Cigar-Makers Union succeeded in eliminating Chinese from the industry. Around the turn of the century, legislation that targeted the work patterns of Chinese eventually forced them out of shrimp and abalone fishing.[13] In San Francisco, white consumers boycotted Chinese-made clothing and shoes. In 1880, Chinese owners and workers in such industries had numbered 1,023 and 4,264 respectively, but their number had decreased to only 84 and 1,694 in 1900. By 1920 there were almost no Chinese makers of boots or cigars left in the city. Chinese also began disappearing from California's agricultural sector during the 1910s and early 1920s as the first generation of farmers began retiring and low rates of immigration and births among American Chinese did not produce a younger generation to take their place.[14]

By 1920, 48 percent of Chinese in the United States worked in small businesses, laundries, restaurants, or stores, and 27 percent were domestic workers. Only 11 percent worked in agriculture, 9 percent in manufacturing and crafts. That year, there were only 151 Chinese miners remaining in the United States.[15]

Despite the dwindling economic opportunities available to them in the United States, Taishanese continued to arrive simply because working as an outcast laundry worker on Gold Mountain still promised a higher income and greater stability than remaining in China. During the 1920s, hired laundrymen could earn US$50 during a good week and support a family in China on just US$100–150 per year.[16] Although incomes fell to about US$25 per week during the 1930s, an immigrant with a little savings could still acquire ownership of a laundry for the relatively low investment of US$3,000, or only US$2,800 if buying from a clansman.[17]

The presence of such friends, relatives, and fellow villagers did much to mitigate the hardships on Gold Mountain.[18] Clansmen were the most likely employers of other Taishanese. When accumulating funds to invest in a business of their own, Taishanese could borrow up to several thousand dollars from cousins and other Taishanese. Kinship also provided the basis for most business relationships. According to a survey conducted by sociologist Paul Siu, 60 percent of Chinese-run laundries in Chicago during the 1930s were owned by "cousins." Partnerships of "strangers" constituted only 10 percent of the total.[19]

Kinship provided other sorts of networks. According to historian Renqiu Yu, circles of friends and acquaintances formed lending societies known as *hui* to pool resources and generate lump sums for investment.[20] Forty or 50 men would band together in groups known as *gongsi fang* to rent apartments that served as safe-houses when any member lost his job or needed a place to stay. The men in these groups helped each other with medical expenses, provided a support network during hard times, kept track of each other, and shared the occasional meal on days off.[21] Larger associations organized on principles of surname or native place, such as the Ningyang Association or the Hehe Association, helped people find jobs, mediated conflicts, lent money, paid for immigration lawyers, provided burials for the indigent, and organized fund-raising drives for charities and war relief.

Taishanese managed to survive in an economically adverse environment primarily because these organizations and kinship networks provided them with the resources and connections needed to find jobs and establish small businesses in the United States. Without these contacts, they could not have found employment on Gold Mountain.

Legal Exclusion

The patterns of migration established before 1882 continued to guide Taishanese in their search for better incomes and higher standards of living for their families even after passage of the Exclusion laws. As the expanding realm of Taishanese economic activities clashed with the protectionist agenda of the American government, immigration became the main site of their conflict.

Signs of anti-Chinese sentiment became evident only a couple of years after the recorded number of Chinese arriving in the United States annually grew to more than a handful. Although a trickle of sailors, merchants, and students had landed on American shores in the late eighteenth and early nineteenth centuries, it was the Gold Rush that jumpstarted the migration of Chinese. In 1851, 2,716 Chinese passed through the San Francisco Customs House. The next year this number increased sixfold, to more than 20,000. That year, California governor John Bigler became the first public official to voice the opinion that measures should be taken to stem the tide of Asian immigration. Despite widespread support, Governor Bigler was unable to act on this notion because an 1849 Supreme Court decision had determined immigration to be a matter of foreign commerce, controllable only by Congress and the federal government. The state of California, therefore, could not pass legislation to police its own borders.

As host to some 70 to 80 percent of all Chinese in America throughout the 1870s and 1880s, however, California remained a hotbed of an anti-Chinese agitation that eventually swept the entire nation.[22] In 1867, California Democrats urged Congress to forbid Chinese from entering the United States, as expressed in the following resolution:

> That the power to regulate foreign immigration being vested in Congress, it is the duty of that body to protect the Pacific states and territories from an undue influx of Chinese and Mongolians, and it is the duty of the legislature of this state to petition Congress to endeavor to obtain the adoption of such regulations as shall accomplish this object, and the legislature should use all its power to prevent the introduction of Mongolian laborers.[23]

As illustrated by comments published in a New York newspaper in 1869, others across the country also believed that Chinese threatened the very existence of the United States as a nation and as a civilization:

> Does not the Chinese question merit more attention than it has received? A little cloud now on the far Western horizon, does it not bid fair to overshadow the whole future of the Republic? The 60,000 or 100,000 Mongolians on our Western coast are the thin edge of the wedge which has for its base the 500,000,000 of Eastern Asia. . . . The Chinaman can live where stronger than he would starve. Give him fair play and this quality enables him to drive out stronger races. . . . [Unless Chinese immigration is checked] the youngest home of the nations must in its early manhood follow the path and meet the doom of Babylon, Nineveh and Rome.[24]

Just a year later, Congress made the first of many decisions to exclude Chinese from the American polity. When discussing legislation that would grant citizenship through naturalization, a process designed primarily to give suffrage to former slaves, Congress explicitly decided that Chinese, or

"Mongolians" as they were known then, would not be eligible. In short, Congress determined that Chinese were incapable of *becoming* Americans. Throughout the 1870s, a national depression exacerbated desires to rid the land of Chinese. Angry white men sought reasons for their unemployment and declining wages and readily found Chinese to blame. At the heart of anti-Chinese sentiment was the fear of Chinese, defined by race, as economic competitors. In a California newspaper, *The Argonaut*, editorialist H. N. Clement espoused the following view:

> I oppose Chinese immigration, not because the Chinaman sells his labor cheaply, but because his civilization is such as to enable him to sell his labor cheaply. . . . The primary reason I oppose Chinese immigration . . . is that they belong to a non-assimilative race—a race which has been among us twenty years and to whom we are, as yet, strangers—a race and a people who come not to escape oppression and to seek a free government, where they can have liberty of thought and freedom of action, but solely for the purpose of making money. . . . They are thus, in every sense of the word, aliens. *I want no accessions from any race or people who bring with them nothing except muscle—who do not aspire at least, to be American citizens—who degrade labor by their stolid and servile habits and manner of living . . . content to be mere machines driven by their employers.* . . . Such a system of labor is semi-slavery or serfdom.[25] [*emphasis added*]

Clement's comments, written seven years after Congress had mandated that Chinese could not become American citizens by naturalization, fed upon pervasive images of Chinese as a race of degraded "coolies" who could never aspire to the higher level of civilization embodied by America's democracy.[26] Some leaders of the anti-Chinese movement asserted that Chinese were not only an unassimilable blot on the U.S. landscape, but also a danger to any Western civilization in which they were allowed to remain. Before Congress, a California spokesman disparaged the fitness of Chinese to live in America:

> They can never assimilate with us . . . [because] they are a perpetual, unchanging, and unchangeable alien element that can never become homogeneous; that their civilization is demoralizing and degrading to our people; that they degrade and dishonor labor; that they can never become citizens, and that an alien, degraded labor class, without desire of citizenship, without education, and without interest in the country it inhabits, is an element

both demoralizing and dangerous to the community within which it exists.[27]

Such stereotypes enabled labor leaders and the Democratic Party to put forth all but irrefutable arguments against Chinese immigration in the aftermath of the Civil War and Reconstruction. The Republican Party had gained ascendancy during the Civil War under the slogans of freeing the slaves and maintaining the Union. In postbellum America, however, Democrats managed to return to power by invoking Jacksonian ideologies of race in which nonwhites were characterized as intrinsically inferior and incapable of participating in America's democratic institutions. Specifically, they argued that free white workingmen had to be protected from unfair and degrading competition from "slavelike" Chinese. In the 1870s, even as they retreated from the original goals of Reconstruction and equalizing the status of blacks and whites, Republicans could not justify refusing to protect the United States from the invading Mongols.[28] In the face of labor's compelling construction of Chinese as threats to white "free" labor, Republican support for a racially equal society had to give way for the sake of a free, democratic, and white America.[29]

The speed and strength with which the anti-Chinese movement spread across the country produced an abrupt change in attitude on the part of the federal government toward Chinese immigrants. As recently as 1868 it had signed the Burlingame Treaty with the Chinese government in order to protect commerce between China and the United States. At the time, the treaty also sought to secure a reliable supply of cheap Chinese labor for the American economy by guaranteeing both Chinese and Americans the reciprocal rights of "free migration and emigration."[30] This formally ratified agreement posed the primary obstacle to congressional passage and presidential approval of any law designed to limit the immigration of Chinese when attitudes changed. Not until Rutherford B. Hayes renegotiated the Burlingame Treaty in 1880 did the United States reclaim the right to "regulate, limit, or suspend" the "coming or residence" of Chinese laborers. Under the terms of the new agreement, only teachers, students, tourists, returning laborers, and merchants retained the right to immigrate. Congress acted swiftly to ratify and proclaim the treaty in October 1881. The first Exclusion Act followed soon after.

On May 6, 1882, President Chester A. Arthur signed into law an

Exclusion act that would remain in force until 1943. The law banned the immigration of Chinese laborers and permitted only six categories of Chinese to enter the United States: teachers, students, tourists, properly certified returning laborers, merchants, merchants' family members, and diplomats and their families. Chinese immigration became increasingly difficult over the next few decades.

Through trial and error, customs and later immigration officials in conjunction with Congress developed new laws and practices of Exclusion targeted at Chinese laborers. Congress passed a series of supplemental laws designed to strengthen Exclusion, primarily by strictly limiting definitions of exempt classes of Chinese and expanding the scope of the term "laborer." In 1884, Congress determined that peddlers and sellers of dried seafood could not claim to be merchants. In 1888 the Scott Act prohibited the entry, or even return, of Chinese laborers for twenty years, forbade the issuance of new Certificates of Return, and declared null and void all certificates of identity previously issued to Chinese laborers then visiting overseas. Thus 20,000 duly registered and certified Chinese who had temporarily departed the United States under the terms of the 1882 act were stranded abroad.[31]

In 1892, when renewing the 1882 Exclusion Act for ten more years, Congress legislated that all Chinese persons legally admitted to the United States must register within one year and carry a Certificate of Residence or be deported. The latter measure was designed to cut down on the number of Chinese sneaking across land borders and working in the United States without undergoing the scrutiny of immigration officials.[32] At the same time, it broadened the legal definition of laborer while narrowing that of merchant. The term "laborer" was clarified to include "both skilled and unskilled manual laborers" and applied to Chinese working as miners, fishermen, peddlers, and laundrymen or in the preparation and preservation of seafood. To claim merchant status, Chinese had to demonstrate that they were occupied solely with the buying and selling of merchandise at a fixed place of business and that they owned at least part of the business. If the individual claiming to be a merchant engaged at any time in any of the activities deemed to be those a laborer, he would lose his merchant status and could be deported from the United States.[33] In practice, the immigration service found that any Chinese not proven to be a merchant, student, teacher, diplomat, or tourist was a laborer and therefore ineligible to enter America.[34]

In 1903, China denounced a treaty it had signed in 1894 that authorized the extension of the Exclusion Act for ten more years. In January 1904, in retaliation, Congress voted without debate to extend the Exclusion laws *indefinitely* by attaching a rider to a routine appropriations bill. Chinese responded to the 1904 extension of the Exclusion laws with a boycott of American goods in 1905. The only effect of this action, taken primarily by merchants in Shanghai and Guangzhou, was that the immigration service's treatment of merchants and diplomats improved somewhat, but the basic goal of excluding Chinese laborers did not change.

Because Chinese were the only people excluded from the United States by race and class, their immigration cases fell under legal and bureaucratic jurisdictions different from those of other immigrants. Only in 1924 was the exclusion of Chinese brought under control of the same set of laws and immigration officials supervising immigration in general. This, however, only made it more difficult to enter the United States. The Immigration Act of May 26, 1924 (43 Stat. 153) was enacted to maintain the ethnic balance of the United States by limiting the number of immigrant aliens—that is, those eligible for permanent residency and later citizenship, to one-sixth of 1 percent of the total number of that group present in the United States in 1890.[35] Because so few Chinese were present in the United States, the quota for immigrant alien Chinese was only 105. Because the Exclusion laws remained in effect for Chinese, immigration authorities claimed to be unable to find enough eligible Chinese each year to fill even this tiny allotment. Those Chinese allowed to enter the United States previously continued to do so without regard for the quota, although the definition of merchants was tightened to include only those engaged in international trade (see Table 5).

The Exclusion laws remained in effect until 1943, when the demands of foreign diplomacy and alliances formed for the purpose of war led the U.S. government to determine that it could no longer afford to exclude citizens of its wartime ally, China.[36]

As illustrated by Table 5, these laws had significantly reduced the number of Chinese entering the United States. The biggest decreases occurred after passage of the first Exclusion Act and the 1924 general immigration bill.

Of the Chinese who managed to come to the United States each year, most did so by taking advantage of a legislative loophole overlooked by

TABLE 5

Chinese Immigrants to the United States, 1879–1940

Year	Chinese Immigrants to the United States	Year	Chinese Immigrants to the United States
1879	9,604	1897	3,363
1880	5,802	1898	2,071
1881	*11,890*	1899	1,660
1882	*39,579*	1900	1,247
1883	*8,031*	1901	2,459
1884	*279*	1902	1,649
1885	22	1903	2,209
1886	40	1904	4,309
1887	10	1905	2,166
1888	26	1906	1,544
1889	118	1907	961
1890	1,716	1908	1,397
1891	2,836	1909	1,943
1892	—	1910	1,968
1893	472	1911	1,460
1894	1,170	1912	1,765
1895	539	1913	2,105
1896	1,441	1914	2,502

(continued on next page)

Congress. The Fourteenth Amendment, originally passed to ensure citizenship for Americans of African descent liberated in the Civil War, declared that any person born in the United States was a citizen and had the right to confer citizenship on foreign-born minor children and, before 1924 and after 1930, foreign-born wives as well. In 1898 the U.S. Supreme Court decided in the case of Wong Kim Ark (169 U.S., 649) that this right extended to Chinese as well.[37] As I will describe later in this chapter, the Fourteenth Amendment would provide a narrow yet unsealable gateway for several generations of Chinese to come to America during the first half of the twentieth century.

TABLE 5   *(continued)*
Chinese Immigrants to the United States, 1879–1940

Year	Chinese Immigrants to the United States	Year	Chinese Immigrants to the United States
1915	2,660	1928	1,320
1916	2,460	1929	1,446
1917	2,237	1930	1,589
1918	1,795	1931	1,150
1919	1,964	1932	750
1920	2,330	1933	148
1921	4,009	1934	187
1922	4,406	1935	229
1923	4,986	1936	273
1924	*6,992*	1937	293
1925	*1,937*	1938	613
1926	1,751	1939	642
1927	1,471	1940	643

SOURCE: Helen Chen, "Chinese Immigration into the United States: An Analysis of Changes in Immigration Policies" (Ph.D. dissertation, Brandeis University, 1980), p. 174, table 12.
NOTES: Years and data in italics show the impact of the 1882 Exclusion law and the 1924 Immigration Act. Data for 1892 are not available.

Enforcing Exclusion

In 1926 the commissioner-general of immigration commented about Chinese immigrants to the United States: "Many, doubtless the majority, have secured admission through false testimony in courts or before the immigration officers at the ports of entry."[38] Both immigration officials and Chinese themselves estimated that of those who entered the United States during the period of Exclusion, 90 percent did so using fake papers.[39]

Language differences, ignorance of Chinese geography, and the inability of immigration officers to distinguish one Chinese person from another made it very difficult to carry out the intent of the Exclusion laws in the face of fierce determination by Chinese to circumvent them.[40] Most important, the immigration service was crippled by the lack of reliable documentary evidence to verify whether events like births and marriages occurred in the United States or in China. The immigration service could demand that merchants, students, and diplomats procure documents demonstrating their status from consuls in Guangzhou or Hong Kong, the Chinese government, and the schools that they planned to attend. But for Chinese immigrants claiming the right to enter as the children or spouses of merchants or U.S. citizens, almost no Chinese birth certificates or marriage licenses existed. The immigration service had to rely on the testimony of supporting witnesses who were, by and large, Chinese. This situation gave immigration officials great cause for unease because they suspected Chinese routinely lied in immigration interviews, as stated in the report filed by the bureau in 1907:

> There is no gainsaying the fact, established by the observations of all
> officers, both administrative and judicial, who have come into close contact
> with the enforcement of the Exclusion laws, that, upon questions affecting
> the admissibility to this country of Chinese, the testimony of persons of
> that race is almost universally unreliable. No matter how trustworthy and
> honorable a Chinese merchant or laborer may be in the conduct of his
> daily business, he seems to have no compunction whatever in practicing
> deceit concerning matters in which the Government is interested.[41]

In cases involving Chinese, immigration authorities attempted to make perjury more difficult by questioning both applicants and witnesses about a wealth of legally irrelevant minutiae concerning everyday life, a process described in a 1926 report:

> The problem now presented is the detection of the fraudulent cases among
> the applicants for admission at the ports of entry. In the case of sons of citi-
> zens and the minor children of merchants, the question of relationship may
> be determined only through long, involved examinations covering family
> history, relationship, village life, and other matters which should be of
> common knowledge to the applicant and his witness.[42]

As early as 1907, immigration authorities had considered this a justifiable strategy: "In cases where the only witnesses are Chinese and there is no documentary record, the court's only recourse is to cast discredit upon the witnesses by showing inconsistencies as to details of their evidence upon the same point."[43] Interviews could last all day for several days running and focus on small details. The following transcript is excerpted from an interview conducted in 1921:

Q: How many houses are there on your row, the first one?
A: Three. One of them is tumbled down.
Q: Which one is that?
A: The third one of the last one of the row.
Q: Who lives in the second one of your row?
A: Mah Sin Ick.
Q: What does he do?
A: He is dead.
Q: When did he die?
A: He died when I was a small boy.
Q: Did he leave a family?
A: Yes, he left two sons. His wife is dead also.
Q: When did she die?
A: I don't remember. She died long ago.
Q: What are the boys' names?
A: Mah Quock You, May Quock Him. I don't know the age of Quock You. Quock Him is over ten.
Q: Is the oldest one married?
A: No.
Q: Who takes care of them in that house?
A: The older brother has gone to Siam. The younger one is now working in Kung Yick village.
Q: Does anybody occupy that house?
A: No, it is empty.
Q: Then your house is the only house occupied on that row?
A: Yes.
Q: Who lives in the first house of the second row?
A: Mah Kong Kee.[44]

The same set of detailed questions was asked of each applicant and their witnesses. Answers had to match.

In delving into personal details that were not directly related to the matter under investigation, this type of questioning exceeded the scope of inquiry allowed to court officials. However, immigration officials justified their irregular procedures by referring to "the gravity of the difficulties inherent in the character of the Mongolian race to be met and surmounted."[45]

The questioning was so detailed and about such irrelevant information in people's daily lives that sometimes potential immigrants made mistakes even when they were trying to tell the truth. According to Ira Lee, who once worked on Angel Island as an interpreter:

> I think it could [happen]. I mean, it's quite detailed. On the other hand you see, what has happened, is that many of the cases where they are really not his real son, where they are paper sons, they are well coached, and so their testimony jibes. Whereas a real case, a legitimate case, where it's not the paper son coming in, they're legitimate, so they haven't gone to the trouble of making up these *hao gong* [coaching papers] you know. And preparing for it. They're the ones that get the wrong answers. Because they think that it's cut and dried.[46]

Despite the hours and energy expended by both immigration inspectors and Chinese, this interrogation system was not an effective means of distinguishing between real and fraudulent identities, if we accept the bureau's own estimated failure rate of 90 percent.

The immigration bureau's attempts to create a paper trail that could be used to trace the familial relationships of immigrating Chinese in the absence of documents like birth, marriage, and death certificates failed because Chinese were fully able to match the bureau's ability to keep records. By adapting existing networks of kinship and native place, Chinese developed informal yet effective strategies for defying the immigration bureau at its own paper-producing game.

Evading Exclusion: Identities and Evidence

Taishanese were well acquainted with the restrictiveness of the Exclusion laws and the zealousness of the immigration bureau. They accepted as a matter of course that in order to enter the United States they would have to assume an identity or status that was not their own. As pointed out by one immigrant, "Most people bought papers, so they were all fake. It was O.K.

as long as it obeyed American rules and regulations."[47] Immigration inspectors were less sanguine about this state of affairs. "There is an openness about the whole matter that is simply astounding. The tremendous fraud is hardly disguised."[48] However, for most Taishanese, there were no other options.

The cheapest method of entering the United States was to avoid immigration scrutiny altogether and cross a land border or jump ship. In 1903 the immigration bureau estimated that it cost $300 to cross the Canadian border into the United States. The money was distributed as follows: $20 for perjured testimony, $20 as commission to the middleman, $20 to the "government interpreters' fund," $80 for the attorney, and the rest for transportation and incidental expenses, members of the ring, and witnesses.[49] By 1909 the immigration service found that Chinese laborers entered the United States "at an average cost to each laborer of about $600."[50] However, this method of entry did not provide the certificates of residence that Chinese needed to have on their persons at all times in order to avoid being deported in case they were arrested by immigration authorities.

More expensive immigration schemes did provide the paperwork needed to remain in the country. Entering as students or as merchant sons gave Chinese the right to remain in the United States. In 1911 one scheme brought over teenage boys as students for between HK$1,324 and HK$2,000.

> An attorney of Seattle with two local Chinese students went to China and gathered together about one hundred boys for whom they secured Section 6 certificates. Sixty-six of these boys were admitted at this port and forty-four at the port of San Francisco, all destined to a private institution of learning of this city. . . . Out of the money collected a certain amount was paid to the men in Hongkong and Canton who gathered together the party, second-class transportation was furnished, and certain other expenses were paid.[51]

The organization of immigration under false pretenses was very systematic. People who made money from helping immigrants dipped into the illegal pot of honey repeatedly, as illustrated by the following account recorded by the immigration service in 1912.

> Between two and three years ago two women professors of a university here went to China and returned with some fifty Section 6 students. These women were assisted in gathering together this body of young men by an

Americanized Chinese student then taking a course at the same institution. It is said that these boys paid approximately $1,000 each, Hongkong currency, to get into the country in this manner. How this money was divided was not known, but one of the teachers admitted that she was paid her expenses and for her time. The other woman has since become a teacher in China, though at the present time she is endeavoring to have landed at the port of San Francisco some seventy-five more students. The fifty first brought in were kept in a private school in Seattle for about four months, when the school was abandoned, the pupils scattering to various parts of the country.[52]

However, Taishanese in the United States with student or merchant-son status risked being deported if caught laboring. In addition, neither students nor merchant sons had the status to earn a little extra money by bringing over other Taishanese as family members.

Establishing status as a merchant required more resources but gave greater flexibility. Before 1924, when merchant status was redefined and granted only to those conducting international trade, merchant papers (*shengyi zhi*) consisted of proof of membership in a U.S. business as well as testimony from two non-Chinese witnesses that the alleged businessman frequented his business premises reasonably often. Evidence of partnership was produced fairly regularly.

> It is a notorious fact that many small grocery establishments have twenty or more professed firm members, each claiming an interest of $1,000 therein, and at no time can the business done furnish support to more than a small minority of such partners, nor frequently can more than four or five members, and sometimes fewer, be found at the business stand. In many instances the other partners are found to be merely laborers, whose callused hands show plainly the nature of their occupation, pointing plainly to the conclusion that the alleged ownership and employment in a mercantile business is a mere pretense to secure them from arrest and deportation as unregistered laborers.[53]

One example of such a firm was Sun Wing Wo in Los Angeles, which listed twenty partners on paper. In reality, these partners were all cousins who started looking for jobs as soon as they arrived in the United States.[54] A firm called Guangfu Chang, located at 30 Waverly Place in San Francisco, was the site of another such ruse.[55] The immigration service acquired a copy of its partnership book that explicitly delineated the costs for providing "investors" with the right status to apply for return papers for themselves or to bring over a "son."[56] Immigrants could also seek out business partnerships for immigration purposes. In the letter quoted below, a Hong Kong broker, Lee Sing Ng, attempted to establish merchant identities with associates, Chin Gin and Chan Kew, in the United States:

> Should you see Mr. Chan Kew, please tell him to send me his address so that I can have him take care of those immigrants with certificates. As newcomers wish to be "New York merchants," it is necessary that the cooperation of a New York merchant be obtained. If Mr. Chan Kew can give the addresses of some of his friends, it will be welcomed. The sum of $60 in gold will be paid upon arrival.[57]

To gain the lesser privilege of permanent residency, the evidence required to prove merchant status was greater than that required to claim citizenship. Merchants had to produce documents showing their investment and membership within a business as well as two white witnesses who could testify that they were frequently on the premises.[58] Once proven, merchant status allowed Chinese men to travel back and forth between the United States and China and to bring over one wife and minor children.

Evading Exclusion: Paper Sons

By far the most flexible and desirable way to immigrate was as a native-born citizen or as such a citizen's son (*tushi zaizhi*) or grandson (*tusheng zaizhi*).[59] Having a status that could lead to citizenship was the most common means of passing immigration inspection, and the paper-son slot system that developed was the most sophisticated mechanism used by Chinese to evade the intent of the Exclusion laws.[60] Between July 1, 1920 and June 30, 1940, 71,040 Chinese entered as U.S. citizens; 66,039 Chinese entered under other statuses, including re-entry (see Table 6).

According to David R. Chan, the system first began as early as the 1880s, with merchants who brought over fake sons.[61] In the 1890s, Chinese began taking advantage of the Fourteenth Amendment right of citizenship to anyone born in the United States and their foreign-born children. Chinese started coming forward in the thousands to claim nativity in the United States, leading one federal judge to comment in 1901, "if the story told in the courts were true, every Chinese woman who was in the United States twenty-five years ago must have had at least 500 children."[62] The immigration bureau collected statistical evidence to support their suspicions of wide-scale immigration fraud being perpetrated by Chinese, as noted in its 1904 report:

> The Twelfth Census [1900] found in the United States 9,010 Chinese who claimed to have been born in this country. But of these, 6,657 were males and only 2,353 were females. It is practically an invariable rule that the two sexes are born and survive to any given age in almost equal numbers. . . . Figures showing that of the native Chinese 73.9 percent were male aroused in the Bureau of the Census both surprise and incredulity.[63]

The first generation of paper sons consisted of Chinese men who claimed to be native-born citizens. Some were actually born in the United States, but many simply crossed a U.S. border and after being picked up by immigration authorities then claimed to be returning from a visit to China. If they were American-born Chinese, they were citizens and had the right to enter. They were able to produce witnesses to verify their claims to birth in the United States. One immigration inspector described such proceedings with disgust:

> At the time set the case of Ah Sing or some other Ah would be called, and with the defendant absent from court throughout the whole session one other Chinese would be put upon the stand to testify to the defendant's having been born in the United States—most likely in the Chinatown of San Francisco, the alleged birthplace of tens of thousands of others that have made the claim at various times and at various places before him. Upon the uncorroborated testimony of this one Chinaman the other Chinaman, awaiting the issues in jail, would be declared a native of the United States. This goes on week after week and month after month, and has been going on for years.[64]

These cases were of particular concern to immigration officials because the word of only one Chinese witness made it possible for another Chinese person not only to enter the United States but also to gain all the rights and privileges of citizenship. In 1902, the immigration bureau noted that "a brisk business has grown up in consequence [of the Fourteenth Amendment], par-

TABLE 6
Percentage of Chinese Admitted to the United States as Citizens, 1900–1940

Year	Number of U.S. citizens entering (% of total)	Total Chinese admitted[a]	Year	Number of U.S. citizens entering (% of total)	Total Chinese admitted[a]
1900		5,799	1921	3,239 (38.9)	8,323
1901		4,064	1922	4,044 (40.3)	10,025
1902		3,768	1923	4,690 (44.4)	10,558
1903		2,982	1924	4,754 (44.4)	10,694
1904		2,676	1925	3,023 (48.5)	6,238
1905	634 (20.1)	3,153	1926	2,396 (44.1)	5,435
1906	915 (33.5)	2,732	1927	3,176 (50.1)	6,339
1907	929 (28.5)	3,255	1928	3,276 (49.5)	6,619
1908	1,609 (34.8)	4,624	1929	3,534 (50.2)	7,045
1909	2,530 (39.6)	6,395	1930	3,220 (49.1)	6,564
1910	2,109 (35.4)	5,950	1931	3,584 (55.3)	6,475
1911	1,639 (32.1)	5,107	1932	3,254 (56.8)	5,724
1912	1,756 (32.7)	5,374	1933	2,785 (60.1)	4,636
1913	2,171 (38.3)	5,662	1934	2,897 (64.2)	4,515
1914	2,201 (38.1)	5,773	1935	3,294 (63.6)	5,178
1915	1,990 (35.2)	5,661	1936	3,311 (64.8)	5,111
1916	1,932 (37.2)	5,193	1937	3,498 (67.7)	5,167

(continued)

TABLE 6   *(continued)*

Percentage of Chinese Admitted to the United States as Citizens, 1900–1940

Year	Number of U.S. citizens entering (% of total)	Total Chinese admitted[a]	Year	Number of U.S. citizens entering (% of total)	Total Chinese admitted[a]
1917	2,018 (42.3)	4,774	1938	5,396 (74.1)	7,282
1918	946 (29.9)	3,166	1939	4,328 (77.2)	5,607
1919	955 (28.6)	3,340	1940	3,351 (73.4)	4,567
1920	1,761 (37.5)	4,690			

SOURCE: This table is based on figures compiled by Helen Chen, "Chinese Immigration into the United States: An Analysis of Changes in Immigration Policies" (Ph.D. dissertation, Brandeis University, 1980), p. 181, table 15.

a. I have excluded tourists and those passing through the United States from these figures. Occasional surges in the number of tourists, for example during years with international expositions, would skew the numbers.

ticularly along our northern boundary, by which, through Chinese testimony solely, American citizens are being turned out in numbers by decisions of United States Commissioners."[65] Few non-Chinese witnesses and even fewer documents existed to verify the Chinese claims. Those living in a largely self-sufficient Chinese American enclave felt little need to register marriages and births formally or to call upon outsiders to officiate over such rites of passage. The 1906 earthquake and fire in San Francisco compounded this problem by destroying those few government documents that did exist in what was a tremendous stroke of luck for illegally immigrating Chinese who came afterward.

Once immigration authorities verified the citizenship of a Chinese man, that man could then bring in his foreign-born children and wife. In 1909, immigration authorities noted that "the second generation of this class is coming forward in such numbers the matter becomes more grave than ever. Thousands of Chinese have availed themselves of this claim and 'established' American birth by fraudulent means."[66] Table 7 illustrates the changing generations of Chinese who entered the United States, first as citizens through nativity, and then as the foreign-born offspring of such citizens. Although the immigration service did not keep count of all categories of Chinese entering as citizens before 1910, the statistics that are available reveal that between 1910 and 1914 the number of Chinese entering as the foreign-born children of citizens began to exceed those arriving as native-born with previously unverified status. Between 1910 and 1920, the largest number of immigrants were returning citizens who outnumbered by far those claiming citizenship for the first time. After 1920, however, the majority of Chinese claiming citizenship did so as the foreign-born offspring of citizens (see Table 7).[67]

The immigration service knew that large numbers of Chinese were fraudulently claiming birth in the United States:

> The largest class of Chinese admitted to this country consists of citizens of the United States, 2,396 having been admitted in the fiscal year 1926 as against 3,023 in 1925. This is a surprising condition, in view of the fact that Chinese cannot be naturalized and the number of Chinese women in this country is small, so that it is physically impossible for any considerable number of Chinese to have been born here.[68]

Although the number of Chinese men claiming U.S. citizenship by birth

(continued on next page)

TABLE 7

Chinese Claiming U.S. Citizenship Admitted to the United States, by Status, 1906–1924

Year	Raw natives[a]	Foreign-born children of natives	Foreign-born wives of natives	Native status previously determined	Native status previously undetermined	Total
1906			7			915
1907			23			929
1908			371			1,609
1909			98			2,530
1910	781	13	110	814	501	2,109
1911	12	173	80	1,051	349	1,585
1912	139	258	88	1,069	188	1,654
1913	495	495	126	1,089	232	2,048
1914	49	725	122	1,155	169	2,098
1915	8	794	106	1,040	109	2,057
1916	22	818	108	955	117	2,020
1917	19	905	110	904	151	2,089
1918	13	331	132	492	98	1,065
1919	15	260	91	471	179	1,016
1920	15	843	141	691	191	1,881
1921	22	2,067	290	812	302	3,493
1922	25	2,292	396	1,239	278	4,230

TABLE 7 (continued)

Chinese Claiming U.S. Citizenship Admitted to the United States, by Status, 1906–1924

Year	Raw natives[a]	Foreign-born children of natives	Foreign-born wives of natives	Native status previously determined	Native status previously undetermined	Total
1923	27	2,399	387	1,610	515	4,938
1924	11	2,136	396	1,912	476	4,931

SOURCE: Based on tables compiled and published by the Bureau of Immigration, 1906–1924, U.S. Department of Commerce and Labor, Bureau of Immigration, *Annual Reports 1906–24* (Washington, D.C.: U.S. Government Printing Office, 1906–1924).

a. This category consisted of Chinese who clamed the right to enter the United States as citizens by birth, returning from visits overseas. They were called "raw" natives because the immigration service had no record of their initial departure.

grew to impossible proportions, once citizenship was acknowledged by immigration authorities or in a court of law it would not again be challenged by immigration authorities. With each trip back to Taishan, Taishanese American citizens reported the birth of as many sons as possible, thereby creating paper slots that could be sold to other Taishanese:

> The trick is this. People came here, they look forward to go back there in about two or three years, disregarding how much money you make. Even you completely poor, you would borrow money to make trip, okay? The purpose of making the trip: you stay there at least one or two or three years to give you a chance to report one or two or three sons. So naturally, they allow you one year to produce one son, okay? So when you accomplish that, then you come back to the United States, you tell the immigration office I have been in China three years, I have three sons, these are their birthdays, the names and so forth. Few years later, maybe ten, twelve, thirteen years later, then if you do have your own, you bring them over here, if not, then you could sell these papers, you know. There's always a lot of buyers ready to buy.[69]

Many paper slots were created in this way, by native-born citizens, by their sons, and by their grandsons.[70] By 1928, immigration authorities had already realized that "the time has now been reached when the grandsons of Chinese born in the United States are old enough to apply in large numbers for admission as citizens."[71] At least four or five generations of Taishanese up to the early 1960s were able to enter the United States through this network of paper sons.[72]

Figure 1 illustrates how the paper-son system functioned. It is taken from the immigration file of one Fong Sun Yin (1), who came to the United States in 1939.[73] This chart records the paper family claimed by Fong's father, Fong Hung Doy (2), as well as Fong's real family. This information is available only because Fong Sun Yin came forward in 1968 to participate in a government program that granted amnesty to Chinese who confessed to immigrating under false identities if they implicated all others involved in the same paper family chain. Without such confessions, it is all but impossible to tell from the files themselves whether the relationships claimed were real or fake.[74]

Fong Sun Yin's right to enter the United States can be traced back two generations to his paper grandfather, a man named Wong Ning Lung (3), from Wing Wah Village in Taishan. Wong was first recorded entering the United States in 1890 as a citizen. Wong brought over a total of three "sons," including Fong's father, Fong Hung Doy (2), of Pak Hang Village in Taishan. Under the name Wong, Fong's father claimed citizenship. He was able to make two trips back to China, during which he claimed to have fathered eight sons and one daughter. In reality, he had only one son, Fong Sun Yin (1), and two daughters. When Fong came of age, his father brought him over as another Wong. Fong's father brought over a total of four "sons," including one actual son, one nephew, and one son-in-law.

This genealogy demonstrates the complexity of the deception needed to enter the United States. Fong Sun Yin had to memorize the names, birth dates, and educational histories of seven nonexistent brothers and one sister as well as details of life in an unfamiliar village as described almost five decades before by a man who was not his grandfather.

In order to produce the memories demanded by such a system, Taishanese had to be able to match the immigration service's ability to keep records and track people. They had to know what had been said in previous interviews as well as how evidence would be interpreted. In using informal systems and networks to exchange information and cooperation, Taishanese more often than not bested the efforts of America's immigration bureaucracy.

Here I quote briefly from a paper that was written to help coach a young man before his encounter with immigration officers:

> Be sure not to say that there are two schools, because your two elder brothers when they came to the United States said their village had but one school. . . . Also do not say that Chang Fook and Chang Look started to go to school at ten years of age, because your eldest brother formerly had said that he went to school for five years, and your second brother had said that he went to school six years. Also your two brothers formerly said your house is in the ninth row counting from the south, No. 3 on the alley. Now the position of the house is changed by two rows.[75]

This document reveals that the interviews tested not so much experiences that applicants for entry might have shared with their relatives, but the immigration bureau's own records of testimony that had been given by earlier immigrants. Such testimony did not necessarily represent actual places or

Genealogy of the Real and Paper Families of Fong Sun Yin

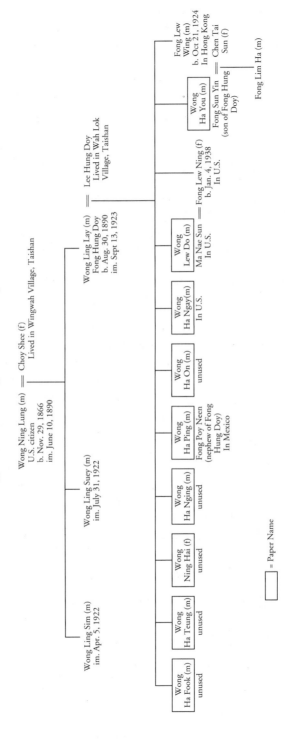

people, merely what immigration officials had previously deemed to be acceptable evidence.

Those using paper identities used coaching books and sometimes maps that provided the details of their paper pasts. Mr. Yuen, a San Francisco old-timer, offered the following description of the writers of these books:

> Normally is a Chinese, for example, I have an uncle, he makes a living doing this. He work with a lawyer, and he would certainly receive some compensation for it. The case is this: you got my case, then if you don't have a book already made, then uncle would help you to make them. He had enough of the basis to make a good book out of it, just by talking to you and your relatives, your father and mother, your grandfather. He might even have to take a trip to Hong Kong. So make sure everything is recorded. Then also, he'll draw a house where you live in the village, showing every room, dimensions, bedroom, kitchen, where you cook. Everything is identified. And also how many stoves you have to cook. Maybe two, maybe three, and you better remember it. It's just fantastic. Just like an architect.[76]

With each new generation of paper immigrants, these books grew thicker. "You compare to what's done before . . . you compile a new one for the newcomer that includes all the previous questioning. As more and more people come this thing gets thicker and thicker, you see?"[77]

Coaching books mimicked the form of actual interviews by feeding immigrants questions and then telling them how to answer:

Q: How often and how much money do you think was sent home each year?

A: I heard my mother say that in the past few years my father sent back HK$500 each year. But I don't know when he sends the money and I also don't know how often. Recently I haven't been at home because I have been studying in Taicheng. My father sends letters home to my mother through the Dexun Company in Hongkong.

Q: Does your family have chickenpox?

A: My family does not have chickenpox. Only my father has a little.

Q: Who in your family is tallest?

A: Of the women in my family, my grandmother is tallest. The second biggest is my aunt who is a little taller than my mother a little. My mother is a medium-sized person, being neither fat or skinny. My father is taller than my younger uncle by about two inches.[78]

As each generation of immigrants entered the United States, there was more to memorize. As recalled by Mrs. Lee, "There was a pile of coaching papers to learn. How many brothers and sisters your father had; names of your uncles; what they did when they came back to China. When did your grandparents die? Where were they born? They asked about three generations back."[79] With so much to remember, immigrants required at least several months to get ready. According to Mr. Yuen, "It took me quite a few months to prepare myself. I had to. I get the book from my uncle probably about six months ahead. I just got out of high school. Then I had about three months preparation time. My duty was just forget about everything, just memorize the book."[80]

Potential immigrants prepared carefully, not just to get into the United States, but also because they did not want to upset the immigration chain for future generations of paper sons.[81] Chang Lam accidentally dropped his coaching papers at the dinner table while on board ship and thereby lost any chance of gaining entry to the United States, not only for himself and his younger brother but also for anybody else claiming to come from the same village of Keow How in Taishan. On the basis of Chang Lam's possession of coaching papers, the immigration bureau determined that his entire line of the Chang family, as well as the village described as their home, did not exist. Because the interviewing process was so complex, however, it was not unusual for even a legal immigrant to possess coaching papers in order to memorize his family history; so simply possessing coaching papers was not an indication of fraudulent entry.[82]

Evading Exclusion: Fabricated Truths and Their Consequences

In order to go to the United States, Taishanese first had to acquire the "slot" or paper identity of someone eligible to come. If lucky, he or she had a father or uncle in the United States who had already prepared such papers or who knew someone else with an available set. Relatives overseas were also helpful because they had greater access to money and could help pay for the papers.

Prospective immigrants without relatives in the United States were forced to ask people in their immediate social circles about the availability of papers that matched in age, gender, and dialect, as recalled by one immigrant who passed through Angel Island: "You try to sell to your own village, or a similar last name. For example, Yuen. Then if you couldn't do that, maybe Chin or Wong in the next village."[83]

In immigration matters, one could not simply post a notice and advertise. As remarked by Roger Tom, immigration matters were conducted by "relatives, friends, mouth to mouth. No advertisement."[84] Strangers who responded to such notices could not be trusted to sell paper identities that gave access to real slots. If the potential immigrant had purchased a dummy set of papers, the deception would not be discovered until detected by immigration officials guarding the borders of America some 5,000 miles away. To immigrate successfully, Taishanese not only had to have a legitimately reported and recorded paper-son identity, they also had to have waiting in the United States, "uncles," "fathers," and "older brothers" who would be able to produce the same set of detailed memories.

The only guarantees that potential immigrants had in purchasing such a complicated set of paper identities and relationships was to buy papers from people they knew, people who could be held accountable in case the immigrant was sent back. In general they turned to relatives, fellow villagers, friends, or friends of friends. Such was the case with Johnny Wong, whose mother purchased papers for him from a friend who lived only a mile away.[85] The genealogy of Fong Sun Yin also reveals that of the four paper slots used by Fong Hung Doy, three went to relatives: his son, a nephew, and a son-in-law.

Even people who ventured beyond the circle of their immediate acquaintances to buy papers usually went to *jinshanzhuang*, the Gold Mountain firms described in Chapter 2. Some managers of Gold Mountain firms had access to paper identities, and they were, to a certain extent, accountable because they depended heavily on maintaining unblemished reputations to attract and retain customers. Because they drew much of their clientele from within the tight networks of shared kinship and native place, *jinshanzhuang* had further inducement to deal honestly with all their customers. Nonetheless, buying and selling papers was a weighty business. According to one businessman who ran a Gold Mountain firm in the late 1940s, Jiang Yongkang, some other *jinshanzhuang* sold papers, but not his. At the time, he had just started in the business and was considered too young to be trusted in such important matters.[86]

Buying a paper identity and all the accompanying evidence was an expensive endeavor. The money was not lightly invested, for "most of them had had to borrow money for their trips to America. Some mortgaged their houses; some sold their land; some had to borrow at such high interest rates that their family had to sacrifice."[87] In the 1930s, papers generally cost US$100 per year of age. The older the immigrant, the more it cost to go to Gold Mountain. At the age of 33, Jeong Foo Louie immigrated in 1928. The papers cost US$3,600, and he was allowed to land after being detained three months at the immigration station on Angel Island in San Francisco Bay. Wong Louie Sue recalled that her husband paid US$1,500 for papers to come to the United States at the age of eighteen in the early 1920s. Prices increased over time such that in 1948, Johnny Wong, then age fifteen, paid US$6,000 to enter the United States under the name King K. Wong.[88]

The debts so accrued were paid off by future labor or by the immigrant's father. Most Chinese in the United States earned US$25 to US$50 per week during the 1920s. If the cost of papers was US$1,500, it would take at least three-fifths to a full year's income to pay the cost of traveling to the United States. Johnny Wong worked two or three years for his paper family to clear his debt, and Wong Louie Sue's husband worked for four.[89]

Despite the high cost and the risk associated with coming to America as paper sons, the networks of kinship and native place that provided the foundation for the system were extremely effective. The estimated success rate of 90 percent cited by both the immigration service and Chinese suggests that far more often than not these networks made it possible for Chinese to circumvent a hostile immigration bureaucracy.

Conclusion

Legislating and implementing national immigration laws is complex and highly contested. Defining who should be allowed to enter and who should have the right to remain or to gain citizenship is almost as difficult as trying to prevent individuals from crossing borders drawn by politicians and bureaucrats on an imaginary map. The decades-long conflict between the U.S. immigration service and Taishanese illustrates the losing struggle of government agents to impose rigid, nation-centered boundaries on the more fluid cultural, social, economic, and political realities of people who move around. Both sides asserted a certain moral prerogative in the fight, with the immigration bureau claiming the rights of a sovereign nation to enforce its borders and Taishanese protesting the unjustness of laws that discriminated against Chinese by race and class while claiming economic hardships at home as legitimate reason to migrate.

During the 1920s and 1930s, Chinese managed to continue coming to the United States at a rate of only a few thousand each year. That so many managed to come at all is testament to their ability to organize and network. By creating slots or paper identities and backing up those slots with "evidence," they gave many the credentials they needed to enter the United States. In short, they were able to beat the immigration service at its own game, playing by rules that the bureau had set itself. Or, as summed up by one Angel Island interpreter, "People might say, we might have come under fraudulent papers but we got in here legally."[90]

The attempts to exclude Chinese had two major effects. Because Chinese found it difficult to settle permanently in such a hostile environment, they continued to look toward China as their home. The discrimination they faced in everyday life was compounded by the reality that most Chinese who came after 1882 could only do so illegally. The crime that marked their entry into the United States ensured that they became even more deeply embedded in the existing networks of kinship and native place that made it possible for them to come.

Success in defying the immigration bureau severely circumscribed the lives of Chinese Americans, for it ensured that most who came committed a crime upon entry. The taint of that crime cast a shadow over the Chinese American community beyond the years that Exclusion was enforced. Chinese did not feel safe relinquishing the paper identities and false statuses under which they had immigrated for fear of being discovered and deported. The danger that their real identities might be discovered placed a barrier between Chinese and white Americans, rendering Chinese the unassimilable presence in America that Congress, and the Exclusion laws, had made them out to be. In front of government agents and most whites, Taishanese could not use their real names and had to maintain elaborate pretenses of convoluted family relationships. Thus while the laws failed to prevent working-class Taishanese from entering the United States, they also made it extremely difficult for those who did to sink roots, establish families, and attempt to become Americans. As Chapter 4 describes, the Exclusion laws trapped Taishanese Americans into an endless commute between jobs in the United States and families left behind in China.

FOUR

Surviving the Gold Mountain Dream: Taishanese American Families

One day in 1934 an unexpected visitor from the United States disrupted the comfortable routine of life in Xiakeng Village in Taishan County. Un-announced, the traveler appeared in Xiakeng accompanied by several porters bearing large trunks. He self-assuredly strode through the narrow alleyways of the village and walked directly to the home of a widow known as Woman Li. Upon catching sight of her guest, Woman Li screamed and ran away, only to return shortly accompanied by all the elders of the village. It seems that the man bore a striking resemblance to the widow's dead husband, Zhen Cheng, a farmer who had passed away from an illness twelve years earlier. Because he had been properly buried and at rest for so many years, and she herself had long since settled into the life of a virtuous widow, Woman Li naturally assumed that the reappearance of Zhen Cheng was the manifesta-tion of a ghost.

Indeed, the "ghost" claimed to be Zhen Cheng and stated that he had not died but had gone to the United States where he had been working as a short-order cook. After twelve years, having become lonely and homesick, he decided to return home to his wife and son. His return was naturally greeted with shock and disbelief. In the face of this explanation, the village elders convened in the local temple to determine whether the man was a ghost, a clever imposter, or really Zhen Cheng.

When questioned, the man claiming to be Zhen Cheng knew without

90

hesitation the dates of Zhen's marriage and his son's birth. The elders closely scrutinized his features and concluded that he also looked like Zhen. As a final test, they sent a messenger to check on the state of Zhen's grave. Upon learning that his skeleton had disappeared, they decided that Zhen had borrowed the bones so that his soul could come back and decided to allow him to remain in the village and comfortably live out the rest of his years with his son and Woman Li.[1]

The story of Zhen Cheng the ghost illustrates many of the ways in which sojourning on Gold Mountain affected the everyday lives and family dynamics of Taishanese. In going to the United States, Gold Mountain guests could dramatically elevate their families' income and socioeconomic status at the cost of remaining separated from them. Few men could bring wives with them because the U.S. immigration laws were even stricter for Chinese women than for Chinese men. Combined with the difficulty of saving enough money to retire, these laws ensured that many family members remained apart for years that stretched into decades until death made reunification impossible. Victor and Brett de Bary Nee captured the plight of many Gold Mountain guests: "Too poor to stay in China and not rich enough to leave America, they lived in California for the duration of their working lives."[2]

For the families of Gold Mountain sojourners, imperfect communication compounded the effects of long-term absence. Although a fairly efficient means of sending letters and money existed in the form of *jinshanzhuang*, illiteracy, discomfort with reading and writing, and men's unwillingness to write except to send money or proclaim success made correspondence sporadic. Even when letters and money crossed the Pacific at regular intervals, years of separation distanced husbands from wives, and children grew up ignorant of the contours of their fathers' faces. In the worst cases, Gold Mountain guests disappeared into the unknown wilds of the United States and abandoned wives remarried other men in Taishan.

Although long-term separation and risk-laden migration did destroy many families in Taishan, during the Exclusion era other Taishanese American households managed to survive and eventually reunite after absences of several months to several decades. Through these long-term separations flexible practices and an understanding of family enabled many of the families of Gold Mountain guests to endure and reproduce even though husbands and wives were united only once every several years.

In this chapter I explore how families split between two continents coped with the pressures imposed by their growing dependence on migration to the United States. I refer to them as "Taishanese American" or "Gold Mountain" families to stress that women and children living in Taishan were bound to life in the United States through the men who provided them financial support. Taishanese men in America were similarly transfixed by people and events in Taishan through the families they continued to support there. The histories of Taishan and American Chinese, although bifurcated by 5,000 miles of Pacific Ocean, cannot be considered complete unless they are written to encompass each other.

During the Exclusion era, Taishanese American lives were framed by immigration laws restricting access to the United States, principles and expectations of family and community, and economic conditions that drove Taishanese men to pursue Gold Mountain opportunities. Despite the difficulties of migration as an economic strategy, many Taishanese American families managed to attain the goals that make Chinese families such enduring entities: mutual support and the generational transfer of financial and spiritual responsibilities. Their trans-Pacific relationships were bolstered by the difficulty for both men and women to abandon an established marriage in order to enter a new one. Legal restrictions and social norms were powerful forces in ensuring that Taishanese American families, once formed, did not readily fall apart.

However, separations did require emotional and practical adaptations and sacrifices. Loneliness, alienation, uncertainty, and self-denial were but a few of the costs. Gold Mountain guests and their families had to accommodate certain insurmountable realities. Wives no longer supported by wayward Gold Mountain guests were forced to defy Confucian norms and find new, more responsible, partners. Long-separated couples found it difficult to have children and adopted sons who could carry on their family lines. Like second marriages for women, adoption was a far from desirable means of ensuring that basic financial and ancestral responsibilities to the family unit would continue to be fulfilled.

Structuring Separation: Chinese Culture and U.S. Immigration Law

Through the 1960s, the term "bachelor society" seemed an apt description of the Chinese American community. Few Chinese women immigrated to the

United States, and most of the Chinese men in the United States lived without either wives or children to give them the appearance of married stability and responsibility. The gender imbalance can be traced to a combination of Chinese practices of sojourning and gendered social and economic roles as well as restrictive U.S. immigration laws and economic conditions. As discussed in Chapter 3, Chinese were not welcome in the United States. The attempts of the U.S. government to exclude all but a few select classes of Chinese made going to America a very expensive proposition for Taishanese. By the first decade of the twentieth century, those planning to immigrate required steamship fare plus at least US$600 to buy the identity papers and supporting evidence that would enable them to enter the United States.

Because only the wealthy or those able to work could afford those costs, most immigrants were merchants and able-bodied men; very few were women. Men of the laboring classes in particular took only sons or nephews in the knowledge that they could work in the United States and pay back the price of immigrating as well as finance their benefactors' retirements back in Taishan. Men who immigrated without the sponsorship of close relatives knew that after arriving in the United States they would be saddled with a debt that would take two or three years of work to repay. Few men could afford to immigrate with women relatives, who had little chance of earning enough to repay the debt.

During the nineteenth century, prostitution was the primary occupation open to Chinese women. This unfavorable economic reality increased men's preferences for leaving women in China. The place of virtuous women was in the home caring for children and in-laws while men supported the family through their activities outside the home. Men in search of gold, building railroads, or draining swampland in the wilderness of the American West found it cheaper, safer, and more convenient to leave their wives and children behind. Ironically, the scarcity of women in the virtuous roles of wife, daughter, and mother produced a highly profitable market in unvirtuous women. According to the sociologist Lucie Cheng, between 1860 and 1870, 70 to 85 percent of the few Chinese women who came to the United States were prostitutes.[3]

The first targets of U.S. exclusion of Chinese were Chinese women, then generally believed to be prostitutes. The Page Act, passed in 1875, was ostensibly legislated to prevent criminals and prostitutes *in general* from entering the United States. In reality, it was primarily enforced against women from

China.[4] The act mandated the deportation of women deemed to be prostitutes and also ordered that persons caught transporting prostitutes be fined and imprisoned. Historian Sucheng Chan argues that the Page Act, in conjunction with police crackdowns on Chinese brothels beginning in 1876, significantly reduced the number of Chinese prostitutes entering the United States by the early 1880s. Giles H. Gray, surveyor of customs for the port of San Francisco, testified on May 27, 1876, before the California State Senate that the number of Chinese women coming through the port had fallen dramatically, from over 250 women per arriving steamer to not more than 250 per year since July 1872.[5] The number of prostitutes had declined from a high of 1,426 in 1870 to a few hundred by the time the 1882 Exclusion Act was passed. Because of these earlier measures, the main impact of this Exclusion Act "fell not on prostitutes but on other groups of Chinese women."[6] The effectiveness of the Page Act and police action in reducing Chinese prostitution did not deter immigration authorities from continuing to regard almost all Chinese women who attempted to enter the United States as practicing or potential prostitutes. This suspicion would define the immigration experiences of Chinese women traveling to the United States throughout the era of Exclusion.

Immigration officials regarded most Chinese women as "slave girls and prostitutes" imported to work in brothels.[7]

> A class . . . to which particular attention should be called is "wives of United States citizens." Such women are admitted upon the theory, not that they are citizens (for not being of a race members of which may be naturalized they can not acquire citizenship by the indirect means of marriage), but that their husbands, being citizens, are entitled to the care and companionship of their foreign wives. Of these "wives," 89 applications were considered, 80 being admitted and 5 deported. The claim is a favorite one under which to import Chinese slave women and girls, who bring an exceedingly high price in this country for use in houses of ill fame.[8]

Chinese women who attempted to immigrate not only faced the humiliating experience of being considered prostitutes, but also found it difficult to prove that they were legitimately married. In 1906 the immigration service declared its skepticism of even "conclusive proof of the claimed marriage, in the form of marriage certificates of undoubted authority" and noted with regret that in such cases "no other course was possible than to land the girls." In other cases, the bureau found ways to deport women who came bearing evidence of their valid marriages.

> It was possible, by a rigid cross-examination of the women and their alleged husbands, to develop evidence sufficient to establish that, if a ceremony were performed at all, it was a mere mock marriage adopted for the purpose of defeating the Exclusion laws, or that the man was already married to another woman before his so-called marriage to the applicant had occurred. Thus it has been possible to deport some of these women to the country whence they came.[9]

These rationales for doubting the legitimacy of Chinese marriages paid little heed to customs that permitted men to take multiple wives and forbade men and women to meet before marriage. It was highly possible that immigrating men had been previously married and all but inevitable that newlyweds knew very little about each other.[10] These social practices could easily be misread by immigration officials predisposed to find vice whenever Chinese women attempted to immigrate. Only the wives of merchants and diplomats were partially immune to such suspicions. Most husbands, however, were discouraged from undertaking the legal and financial risks of bringing their legitimate wives to the United States for fear they would be deported or debarred as prostitutes.

By 1900, the only Chinese women who could legally enter the United States were the wives and daughters of merchants, diplomats, and U.S. citizens. In 1900 the Supreme Court ruled in the case of *United States v. Mrs. Gue Lim* that the wives and children of merchants, although citizens of China and not one of the designated classes of acceptable immigrants, were allowed to enter and reside in the United States. That same year, the Supreme Court used the same logic to rule that laborers' wives, although themselves not laborers, acquired their husbands' status and could not enter the United States. Moreover, even those who had the proper status had to lay to rest the suspicions of immigration officials that they were not prostitutes. They faced interrogation by white male officials concerning their marital relationships, incarceration for weeks and occasionally even years at the immigration station, medical tests for hookworms that required stool samples, as well as the possibility that they would, after all, still be turned back.

Most of the women who managed to enter the United States did so as the wives and daughters of merchants, in part because upper-class women were treated with more consideration and also because merchants were the only ones who could afford to finance the immigration of individuals who could not go out and work. Although many working-class men could support their families back in China in some comfort, few could accumulate the funds needed to pay for their wives and daughters to join them in America.

During the 1920s, immigration legislation became even more restrictive. In 1921, Congress passed a new law (57 Stat. 601) stating that foreign-born wives of U.S. citizens could not themselves gain citizenship by derivation. The search for a wife became even more difficult for Chinese men with the Cable Act of 1922. This law dictated that any woman with U.S. citizenship, even if native born, would lose that citizenship if she married a man who was an alien ineligible for citizenship. The sweeping Immigration Act of 1924 specifically excluded "Chinese women, wives, and prostitutes" and explicitly stated that the foreign-born wives of U.S. citizens were ineligible for citizenship and could not enter the United States. On May 25, 1925, the day before the enactment of the 1924 Immigration Act, the Supreme Court upheld the exclusion of Chinese alien wives of U.S. citizens in the *Chang Chan et al. v. John D. Nagle* decision. That same day, however, the court also determined that the alien Chinese wives and minor children of domiciled alien merchants could enter the United States for permanent residence (but not citizenship) as nonquota immigrants in *Chan Sum Shee et al. v. Nagle.* Any woman marrying a racially Chinese man (so defined if 50 percent or more of his genetic heritage was Chinese) would lose her U.S. citizenship. After 1924 only the wives of merchants and diplomats could enter the United States legally.

Table 8 indicates a steady decline in the number of Chinese women coming to the United States in the first half of the twentieth century.

The hardships generated by these laws were mitigated somewhat by a 1930 act (46 Stat. 581) that recognized that U.S. citizens had the right to live with their wives and so permitted Chinese American men married before May 26, 1924, to bring their alien Chinese spouses to the United States. American-born women won the right to reacquire the U.S. citizenship they had lost when they married men ineligible for citizenship. Despite these legal

TABLE 8

Chinese Women Immigrants Admitted, 1900–1932

Year	Total Chinese admitted	Women admitted	Percent of total
1900	1,250	9	0.7
1901	2,452	39	1.6
1902	1,631	44	2.7
1903	2,192	40	1.8
1904	4,327	118	2.7
1905	1,971	88	4.5
1906	1,485	88	5.9
1907	770	64	8.3
1908	1,263	86	6.8
1909	1,841	135	7.3
1910	1,770	172	9.7
1911	1,307	183	14.0
1912	1,608	241	15.0
1913	2,022	330	16.3
1914	2,354	302	12.8
1915	2,469	287	11.6
1916	2,239	277	12.4
1917	1,843	280	15.2
1918	1,576	300	19.0

(continued on next page)

changes, however, only about 60 nonmerchant wives entered the United States each year between 1931 and 1941.[11]

These convoluted rules and categories made immigration a difficult process. Mrs. Lee, originally of Lung Do Village, recalls attempting to join her fiancé in 1938 using papers belonging to a woman named Wu: "My papers were not in order. They were purchased by the young fellow. It was very crooked. . . . There was a lot to memorize in preparation for the interrogation, such as your grandparents, neighbors, distances from hills, surnames, ponds, temples, etc." Despite her efforts and her fiancé's expense, Mrs. Lee was turned back. The couple had to wait until 1947, after laws were

TABLE 8   *(continued)*
Chinese Women Immigrants Admitted, 1900–1932

Year	Total Chinese Women admitted	Women admitted	Percent of total
1919	1,697	272	16.0
1920	2,148	429	20.0
1921	4,017	713	17.7
1922	4,465	843	18.9
1923	4,074	835	20.5
1924	4,670	938	20.1
1925	1,721	195	11.3
1926	1,375	193	14.0
1927	1,051	221	21.0
1928	931	263	28.2
1929	1,071	271	25.3
1930	970	249	25.7
1931	748	225	30.1
1932	534	228	41.8

SOURCE: Based on Fu-ju Liu, "A Comparative Demographic Study of Native-born and Foreign-born Chinese Populations in the United States" (Ph.D. dissertation, School of Graduate Studies of Michigan, 1953), p. 223; and Helen Chan, "Chinese Immigration into the United States: An Analysis of Changes in Immigration Policies" (Ph.D. dissertation, Brandeis University, 1980), p. 201.

passed permitting the immigration of Chinese war brides, to be reunited and finally marry in the United States.[12]

In the face of all these legal obstacles, some Chinese men remained determined to reunite with their families in the United States but very often did not have the proper status to do so. For example, in 1907 a Chinese resident of New York attempted to bring his wife and daughter over from China by claiming merchant status. The inspector in charge found him not to be a merchant and denied his case. The man persisted and arranged passage for his wife and daughter to Boston. He went to the commissioner of immigration there with the evidence needed to demonstrate that he had been an active member of a Boston firm for the preceding year. This time he called

TABLE 9

Married Chinese Men Living as Bachelors in the United States, 1890–1940

Year	Number of Chinese men	Number of married men[a]	Number of married women	Number of husbands living as bachelors	Percentage of Chinese husbands living as bachelors[b]
1890	103,620	26,720	1,951	24,769	24.2
1900	86,341	31,794	2,157	29,637	35.4
1910	66,856	26,449	2,016	24,433	37.9
1920	53,891	24,782	3,046	21,736	43.6
1930	59,902	23,868	5,574	18,294	35.5
1940	57,389	25,790	7,155	18,635	38.3

SOURCE: S. W. Kung, *Chinese in American Life: Some Aspects of Their History, Status, Problems and Contributions* (Seattle: University of Washington Press, 1962), p. 35, table 2.

a. These figures should be read to include small numbers of men married to Mexican, Caucasian, and black women. See Lisa See, *On Gold Mountain* (New York: St. Martin's Press, 1995) for an account of a rare contract marriage between a Chinese man, Fong See, and a white woman, Letticie Pruett.

b. My calculations are based on Kung's figures and should be read as approximate percentages that do not account for men married to Mexican, black, or Caucasian women.

on white witnesses. Although the commissioner determined that the woman and girl were indeed his wife and child, he found that they could not enter the United States because the man did not have the proper status. He also persisted in investigating the man's fraudulent attempts to prove himself a merchant, thereby leaving the man at risk for deportation.[13]

Split-Household Families

From 1890 to 1940, perhaps two-fifths of Chinese American men were married men living apart from wives and children (see Table 9). In addition, a

1930 U.S. census reveals that there were four times as many married Chinese men in the United States as there were married Chinese women, and that there were only two children for every three married men.[14] These statistics suggest that many Chinatown "bachelors" found themselves trapped between the rock of economic hardship at home and the hard place of immigration laws that made it difficult and expensive for Chinese women to enter the country. These conflicting realities produced the "split-households" that characterized so many Chinese American families during the Exclusion era.

Sociologist Evelyn Nakano Glenn has described a family for whom the physical separation of male workplace and female domestic sphere altered the patterns of Chinese American family life. In this particular family, men had immigrated to the United States for over 60 years without a single member being born in the United States. The family's American connection began with a man who came in the 1890s as a paper son and worked as a laborer for about twenty years. This man then sent for his son to help him run a small business. The father then retired to China, leaving his son in charge of the business and responsible for sending money back. The son in turn brought over his own son during the 1940s. Up to that point, not one of the men's wives joined him in the United States. Only in the late 1950s, when the third-generation Gold Mountain guest brought his wife to the United States, was a child finally born in America after nearly 70 years of traveling back and forth.[15]

Surviving Separation: Working on Gold Mountain

Glenn's example of the split-household family demonstrates how Taishanese American families accommodated the long separations demanded by transnationalism. Their desire to establish and raise families overcame the difficulties of maintaining a family unit and suggests the importance of family to Taishanese Americans. In a society where "people married because it was the normal and unquestioned thing to do" and "a son must marry in order to carry on the genealogical line and ensure the worship of his ancestors . . . [and] a daughter must marry in order to guarantee some type of old age security for herself," living singly was not an acceptable choice for most. Most Taishanese Americans would leave Gold Mountain families only if

TABLE 10

Chinese Population in the United States by Gender, 1900–1940

Year	Total	Male	Female	Males per 100 females
1900	89,863	85,341	4,522	1,887.2
1910	71,531	66,856	4,675	1,430.1
1920	61,639	53,891	7,748	695.5
1930	74,954	59,802	15,152	394.7
1940	77,504	57,389	20,115	285.3

SOURCE: Judy Yung, *Unbound Feet* (Berkeley: University of California Press, 1995), p. 293. Based on U.S. Census Bureau publications. Taishan, in contrast, had a relative shortage of men. According to the 1953 census, the ratio of men to every 100 women was only 88.5. That year, the national average was 107.5. In 1964 this figure had risen to 99.1, but it was not until 1982 that Taishan's ratio began to approach national standards by reaching 105.5 to 1. That year, the national average was 106.1. See Chen Yintao and Zhang Rong, *Guangdongsheng Taishan, Shunde liangxian nuxing renkou guoji qianyi ji qi yingxiang bijiao yanjiu* [Comparative research into the international migration of women from the two counties of Taishan and Shunde, Guangdong Province, and their effects], p. 112.

they could enter another family arrangement. And remarriage was not an easy matter for men in America or for women in Taishan.[16]

The gender imbalance among Chinese in America left Chinese men with few attractive and available marriage partners. In 1920 there were 695 Chinese men to every 100 Chinese women in the United States, a ratio that had already improved considerably since the nineteenth century with the birth of a second generation in the United States (see Table 10).[17]

American-born women tended to be few in number and were inclined to accept only husbands from wealthier backgrounds.[18] Antimiscegenation laws inhibited Chinese men from looking outside the Chinese community for brides. In California the first antimiscegenation law was passed in 1872 to prohibit marriages between whites and blacks. In 1906 it was amended to include Mongolians, the racial category that included Chinese. Not until 1948 was this statute repealed. Moreover, after 1921 any woman marrying a Chinese man without U.S. citizenship would be stripped of hers.

Even in New York, which had no antimiscegenation laws, Chinese overwhelmingly married other Chinese.[19] Their preference for other Chinese meant that few married while abroad, and even fewer married interracially. In 1930, out of approximately 10,000 Chinese in New York City, there were only 500 complete conjugal families. Between 1931 and 1938, only 254 legal marriages occurred that included a groom of Chinese descent. Of these marriages, less than 26 percent were with non-Chinese women. This preference is even more marked when we consider that according to the 1930 census for New York there were 5,112 unmarried Chinese males age fifteen or older, and only 122 females in the same category. Single Chinese men outnumbered single Chinese women by a ratio of almost 42 to one and yet continued to seek out Chinese brides.[20]

In marriage matters, women born in China were considered better potential wives because they were thought to be more virtuous than women born in the United States. One Chicago laundryman pondered his options:

We Chinese are not even allowed to become citizens. If we were allowed, that might be a different story. In that case, I think many of us Chinese would not think so much of going back to China. It is indeed comfortable to live in this country as far as material things are concerned. . . . Many would get a woman and settle down here. . . . Yes, indeed, the problem is where you can get the woman. For me, I would never marry a white woman. It just won't match. You have every difficulty; people look at you when you go out on the street, making you very uncomfortable. They won't let you live in a decent place. . . . I would rather marry a Chinese woman if I choose to stay in this country. . . . These Chinese girls born in America are not trustworthy. They are good money spenders and yet not good wives. They might deceive you. As a matter of fact, they are not willing to marry a *wah-chao* [overseas Chinese]. Very few of them are virtuous.[21]

An American-born Chinese woman jilted by her fiancé at his parents' urging described the stereotypes: "They thought American girls will be bossy; she'll steal the son and go out freely. They said, 'She will ruin your life. She'll be free spending with money.' Also, she won't support the parents the rest of their life. They want a typical Chinese girl who will do what the father wants."[22]

In this predilection for China-born brides parents of overseas Chinese men wielded a great deal of influence. The choice of daughter-in-law was of vital importance, for an extravagant or selfish woman could divert a son's attention from the support of his parents in their old age. As discussed later in this chapter, parents raised sons to provide for their declining years in a chain of shifting responsibilities that enabled families to survive one generation in order to reproduce the next. In this system, a young woman raised in the village who would remain in Taishan and take care of her in-laws was considered far superior to an American-born miss, who was assumed to be of uncertain character and moral values.

The case of Don Hang Wang illustrates many of the concerns. Wang's father brought him to the United States in 1915 when he was only fourteen years old. Wang soon acquired a girlfriend, the daughter of a wealthy Chinese American family, and they dated for six years. His father, by then retired to Taishan, heard of the relationship and took steps to prevent a potentially disastrous marriage. Feigning a mortal illness, he summoned Wang back to Taishan via telegram, expressing a desire to see his son before he died. In the meantime, he completed negotiations for Wang's marriage to a local girl. Wang returned to Hong Kong in 1921, where he learned of his planned fate from a first cousin. He was deeply unhappy at the prospect of marriage to an unknown woman and even thought of committing suicide. In the end, he agreed to the match if the woman was willing to meet him in Hong Kong and to have a Christian ceremony. The woman agreed and the match was made.

However, Wang's mother cried throughout the ceremony, upset that her son would not celebrate according to any Chinese rituals. Wang offered her the reminder that he was a good person. He asked "whether she preferred a good Christian who sent her money and remembered her but did not worship his ancestors or a son who worshipped ancestors and committed crimes." According to Wang, "Mother understood his point" and accepted both his marriage and his religion. Wang took his wife back with him to the United States and continued to send money back to his mother every year.[23]

With such strict limits on bringing wives to the United States, responsible Chinese American fathers and husbands could not help but be sojourners because they had to look to Guangdong in order to marry and establish families. Unless they were willing to forgo one of their primary responsibilities to their ancestors and to themselves, they could not consign their lives to the options available in the United States.

Surviving Separation: Living in Taishan

The eagerness of Gold Mountain guests to find marriage partners on the other side of the Pacific was reciprocated by women in Taishan. As recalled by one man, "See when I was nineteen or eighteen, my mother insisted I go back to China to get married. So I went back to China to get married. I went as a *gum-san hock* [Gold Mountain guest] as a young man so I had a lot of offers."[24] Earning-power was the main attraction, and money did much to compensate for husbands who were absent most of the time. Judy Ng, who lived as a "grass widow" for nine years after only ten months of marriage, described the relatively satisfying conditions of her long-distance marriage: "My husband loved me, and my father-in-law always mailed me the money." With remittances in hand and a compatible relationship with her in-laws, her husband's absence did not greatly matter. Only with the outbreak of World War II and a forcibly imposed silence of three years did Mrs. Ng begin to worry for the well-being of her distant spouse.[25] For a Gold Mountain wife, a good marriage consisted of receiving a steady stream of letters and enough money to build a new house, educate children, and perhaps buy land.[26]

These material benefits did much to incline women to remain in partnership with Gold Mountain husbands. Social, economic, and religious realities also nurtured fidelity. Only within the institutions of marriage and motherhood could women be guaranteed life-long economic support as well as descendants to worship their ghosts after death. Women could not leave the security of a Gold Mountain family unless they entered into a new marriage with another, equally eligible, partner. However, in a society where ideals of proper Confucian behavior dictated that even the fiancées of dead men should not marry other men and erected public monuments to chaste widows, Gold Mountain wives learned from birth to believe that virtuous women became engaged and married only once in their lives. In 1893 the county gazetteer had already begun honoring women who remained chaste after being "widowed" by overseas migration. Of the thirteen women honored, the most extreme example was that of Woman Huang, who remained loyal for over 50 years to a fiancé whom she had never met.[27]

Social and material conditions reinforced Confucian norms. Upon marrying, women moved to the villages of their husbands, where they lived with their in-laws surrounded by their husbands' fellow villagers and clansmen. There was not much need to venture far beyond the village, for the surrounding fields and the nearest market town provided most of the necessities of everyday life. Villagers kept a close watch on married women and gossiped about those who ventured outside the village too often, even if only to visit their mothers. Under such restricted circumstances, Gold Mountain wives had few chances to encounter alternative marriage partners. While living in the village in Taishan, women found it difficult to be anything but virtuous wives.

With a few acres of paddy, villagers could cultivate rice, taro, water chestnuts, a variety of vegetables, melons, and fruits while raising chickens, geese, and pigs at home. The ponds found in front of most villages supplied fish, shrimps, and tiny crabs. On market days, villagers walked up to five kilometers to the nearest town to sell their extra produce or poultry in exchange for cash, which could then be used to buy manufactured or processed goods such as oil, soy sauce, salt, sugar, cloth, salted fish, and tofu. In the winter months, they survived on stored or preserved foods such as salted vegetables and shrimps while spinning and weaving to generate some supplemental income. With enough land and some willingness to work, it was possible to spend one's days within five square kilometers and never need for anything else.

Hilda Wong recalls the self-sufficiency of her grandfather's village:

Grandfather's home that really practically have everything. He doesn't really have to go to the market. He has his own fish pond. He raise enough fish for the whole year. And he has vegetable garden. He has chicken and ducks. Don't have to go out for food, if he doesn't have to. And then he also has raise pig. So he will have a pig killed once a year for the holiday. . . . And then they have, extra houses build only for restore the rice there for every season. And then they have their own water well. So they never have to go out anywhere to get water.[28]

Villages in Taishan were laid out on gridlike patterns with all the houses confined to the same ground-floor dimensions, approximately ten meters by twelve. These gray brick houses were stacked like boxes running in straight rows from the front of the village to the back, separated only by narrow lanes edged by shallow ditches. On both sides of each house doors opened onto the lanes. These doors remained open all day to the traffic of domestic livestock and village neighbors. Only when a family moved away were the gates shuttered and locked. These densely packed houses presented to the outside world forbidding facades of brick walls and narrow windows. The hills and trees that protected the backs and sides of each village and the threshing grounds and fish ponds that shielded their fronts further inhibited access by unwelcome strangers. Footpaths meandered between the irregularly laid-out fields and around low hills, allowing only those familiar with every twist and turn to find particular villages. These paths and fields ended at the foot of hills that held in their protective embrace the villages in which Taishanese ate, slept, and dreamed of better lives.[29]

This physical impression of consolidation reflected social realities. Sharing the same birthplace conferred upon Taishanese loyalties and responsibilities to each other that served as the basis for cooperative action when interacting with village outsiders. For many Taishanese, these native-place ties were strengthened by the fact that many villages were single surname settlements, whose inhabitants were further bound to each other by the ties of fictive kinship. Within these self-contained societies, women had few chances to meet men with no connections or loyalties to their husbands.

Women also had to be careful not to fall victim to the main village pastime—gossip. Johnny Wong recalls that his grandmother joined other women at the front of the village to gossip and watch the children. They talked about their children and husbands, the price of goods, and the crops they planned to plant. They kept an eye on each other's activities and secretly competed to do better than their neighbors. They told tales of husbands meeting prostitutes in nearby cities, sons joining bandit gangs, men who took concubines, and Gold Mountain wives, the only women in the village who did not live with their husbands.[30]

The power of these chatting circles was considerable, and women feared becoming their target. Women who left the village too often or wore cosmetics drew unwelcome attention to themselves. They could visit relatives but had to return within a respectable amount of time.[31] There were always people keeping watch, and Gold Mountain wives like Judy Ng had to be careful to maintain the appearance of propriety. When asked if she ever went to teahouses, Mrs. Ng replied, "A young girl doesn't do that. What would people say? I am afraid of gossip. In my village I don't even know what a tea house is."[32]

1. The People's Movie Theater. Constructed with overseas Taishanese capital and expertise, this building opened in 1928 as the Guangsheng Movie Theater. Note the Doric columns and classical facades that adorn its top two floors. (Author's photograph)

2. Six houses constructed by Chen Yixi for his six wives. Upon returning to Taishan to build his railroad, the sexagenarian Chen Yixi settled down with six wives and built a house for each in a new village close to his ancestral home of Langmei Village. Rising three stories high in the countryside, these houses provided visible proof of Chen's American-found prosperity. (Author's photograph)

3. The Taishan City Zhihua School of Culture and Technology. Tucked away on a narrow street of Taishan City, this building illustrates the classical architectural motifs found on many products of overseas Taishanese money. (Author's photograph)

4. Watchtower constructed to defend villages against bandit raids. An ugly side effect of remitted prosperity was a proliferation of bandit attacks. Called *paolou* by local residents, structures such as this dotted the Taishanese landscape by the 1930s and served as watchtowers, guardhouses, and barred fortresses in times of attack. (Author's photograph)

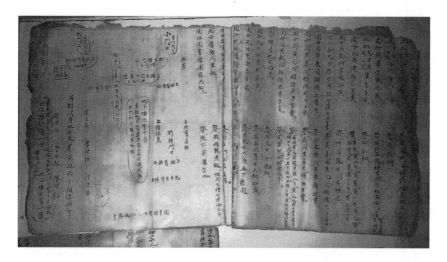

5. Coaching book. Immigration officials' close questioning of potential immigrants about the minute details of village life required most Chinese to memorize coaching books in preparation for their ordeal. On the right, the vertical lines of prose replicate actual interview questions and provide the correct answers. On the left, the coaching book provides a detailed layout of the village school, complete with the location of windows and students' seats. (Courtesy of the Taishan County Museum of Overseas Chinese)

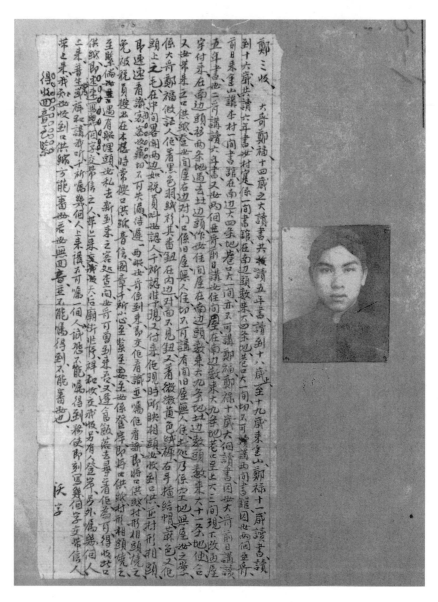

6. Coaching letter and photograph. When found aboard ship, this coaching letter and photograph of Chang Sam's alleged brother, Chang Fook, ended the chances of would-be immigrant Chang Sam. Although most immigrants, whether using real or paper identities, had to use coaching materials to prepare for the detailed questioning they faced upon arrival, immigration authorities assumed outright that the existence of such documents demonstrated false status. (Chinese Exclusion Case File #12907/5-1, Record Group 85, Immigration and Naturalization Service Records, National Archives, San Bruno, California, branch)

7. Grid layout of a typical Taishanese village. Taishanese villages were laid out in gridlike fashion with all houses built on identically sized lots. Narrow alleyways separated each column of houses. Considerations of *feng shui* and pragmatism combined to locate villages against hillsides protected in the back by groves of trees and in the front by a fishpond. *Yanglou*, the newly built homes of Gold Mountain families, occupied formerly empty lots toward the back of villages and towered over their less magnificent neighbors. Note the guard tower at the lower left. (Reproduced with permission of Jonathan Hammond from *The Village as Place*.)

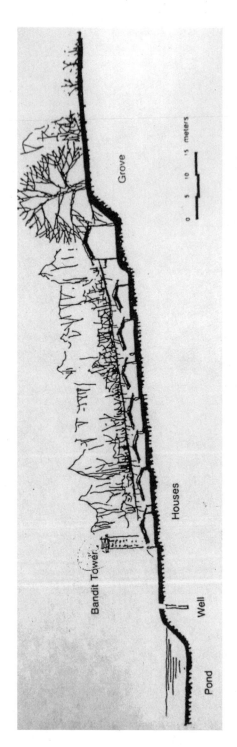

8. Section view of a typical Taishanese village. This drawing illustrates the regular layout of most Taishanese villages, as well as the sandwiching between pond and tree-covered hillside. Note the taller *yanglou* built at the back of the village where there was more space. (Reproduced with permission of Jonathan Hammond from *The Village as Place*.)

9. View from alleyway of one village across fields to a neighboring community. Separated only by narrow alleyways and small patches of farmland, Gold Mountain wives lived in close proximity to neighbors, who were usually their husbands' relatives. The physical space of village life limited privacy and encouraged gossip. (Author's photograph)

10. *(Above)* View of *qiaoxiang* with *yanglou* and older, shorter neighboring houses. This view from the guard tower at the back of this village in Baisha district overlooks both the ornately decorated *yanglou* homes of Gold Mountain families and the humbler, older houses at the front of the village. (Author's photograph)

11. *(Opposite)* Taishan County Middle School. Publication of *Xinning Magazine* began with fundraising drives to build this school in 1909. Both U.S. and Canadian Taishanese donated generously to establish and then expand what remains one of the grander structures in Taishan County. (Author's photograph)

12. *(Above)* Advertisement for Heavenly Longevity brand fertility medicine. Only advertisements for banks and remittance agencies appeared more often than those for fertility medicines in the pages of *qiaokan*. This particular brand guaranteed the birth of a child by the following year. (*Taishan Overseas Chinese Magazine* 3, no. 1 [1934]: frontispiece)

13. *(Opposite)* Advertisement for Hong Kong brand fertility medicine. This advertisement reached for the hearts of many Gold Mountain guests by holding out the promise of multiple generations living under one roof. (*Xinning Magazine* 22, no. 34 [1930]: back cover)

14. Statue of Chen Yixi in the town square of Taishan City. This statue was erected in 1984 to honor Taishan's most celebrated local son. The bottom inscription reads: "Bronze statue of Mister General Manager Chen Yixi established with contributions from the board of directors to express their deep respect and to commemorate [Chen's] achievements." (Author's photograph)

15. Main terminus of the Xinning Railroad. Taishan City's main bus station remained the focus of Taishan's communications network even after the railroad was dismantled in 1939. In 1996, however, a new bus station located several hundred meters to the north became the center of travel and commerce in Taishan. (Author's photograph)

16. Remains of the Xinning Railroad. The only physical remnants of Chen
Yixi's dreams of a railroad empire are a few scattered ruins as viewed from the edge of
the main highway. (Author's photograph)

By definition, a virtuous woman could not be associated with even a hint of gossip. In 1934, *Xinning Magazine* held up Woman Huang of Mamen Village as a chaste woman, her unassailable virtue manifested in the lack of gossip about her within her village.[33] In another instance, Woman Xu of Hua'an Village defended herself against attempted libel by reporting the incident to the police and noting that once a woman's good reputation had been destroyed it would be difficult to avoid disaster.[34]

The daughter of Wu Hong of Chonglou found her engagement to one Mr. Liang broken off by her fiancé once he learned that her cousin and close friend was reported to have run away from her husband.[35] Chen Xiangyuan of Sanxi Village near Taishan City received a letter reporting that his wife was conducting herself in an unseemly manner at home. Believing the rumor, he returned, and upon arrival, without a word to his wife, started to beat her. When neighbors learned of the reason for Chen's attack, they informed him that he had been misled by hearsay.[36]

Occasionally villagers actively enforced moral codes of behavior. Village security forces arrested illicit or unmarried couples seen walking on the street.[37] In West Village, angry neighbors reported a gambling party for village women arranged by the bored wife of overseas guest Qi Hu. The local security team arrived to break up the party and forced the women to scatter in all directions.[38] Residents of Namou Village in Xinchang District became angry that one of their neighbors, a widow known as Woman Kuang, was having an affair with a returned Gold Mountain guest who ran a gambling parlor in Taishan City. When Woman Kuang became pregnant, fellow villagers drove her from the village.[39] Other stories of village retribution against adulterous women include that of Woman Ma, the wife of Huang Chuanmou, who was working in England. Woman Ma took up with a fellow villager and clansman of her husband's, Huang Mouqiang. When the rest of the village learned of the affair, they accused Mouqiang of rape and surrounded the house while the two were inside. Mouqiang, realizing the danger of his situation, escaped the house and fled the village. His indiscretion rendered him unable to call upon the aid of fellow villagers or relatives, and at the time the incident was reported he was reputed to be destitute without clothing or food in the nearby town of Shuixu.[40]

Villagers also enforced moral codes by reporting the misbehavior of Gold Mountain wives to their husbands. Chen Mingrui, who ran a laundry in

New York, returned to Taishan in 1934 after hearing that his wife of twenty years had been having an affair while living in Guangzhou. Chen returned first to his village to confirm the rumors. He learned that not only had his wife been unfaithful, she had also become pregnant in his absence. In a rage, Chen traveled to Guangzhou and at the first opportunity shot his wife in the back with a revolver.[41]

Taishanese American families could also prove to be astoundingly enduring. The longest separation and reunion that I encountered in my research was that of Mei Shiming and his family. In 1922 at the age of 38, Mr. Mei went to the United States, leaving behind a wife and five children. He lived alone and worked as a laundryman while sending money nearly every month to support his family. His wife, who was illiterate, could respond only by affixing her thumbprint to letters written by their sons to let her husband know that things were all right. Matters continued in this way for decades. It was Mei's great fortune that his family is so long-lived, for only by surviving to the age of 100 was he able at last to return to China in October 1984, after the Cold War, Cultural Revolution, and normalization of relations between China and the United States, and reunite with his 98-year-old wife and their four surviving sons and daughters. After a separation of more than 60 years, the family of Mei Shiming was still intact and bound to each other.[42]

Sojourning and Chinese Families as Economic Entities

From the vantage point of a society accustomed to divorce by the late twentieth century, it is easier to assume that many Gold Mountain families also shattered, broken into pieces scattered at opposite ends of the Pacific. However, a surprising number of Taishanese American families managed to survive their years apart and reunite, sometimes decades later, in Taishan, Hong Kong, or America. Anthropologist Sandra Wong interviewed 40 Chinese who lived in the United States without their families, fully 60 percent of whom were reunited with their fathers, mothers, or spouses after separations of more than three years.[43] Of the total, 40 percent were reunited with their transnational families after separations of more than ten years.

As noted earlier, Asian American sociologists have coined the terms "split-household families" along with "separated families" and "mutilated families" to describe the domestic experiences of Chinese Americans living under Exclusion.[44] According to Evelyn Nakano Glenn:

> The sojourning strategy led to a distinctive family form, the *split-household family*. . . . In the split-household family, production would be separated from other functions and carried out by a member living far away (who, of course, would be responsible for his own consumption needs). The other functions—reproduction, socialization, and the rest of consumption— would be carried out by the wife and other relatives in the home village. The family would remain an interdependent, cooperative unit, thereby fulfilling the definition of a family, despite geographical separation.[45]

The practice of physically dispersing family members in pursuit of a broader range of economic opportunities is not a new one in China. Despite the depictions of nineteenth-century sinologists that have emphasized the all but unbreakable bonds linking Chinese peasants to their land, eking out a meager existence for generations on one plot, Chinese could, and did, migrate when need or opportunity dictated.[46] As described in Chapter 1, patterns of sojourning and split-household families existed in China at least as early as the Tang dynasty (618–907).

The connections between migration and family structure and how they configured the lives of Taishanese American men, women, and children requires families to be analyzed as economic entities. Glenn points out that "[a] common sociological definition of a family is a group of people related by blood or marriage, cooperating to perform essential domestic tasks such as production, consumption, reproduction, and socialization."[47] For this more functionalist interpretation of Chinese families, it is helpful to review Myron Cohen's discussion of the economic family, *jia*, and his argument that families can have inclusive economies while existing as physically dispersed groups.

Cohen identifies three elements of the economic family: the family estate, the family group, and the family economy. The economic family shares an *estate*, corporate property that is subject to division among members of the *family group* in case the economic family splits up; members of the *family group* contribute to and partake of the *family economy*, which comprises a budget based on their pooled incomes; reserves from the *family economy* can be used to build up the *family estate*.[48] Cohen contends that these three components can be used to understand the simplest of conjugal families, more complex stem families, and even the most elaborate of joint families.

Joint family households consisted of parents, two or more married sons, and their wives and children. In such family groupings, all the brothers could make claims on the family estate, and all the brothers and their wives contributed to the family economy. If the brothers could not get along, the family estate and economy would be split, with each brother establishing his own conjugal family, including himself, his wife, and unmarried children. The brother who ended up caring for their parents lived in a stem family of three generations.

The Confucian standard of five generations living under one roof fell under the category of joint family and was an ideal almost never achieved in Taishan, or indeed in China in general. Poverty and high mortality rates ensured that families remained small and that simple stem or conjugal families predominated. During the 1930s, the average family in Guangdong had 5.8 members with no more than three generations living under one roof.[49] Taishanese American families were probably even smaller because children tended to be fewer in number and spaced according to the Gold Mountain guest's visits home.[50] Although Cohen's concept of the family estate does not reflect the Taishanese American experience because such families were too poor to own corporate property, the principles and practices of family group and family economy played prominent roles in their lives:

> Unlike the agrarian Chinese family, the Overseas Chinese family cannot be defined in terms of a corporate property-holding unit. . . . Its bonds are more elusive but just as real and important. . . . Members of an Overseas Chinese family are bound by ties of expectation and feelings of obligation to provide a better life for those left behind—limited to include one's parents, siblings, spouse and/or children.[51]

Within the family group and the family economy, Taishanese Americans attempted to maintain the ebb and flow of a family over time. From generation to generation, the able-bodied cared for the old and nurtured the young, who would eventually grow up to care for their own aged parents while raising yet another generation of caregivers. It was a system that satisfied both material and spiritual needs. A family that perpetuated itself both ensured lifelong material security for all its members and provided descendants to worship the spirits of ancestors who would become wandering, starving, vengeful ghosts if not fed by male heirs in the material world. By emphasizing collective interests rather than individual needs, the family group and the family economy provided the rules by which men and women of different generations could coordinate their efforts and provide mutual security for themselves and for each other.

It is important to note, however, that remaining part of the same family economy did not require that members live and work in the same place. Put another way, physical dispersion did not signify that the family had divided.[52] Upon going separate ways, some newly formed families did permanently divide the family estate and use their share to move elsewhere. In many other instances, however, individuals and even entire conjugal households elected to move away from the primary household, thereby diversifying and strengthening the family's economic base, while still contributing to and benefiting from the family economy and estate.[53] Such sojourners or migrants remained "concerned with promoting the *chia's* [*jia's*] survival and advancement."[54] They sent money back to the primary household and, if possible, helped to expand family holdings of land or other kinds of property and investments. If by their efforts elsewhere the family estate could be expanded enough to provide the sojourner with a job, or if local economic conditions improved, the dispersed family member or household might be able to return home. According to Cohen, "the *chia* group . . . was distinguished by the potential of its membership to rejoin the *chia* economy and household [after going away to work], as well as by the possession of an estate."[55] Individuals could move away, relocate, and relocate yet again, and still remain contributing members of the original economic family unit. Even those who failed to earn enough to send back remittances had the option of returning to Taishan.

These principles of economic family organization provided the social context for Taishanese men and their pursuit of the Gold Mountain dream. In times of need or when presented with good opportunities, men could and did choose to support their dependents from afar, secure in the knowledge that their absence was merely part of the regular ebb and flow of family life. Even without commonly held property, Taishanese American men continued to feel loyal to those they left behind, bound by "the deeply ingrained expectation and feeling of obligation to provide a better life for one's parents and siblings."[56] One of Sandra Wong's informants voiced his sense of responsibility to those at home:

> Most families of Overseas Chinese live in very poor conditions; peasants don't have very much. They are my family, don't you think I should help them out? That's my father and mother, you know, they're not friends. I've always sent them money. It is a way to pay respect to your ancestors. It is not a matter of whether you have money or not. It is a matter of responsibility and respect. There is no old age pension in China. You have to have a family line for security. If not, you may well starve in your old age. So it is the younger people's responsibility to help the family out.[57]

Those in America remained committed to the family group and the family economy despite their extended residence in the United States:

> We had been educated ever since we were little. It was family training. While we were young, my father worked very hard and sent money to support us until we could get out of China. My older brother did too. Recently my father was no longer able to work, so it was our turn to provide for him. We have to keep the family together; we have to help each other out. Before, he helped us until we could stand on our own. Now, we should help in whatever way we can.[58]

The 60-year separation of the family of Mei Shiming illustrates how well the economic family could survive the experience of sojourning on Gold Mountain. After his return, Mei helped two of his sons immigrate to the United States before settling into retirement with his wife in Taishan. When I went to interview Mr. Mei in 1993, I was met by his 85-year-old son, who had returned to Taishan to look after his 108-year-old father who was then in ailing health. After a separation of more than 60 years, the economic family of Mei Shiming was still intact.

Living the Gold Mountain Dream

This discussion of Chinese principles and family practices suggests how Gold Mountain families survived extended separations and limited communications. It does not, however, reveal the strains of actually being part of such a family as a "bachelor" father or a virtual widow. For Gold Mountain families, there were the obvious advantages and profound disadvantages already discussed. But the main quality that most Cantonese associated with sojourning on Gold Mountain was wealth.

Despite the bureaucratic and legal obstacles posed by the immigration service and the Exclusion laws, Taishanese continued to regard going to America as one of the more reliable and profitable ways to make a living. This belief motivated thousands of Taishanese American men and their families to separate willingly for decades at a time in pursuit of upward social and economic mobility. The scanty statistical evidence that is available for this period confirms that the families of overseas Chinese did indeed become a highly visible class of the newly well-to-do.

Although there are no figures detailing the incomes of Taishanese American families specifically during the 1920s and 1930s, information collected by the American-trained sociologist Chen T'a does shed some light on how well the families of overseas Chinese lived in comparison with their nonmigrating neighbors. In 1936, Chen sent a group of students to gather data from communities in western Fujian and eastern Guangdong with high levels of migration to Southeast Asia. Although these figures do not apply specifically to Taishan and remittances from America, they provide some sense of the patterns of production and consumption among the families of overseas Chinese. When looking at these numbers, however, it is important to remember that Chinese in the United States were known to send back even greater amounts than their Southeast Asian counterparts.[59]

According to the figures collected by Chen's students, overseas incomes made tremendous differences to the families of overseas Chinese (see Table 11).

From these tables we can see that the average income of the 100 overseas Chinese families interviewed was Ch.$54.38, whereas the average monthly income of the 100 nonoverseas Chinese families was less than one-third that amount, or Ch.$16.95. If we exclude the wealthiest class of emigrant families—those whose incomes were more than double the average income of other families with overseas connections—the average overseas Chinese family still made more than double that of those without ties abroad, or Ch.$35.43. The families of overseas Chinese devoted a greater percentage of their incomes to rent because property values were higher in areas with large numbers of emigrant workers. Both categories of households allocated about

TABLE II

Household Budgets in Emigrant and Nonemigrant Communities, 1934–1936

Monthly Expenditures per Family

Monthly income per family (Ch.$)	Number of families	Rent (%)	Food (%)	Clothing (%)	Light and fuel (%)	Miscellaneous (%)	Average income (Ch.$)
Emigrant Families, October 1934 to September 1935							
Below $20	17	10.1	62.7	5.2	13.0	9.0	14.88
$20–49	49	9.4	59.5	6.2	12.0	12.9	25.82
$50–124	21	15.6	53.8	5.0	7.1	18.5	74.48
$125–250	13	19.9	43.0	3.1	5.7	28.3	181.20
Total	100	15.9	50.6	4.4	7.8	21.3	54.38
Nonemigrant Families, March 1935 to February 1936							
Below $15	52	6.7	59.2	5.5	11.2	17.4	11.73
$15–24	23	6.1	58.2	5.4	9.5	20.8	17.45
$25–34	16	6.0	56.5	6.3	8.0	23.2	24.00
$35–80	9	13.9	49.5	8.5	6.7	21.4	33.28
Total	100	7.7	56.6	6.2	9.3	20.2	16.95

SOURCE: Chen T'a, *Emigrant Communities in South China: A Study of Overseas Migration and Its Influence on Standards of Living and Social Change* (Shanghai: Kelly and Walsh, 1939).

the same percentage of their budgets to food, fuel, and miscellaneous purchases. However, because they had larger overall budgets in absolute terms, overseas Chinese families spent more on food and miscellaneous items such as jewelry and educating children. These figures suggest that even those overseas Chinese families that did not become dramatically wealthy at least led more comfortable lives.

Chen's survey also revealed that overseas Chinese derived between 75 and 80 percent of their incomes from abroad.[60] This extreme dependence upon overseas incomes made it difficult for the men who provided them to stop working abroad and go home. Unless they could save enough money to retire, some men could be good fathers and husbands—that is, good providers—only by staying away. After leaving behind his family in the 1920s, Xiao Dexing never earned enough either to bring his family to the United States or to retire at home. However, he did make enough to enable his wife to live comfortably in Hong Kong and give all three children, two daughters and one son, a high-school education.[61]

It was not easy to accumulate enough reserves to forgo working on Gold Mountain altogether. As described by one Gold Mountain guest who had retired but was then forced to return:

> Oh, I brought home about forty thousand dollars American money. With that much I thought I would not have to come back here anymore. Finally I spent it all. I stayed in China for about six years until I was forced to get a paper for me to come back here. . . . See, for the six long years I had no income but outgo and with a family of five mouths to be fed I could find nothing suitable for me to do in Hong Kong. . . . If I had about five or six thousand American money now, I would like to go back right now.[62]

Gilbert Leung recalls that in the 1930s, Chinese men believed that they could retire with savings of about $10,000. This "small fortune" took most of them some 30 or 40 years to accumulate. Many of the men who faced such odds before leaving knew that they would never be able to return.[63] Mai Yizhao recalls that his parents were married only two months before his father left to sneak into the United States from Canada in the 1930s. His father knew that he probably would be unable to return, given his mode of entry, but continued to send back money and letters nonetheless. In partial recognition that he would never come back, Mai's mother made the decision to adopt Mai when she was only twenty years old, a relatively young age at which to make such a drastic decision. Her choice proved to be the correct one, however, for she never saw Mai's father again. Until his death, he continued to send money regularly to a wife he barely knew and, later, to support an adopted son that he had never seen. These remittances were crucial to Mai and his mother, for they had no fields and no other source of income.[64]

This dependence upon foreign incomes transformed Taishanese families into transnational entities characterized by the long-term absence of the primary male breadwinners in the United States. If possible, the burden of working overseas was transferred from one generation to the next. The story of the following Chicago laundryman represents this pattern:

> I came to this country when I was a young boy. My father was here before me and I worked with him and my older brother in a laundry in New York. Right after the First World War, we made over four hundred dollars a week.
>
> We worked about seven years, and the money earned by the three of us was quite a sum. My father took it back to China, retired when he was less than fifty. In the village, he built a house and got two or three concubines, enjoying life. He had money to live on until his death several years ago.
>
> I have been back to China five times. The first time I got married. . . . [I have a] wife, and three sons and a daughter. My oldest son is now seventeen, but the youngest one is only eight. . . . They have no financial resources unless they received money from me.[65]

In most families, men were the only ones to go to America. Women remained in Taishan, where babies were born and where children were educated and raised to young adulthood.[66]

In Taishan, women became the de facto household heads. In her 1979 interviews with 40 first-generation Chinese Americans, Sandra Wong found that 50 percent had lived in households headed by women.[67] In such households, the fathers or elder brothers of Gold Mountain guests had passed away or lived elsewhere, leaving either the mothers of the Gold Mountain guests or their wives as the designated recipients, and main spenders, of remitted incomes. Dick Tom recalls sending the bulk of his remittances to his mother, who used the funds to buy five or six *mu* of land to rent out.[68] Another Gold Mountain guest, Xiao Dexing, carefully divided his remittances equally between his wife and his older brother.[69]

Remaining alone in Taishan, in charge of the household and in control of remitted finances, was for many women preferable to joining their Gold Mountain husbands in the United States, where they would be required to work hard. The wife of one wealthy herbalist elected to remain in Taishan, where she lived comfortably with two servants to take care of the cooking and housekeeping while her husband's concubine in the United States struggled without household help to take care of several children, keep house, and mind the store.[70] Women who did accompany their husbands to the United States frequently returned to China, where life was less arduous.

Women who remained in China also gained greater control of their children's upbringing. After Xiao Dexing left for Chicago, his wife chose their children's schools and made all their marriage arrangements, sometimes over Xiao's objections. She paired their second daughter with a U.S.-born Taishanese man, believing it to be a good match. Xiao objected, stating from personal experience the belief that foreign-born Chinese were "no good." However, the marriage went ahead as his wife had planned.[71]

Men found themselves reduced primarily to the role of financial providers. Children grew up estranged from their fathers. Xiao Jinliu and Xiao Jinrong, the daughters of Xiao Dexing, never saw their father after the ages of five and six and never even attended his funeral because he died in America while they were still in their teens. Even those men who managed to reunite with their families in the United States or in Taishan found that they had become strangers to their own families: "Sons indulged by their mother looked upon their fathers as intruders into their close family circle. Wives had to relinquish their control over the purse strings and their authority as heads of the household. The men had to get to know their women and children, some of whom they had never seen before."[72]

Sporadic communications and lack of personal contact had other repercussions. Adults became distant from one another and lost earlier feelings of familiarity. Cousins of Xiao Dexing recall that before he went to the United States he was known as an honest and loyal man. They lamented, however, that despite constant correspondence and regular remittances from him, they "didn't know what he became after going" or whether his personality had changed.[73]

Breakdowns in communication occurred for a multitude of reasons, good and bad. Woman Huang of Nancun in the eastern district of Taishan

City received regular remittances from both a husband and a son in the United States. During the economic woes of the 1930s, however, they lost their jobs, and in 1932 both stopped sending either letters or remittances. After several months of silence, she began to suspect that both were having affairs with other women in America, and in desperation she drew upon the only resource at her disposal. She consulted a local shaman who promised to restore the affections of her son and husband for a payment of $200. Fortunately, Woman Huang's son returned a few days later and explained that he and his father had no jobs and no money to send but that they had not abandoned her. Woman Huang was greatly relieved to have her fears dissipated, and her son promptly demanded that the shaman return her $200.[74]

Extended silences made possible other kinds of pressures. Women were vulnerable to many kinds of gossip and hearsay about their husbands and sons living overseas. When Li Mougui of Anhe Village failed to extort money from the wife of a Gold Mountain guest, he exacted his revenge by spreading rumors that her husband, Li Yanwen, had died while overseas. This method of retaliation was possible because Li Yanwen had not been in touch with his wife for several months. The scheme worked, for Li Yanwen's wife had heard of her husband's death and become extremely despondent. She even contemplated committing suicide. Fortunately, her in-laws managed to stop her, and of course Li Yanwen himself returned unannounced soon thereafter, laden with Gold Mountain riches.[75]

Adaptations to Absence: Remarriage

The story of Chen Mingrui indicates that women who committed adultery were irredeemable in Chinese village society. Women who had love affairs simply could not be tolerated. However, if a Gold Mountain guest abandoned his marital responsibilities by failing to send money or even letters, villagers were much more willing to forgive Gold Mountain wives who sought out new husbands who would be reliable providers. Such women often were left with no recourse but to remarry. Despite Confucian mandates defining the virtue of women by their fidelity to dead husbands and fiancés, anecdotal evidence from southern Guangdong suggests that it was socially acceptable for abandoned Gold Mountain wives to find new husbands who would be more responsible.

In the faraway land of America, a rarely seen and barely known husband was easily lost to a variety of evil forces. Abandonment was signified by no letters and no remittances. Sometimes men remarried and established new households overseas.[76] Others never saved enough to return to Taishan, and the even less fortunate did not earn enough even to send money home. Men in that unfortunate situation occasionally elected to break off contact simply because they were ashamed of their inability to support their families.[77]

No one knows exactly how many Gold Mountain guests returned to China successfully. Glenn suggests that about two-thirds managed to return before 1882, based upon Stanford Lyman's observation that there were never more than 110,000 Chinese in the United States at any one time and that between 1852 and 1882 more than 300,000 Chinese arrived in the United States from Guangdong. However, because this estimate does not account for those who died while in the United States, the rate of return was likely somewhat lower.[78] June Mei estimates that less than one-fourth of immigrants managed to return to China, based on Senate estimates made in 1877 that Chinese in California numbered about 148,000 and that around 200,000 had arrived.[79] Nai-ming Ginn, a Los Angeles old-timer, offered a more personal estimate: "Before World War II, I believe 40 percent went gambling, 60 percent were good people and these people saved money and went back to China to see their wife and family. But these 40 percent, they found it hard to go back because they worked but they lost their money in gambling."[80]

Johnny Wong's grandmother was one of the women whose husband stopped sending money and never returned. Her situation was made worse by the other village women who "were kind of laughing at her," making little remarks and asking needling questions about when her husband would come back. In general, there was a low opinion of Wong's grandfather in the village, and suspicions abounded that he might have found a new wife in America. Wong's grandmother was relatively lucky, however, because she had a son to live with and support her. However, she remained "mad all the time" at the husband who had abandoned her.[81]

Other grass widows were less fortunate and faced the decision of whether to live in destitute chastity or marry a second time. According to circumstances, fidelity was a virtue that could easily be shed in the face of practicality. In Taishan City, town officials were amazed by the refusal of a 35-year-old beggar woman with seven-year-old twin daughters to marry an elderly returned Gold Mountain guest, Liu Jia, who was willing to support both her and her daughters. The virtuous woman refused to remarry and refused to sell her children, leading residents of Taishan City to deem her extremely odd.[82]

A woman's decision to remarry or to remain chaste depended in large part on the relationship between the Gold Mountain wife and her husband's family. If they were compatible (and here it helped if the Gold Mountain wife had produced a son to contribute to her husband's line), she could continue to live with her in-laws. If they did not get along, however, or the in-laws were too poor to provide for an extra mouth, the Gold Mountain wife found it more practical to find a new husband.

Second marriages, despite their bad reputations, were easily achieved. The abandoned Gold Mountain wife, usually with the permission of her husband's family, moved away from the village and contacted a matchmaker to begin new marriage negotiations. If there were children, she would leave them with her former in-laws or sell them for $1,000 or more.[83] Because it was not always easy for men to find wives in Taishan, they were not always particularly selective. For example, The 47-year-old wife of Xu Dacun of Panlong Village in Datang Xiang was ordinary in appearance and almost certainly beyond childbearing age. Nonetheless, through a matchmaker, she managed to find a new husband in nearby Xinhui County. Unfortunately for the new husband, she still had a first husband providing for her, whose family was able to nullify the new marriage.[84]

Li Yalian of the western district of Taishan City returned from the United States and through the services of a matchmaker married the daughter of one Liao Yaquan. Ten days after the ceremony, Woman Liao gave birth to a child. Li was, of course, very surprised and asked for an explanation. In tears, Woman Liao confessed that she had been married once but that her husband had died suddenly on a trip to Guangzhou. She had remarried at the urging of her parents and the matchmaker. Li was justifiably angry and reported the matter to the authorities, but Woman Liao's parents intervened on her behalf. Li hesitated in his pursuit of the case and then decided, upon reflection, that he had grown fond of his wife and let the marriage stand.[85]

Villagers usually realized that women who remarried had few alternatives. Such was the situation of the wife Wu Yusheng of Sanxi Village in the eastern district of Taishan City. Mrs. Wu had not heard from her husband in over twenty years but had managed to survive alone and raise his son to adulthood. Their son died before he was able to marry and have a child, however, and then she heard that Wu had passed away as well. Reluctantly, she agreed to a new marriage. Overseas, Wu finally received word of his son's death as well as his wife's remarriage and returned in haste only to find that his family had completely disappeared. Depressed and alone, Wu then attempted suicide.[86]

The stories of these women illustrate that when the bonds of family failed to bond Gold Mountain guests to their wives, it was possible for women to build new lives for themselves and remain with the structure of a family unit. It was a less socially acceptable solution than remaining a loyal Gold Mountain wife but one that recognized the problems inherent in marriage to a Gold Mountain man.

Adaptations to Absence: Adoption

The absence of Gold Mountain guests from Taishan also made it difficult to produce the children, and especially the sons, that were essential to perpetuating the family line and continuing the generational exchange of support.

Extended separations greatly complicated the fundamental act of procreation. In Gold Mountain families, the natural difficulties of barrenness and infertility were compounded by the few opportunities men and women had to meet in order to procreate. The main strategy for dealing with this problem was adoption.[87]

The importance of sons, and the popularity of adoption as a means of acquiring them, is suggested by the actions of four of the thirteen women honored in the 1893 gazetteer as virtuous women. These four women, who had merely been engaged to men who had disappeared or died, decided to adopt sons to carry on their fiancés' legacies as well as provide for themselves in the future.[88] In letters to Gold Mountain guests during the 1930s, the most frequently voiced request, after pleas for more money and return visits, was for permission to adopt sons.[89]

Choosing to adopt was a difficult matter, for according to Confucian tradition it was an unsatisfactory way of fulfilling the needs of ancestors for male descendants and worshippers.[90] Qing law codes also forbid the adoption of male heirs across surname lines. The material and spiritual importance of "getting an heir," however, led many to ignore such prohibitions.

In Taishan, the problem was even more acute. Mai Yizhao, the adopted son described earlier in this chapter, was actually the second generation of adopted sons in his family. His grandfather, who had gone to the United States to work on the railroads, adopted Mai's father, who in his turn also went to the United States and adopted a son. But for the death of his father overseas and the intervention of World War II, Mai Yizhao himself might have followed the path of his immediate ancestors and journeyed to America.[91]

In Taishan, most of those who adopted sons were Gold Mountain guests. A Gold Mountain wife, Mrs. Wu, recalled that before World War II the richest man in her village was a returned overseas Chinese who used his savings to open a general goods store. He chose not to remarry but did adopt two sons. She added that many such men did not find it easy to have sons of their own because they returned after the age of 50.[92]

Older Gold Mountain guests ran extra risks when they adopted because they tended to choose adult men as their sons. The greatest danger in such cases was that the adoptee would decide to abandon his new parents and return to his original home and family. The best way to prevent such an eventuality was for parents to adopt while both they and the child were still young, as Mai Yizhao's mother did, and carefully guard the identity of the child's first parents. Older couples, however, had fewer options because they needed adult children who could provide care for them in their waning years. These rather difficult circumstances occasionally resulted in tragedy. Wu Shihui of a village near Chonglou returned from the United States after several decades of life abroad. Thinking himself old, he and his wife decided to adopt a son from Enping as their heir. They renamed the man Shengwang and found him a bride. When Shengwang and his wife had a son, the old couple thought they could rest assured that the family line would continue (*manxin huanxi yiwei xuhou you ren*). However, this satisfying state of affairs abruptly ended when Shengwang suddenly returned to his original home, taking his wife and child with him.[93]

Misfortune also befell Ma Guangzhan of Longhua Village in Daliang Village. After doing business in the United States, he returned in 1934 laden with riches. He was old but wanted to fulfill his duties to his ancestors, so he adopted a son through a matchmaker. He called the man Chijin and found him a wife. However, Chijin was a disreputable character, and one day, when Ma and his wife were in Guangzhou, he and his wife stole 400 dollars in silver, two gold rings, and some clothes before running away, never to be seen again.[94]

For the Mas and the Huangs, adoption was an unsatisfactory solution to the problem of childlessness. These unfortunate couples found that no matter how adaptable they might be in striving to guarantee the continuity of their family line, they still could not overcome all of the obstacles posed by extended separations. In the long run, Gold Mountain dreams provided the Mas and the Huangs with material wealth but led to the end of their family lines.

Conclusion

In light of the prevalence of adoption and remarriage in southern Guangdong, we can consider Zhen Cheng a relatively successful Gold Mountain guest. Although he was absent for twelve years and never sent his wife any money or letters, supporting the misperception that he was dead, he did, in the end, return to China bearing a small fortune. He came back to find his wife still living in the village, faithful to his memory, and his son still alive, prepared to carry on his family line. Zhen's pursuit of riches in the United States enabled him to accumulate a substantial nest egg without failing in his duties to his family or to his ancestors. He was able to fulfill all of his familial responsibilities because he, his wife, and son remained committed to their family unit even in dispersion. Such loyalty to family as an institution enabled generations of Chinese American families to endure and survive the separations imposed by economic hardship and racist immigration laws in the United States.

FIVE

Magazines as Marketplaces: A Community in Dispersion

In the physically dispersed community of Taishan, the most enduring relationships were those of the immediate family—the loyalties and institutions that bound husbands and wives, parents and children. In addition, connections to clan and native place also compelled the loyalty and support of overseas Taishanese. The responsibilities associated with these bonds were, however, less clearly defined; they needed reinforcement and organization in order to be of systematic benefit to native place and clan. Within the far-flung borders of these transnational circles of community, material expressions of belonging appeared in the form of magazines known as *qiaokan*.

Translated literally, *qiaokan* means "overseas Chinese magazines." They were and continue to be published by organizations in China and distributed internationally for the purpose of maintaining a sense of community among Chinese overseas. Given Taishan's heavy dependence on migration, it should be no surprise that the county of Taishan was the first to produce a *qiaokan*, *Xinning Magazine*.

Xinning Magazine and its many imitators were written and published locally and distributed to Taishanese internationally with the goal of nurturing a sense of connection and responsibility to Taishan among émigrés and their descendants. At the heart of this relationship was an understanding of native-place loyalty that defined the most fortunate, most capable, and most accountable Taishanese as those who had left Taishan to work over-

124

seas. *Qiaokan* regularly stressed that the greater opportunities and possibilities attained by physically leaving their native place imbued Taishanese overseas with even greater responsibilities to support the home they no longer inhabited. Through their absence, émigrés in fact gained stature and importance in Taishan. Over the duration of the Republican period, *Xinning Magazine* propagated this vision of community with such success that other Taishanese organizations would produce roughly 120 other *qiaokan* as a form of outreach to overseas Taishanese.

This proliferation of *qiaokan* indicates the essential roles played by overseas Taishanese in the economy, culture, and society of Taishan. The magazines provided a lively forum for the sharing of ideas, information, and projects of concern to the entire community. In an era without air travel, fax machines, or electronic mail, *qiaokan* were the means by which a migratory people overcame the obstacle of separation and nurtured commonly shared interests and aspirations. Cheaply printed and readily accessible, these magazines in form and content helped local communities defined by kinship and native place maintain themselves in spite of physical dispersion.

Deeply embedded loyalties to clan and native place became even more important amidst the often hostile conditions of life in foreign lands. According to one scholar of China, "Among the most important needs of Chinese sojourners, including peddler merchants and seasonal laborers, were networks of protection and introduction as they endeavored to make their way in alien communities."[1] Within four years of arriving in the United States in significant numbers, Taishanese had established their own native-place organization. In 1853 they decided to break away from the Four Counties Association (*siyi huiguan*) to establish the Ningyang Association for Taishanese alone. With its more narrow focus, the Ningyang Association would be better able to coordinate the specific interests of its members.[2] Eventually, through force of numbers alone the Ningyang Association achieved a dominant position within Chinese American society. By 1875 at least 70,000 of the 150,000 Chinese in the United States were members of the Ningyang Association. Up to 20,000 more Taishanese were members of the Hehe Association, which served those surnamed Yu.[3]

Organizations such as the Ningyang Association and the Hehe Association provided their members with a variety of vital services: preferential access to employment opportunities, potential business partners, and temporary lodgings. Associations also retained immigration lawyers on call and occasionally intervened with government authorities on behalf of members in emergencies. For Taishanese in the United States, survival required the help of fellow county- or kinsmen even to acquire the papers needed to enter the country. Upon arrival, they turned to other Taishanese to provide the testimonies that would secure their release from immigration detention, connections to find jobs, a place to stay, and perhaps later even loans to acquire new businesses.[4] Although native-place and kinship connections were essential to Taishanese survival in the United States, their dependence on fellow Chinese only fueled widespread criticisms of Chinese as clannish and nonassimilating.

Native-place and kinship organizations provided services that also reinforced the bonds linking expatriate Taishanese to Taishan. The Ningyang Association organized religious festivals that were celebrated according to the customs of Taishan. It provided the funds for even the most destitute of Taishanese Americans to fulfill their final duty to their ancestors and be buried in their native place. In conjunction with kinship associations, the Ningyang Association arranged fundraising drives for projects and disaster relief in Taishan. Expatriate Chinese assumed as a matter of course that they bore at least some responsibility for conditions at home:

> The substantial involvement of native-place associations in native-place affairs meant that when the native place suffered, association directors and sojourners reached deeply into their pockets. Guangdong province was beset by both natural and militarily induced disasters throughout the early Republican period. . . . In the event of small and localized disasters, each Guangdong *huiguan* assisted its home area.[5]

Amidst the flurry of reformist and revolutionary zeal that consumed Chinese in the years before the 1911 Revolution, Taishanese loyalists participated in the political fervor by publishing *Xinning Magazine*, which was intended to inspire fellow Taishanese to contribute to the rebuilding of local state and society. The main audience that *Xinning Magazine* attracted was largely overseas Taishanese. In this fashion, a new category of publication appeared. This and other *qiaokan* were published in the home communities of overseas Chinese for the benefit of audiences abroad. Magazines were a readily transportable means of conveying news, ideas, and aspirations to a widely dispersed audience. *Qiaokan* strengthened transnational ties to Taishan by making it possible for Taishanese around the world to share the same pool of information and partake of the same local events, in detail within roughly the same time frame.[6]

Like the networks of trade that bound *jinshanzhuang* (Gold Mountain firms) in Hong Kong to businesses in Taishan and Taishanese-run mercantile establishments around the world, publications could travel.[7] They had the added advantage of being accessible to all who could read, an estimated 90 percent of male Taishanese in 1910, and were therefore available to many outside the wealthy elite of expatriate merchants.[8] The utility of this form of communication for a transnational society led other groups to emulate it. Before World War II, dozens of organizations began to publish *qiaokan* using varying considerations of native place and kinship to define common interests.

Principles of native place and kinship, as signified by shared surnames or membership in the same clan, provided flexible guidelines for different groups of people to define and promote shared interests and communal goals. In the case of the Ningyang Association and *Xinning Magazine*, the county of Taishan was the defining marker. For the Hehe Association, the surname Yu was the determinant of membership. Other organizations that produced *qiaokan* were also formed on the basis of geographic entities of varying size and sometimes in combination with surname restrictions: the *Four Counties Magazine* (*Siyi zazhi*) targeted people from the Four Counties of Enping, Kaiping, Xinhui, and Taishan; *Haiyan Magazine* for those from the Haiyan district of Taishan; *Huang Clan Monthly* for those surnamed Huang; *Duanfen Monthly* for members of the Mei clan from the central district of Duanfen; and *Longgang Magazine* and the *Longgang Tri-Monthly Report* published for members of the Four Brothers Association (*Longgang gongsuo*) who were all surnamed Liu, Guan, Zhang, and Zhao.[9] By and large, these variously defined organizations, or communities, used *qiaokan* to share news of local affairs as well as to inform expatriate members of the need for their contributions to improve life at home in the form of schools and hospitals. Each *qiaokan* served a differently defined community of local and expatriate Taishanese. Each provides a glimpse of the different but not necessarily competing circles of transnationality and inclusion that encompassed Taishanese Americans and connected their lives to Taishan.

Copies of at least 122 different pre-Liberation *qiaokan* are extant today. The magazines vary in the degree to which they have survived the ravages of time, humidity, neglect, and the Cultural Revolution. In some cases, only one dilapidated issue of a particular *qiaokan* still exists. Others were purged by unknown archivists and survive only in sections. It is impossible even to determine the date of initial publication for some *qiaokan*. The earliest complete copy of a *qiaokan* still available is a 1912 issue (no. 22) of *Xinning Magazine*. Despite the scarcity of these sources, they illuminate the nature of the bonds between Taishanese at home and those abroad and provide a means of exploring the tensions of a community whose members were physically separated yet remained socially and economically entwined. From the tattered remains of these Republican-era *qiaokan* it is possible to reconstruct varying visions of transnationality in Taishan.[10]

Origins: Political Mobilization

Qiaokan were born amidst the flurry of politically motivated publishing that ensued in the wake of China's humiliating loss to Japan in the Sino-Japanese War of 1895 and the abortive Hundred Days' Reform. After 1898 a widespread sense of national crisis permeated all levels of Chinese society and motivated local gentry and merchant leaders as well as teachers and students to agitate actively for the salvation of China. These idealistic reformers and revolutionaries believed that it was necessary to involve all Chinese in the project of reconstructing a modern and strong China. In the first years of the twentieth century, one of the main accoutrements of politically active Chinese was a printing press for propagating a multiplicity of competing visions concerning the best ways to build a better and brighter China.

Many reformers believed that to construct a stronger nation one should begin from the ground up—that is, with one's native place. When Chen Jiongming, an avid reformer and soon-to-be warlord, returned home to Haifeng County, Guangdong, after the enlightening experience of studying in Guangzhou, he started publishing the *Haifeng Self-Government Newspaper*.[11] In Shanghai, many native-place associations also began publishing reformist and revolutionary journals: "Journals like the *Ningbo baihua bao* (Ningbo vernacular) . . . featured articles about native-place industries, customs, education and literature, they also criticized national corruption." Through the expression of loyalties both to native place and to nation, these magazines defined "love for the native place and activism in the interest of local self-government . . . as integral to national strengthening, creating local building blocks for a modern constitutionalist state."[12]

The links between nation and native place also inspired Chinese overseas to begin publishing. After the failure of the Hundred Days' Reform, Kang Youwei traveled abroad in search of new supporters. His followers in North America founded a series of newspapers to argue the revolutionary cause, including the *Revive Civilization Daily* (*Wenxing ribao*), later the *World Daily Newspaper* (*Shijie ribao*) of San Francisco; the *Renew China Newspaper* (*Zhongguo weixin bao*) of New York City; the *New Day Newspaper* (*Rixin bao*) of Vancouver; and the *New China Newspaper* (*Xin Xhongguo bao*) of Honolulu. A few years later, revolutionary supporters of Sun Yatsen would establish *Young China* (*Shaonian Zhongguo chenbao*) in San Francisco and the *Liberty News* (*Ziyou xinbao*) of Honolulu.[13]

Taishanese also partook of this publishing frenzy, believing newspapers to possess almost transcendental qualities:

> It is established above society, like a telescope that illuminates objects, a conduit that produces civilization, sufficient to view the good and the bad and distinguish between them, erecting righteous dialogue and encouraging evolution. What is this object? Newspapers. It is established under the unifying power of the nation, freedom of movement, disciplining the government above and promoting the spirit of the people below, and causes the foundations of the nation to become more solid, and the nation's power to become more developed. What is this thing? Newspapers.[14]

With the power of publishing in mind, several local scholars and forward-minded gentry decided to publish a magazine that would inspire and guide reform in Taishan, noting, "The newspaper is a beneficial tool and if we wish to improve county customs, we particularly cannot do without this county's own newspaper to act as leader."[15]

At the heart of this publishing endeavor was the belief that providing modern education for the young was essential to building a stronger nation. The founders of Taishan's first *qiaokan* began their publishing careers as idealistic reformers concerned with upgrading Taishan's educational facilities.

They were all members of the Anliang Bureau, later renamed the Education Committee (*jiaoyu hui*) in 1908. One of their responsibilities was to raise funds from overseas Chinese in order to build a modern middle school in Taishan.[16] With education as the cornerstone of their quest for broader social and political change, Tan Yuzhi, principal of the Tan Clan School, Zhao Gongchen, Liu Richu, and Liu Xiaoyun decided to publish a magazine that would inspire their fellow Taishanese to become active in building a better Taishan.[17]

Their first publication appeared in the middle of 1908 under the title *Xinning Public Newspaper* (*Xinning gongbao*). Despite the support of the county magistrate, Tan Xiaofang, this initial effort quickly folded.[18] Undaunted, Tan Yuzhi, Liu Richu, Liu Xiaoyun, and Zhao Gongchen revised the project and started again in the first month of 1909. They named their second effort *Xinning Magazine* (*Xinning zazhi*).[19]

Tan Yuzhi, Zhao Gongchen, Liu Richu, and Liu Xiaoyun invested the project with great hopes and expectations:

> Although its starting point is slight, aspirations are great. During these times, if we do not have a newspaper that uses interpretive and investigating words to record this, these affairs will dissipate without record, pass, and no longer exist. And if there is no newspaper to comment rigorously and restrain them, obstructionists will run amok and the fearful will not advance. How great will be the regrets? My colleagues have witnessed this situation and so have organized the Xinning Magazine Society.[20]

The editors believed that it was their duty, as concerned Taishanese and Chinese, to start a magazine that would inspire the public debates and lead to saving changes in the government, economy, society, and educational system of Taishan.

In addition to education, one of their more strongly advocated reforms was the establishment of local self-government (*zizhi*): "The native place serves as a necessary and familiar place to begin. By addressing reform in the native place, the abstract and enormous task of reforming the nation becomes concrete, manageable, and familiar." The idea had broad appeal. The Education Committee was drawn to the words of reformers like Feng Guifen and Huang Zunxian, "who advocated the mobilization of local elites and resources in the interest of strengthening the state." In articles such as

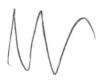

"Discussing That Self-Government Offers Benefits Without Harm," Tan Yuzhi, Zhao Gongchen, Liu Richu, and Liu Xiaoyun advocated the responsibility and greater suitability of Taishanese to contribute to the betterment of China by improving Taishan.[21] In their eyes, "This type of localism was not seen as separatism (opposed to the state) but was viewed, instead, as necessary for the health of the polity. These connections between native place and nation were both sincere and pragmatic, justifying the obvious and convenient native-place networks which underlay effective social organization in this period."[22]

In his preface to the magazine, their main supporter, county magistrate Tan Xiaofang, traced this political ideal back to the days of Mencius, when "the way of kings began with silkworms, mulberries, chickens, and pigs and culminated in the people living and dying without regrets." He stressed that restoring this "natural" form of society was not a task that one official could accomplish alone and urged scholars, local gentry, and merchants to assume responsibility as well.[23]

The first issue of *Xinning Magazine* raised many other issues that Tan and the Xinning Magazine Society targeted for reform. The articles "Self-defense Corps for Every Area," "That Reviving Industry in Taishan Should Emphasize Agriculture and Forestry," and "The Reasons Education in Xinning Is Lifeless" suggested specific areas requiring change and improvement. Education, of course, received considerable attention. In his preface to the first issue, Liu Xiaoyun asserted that "the ambitious men in this county seek that which reforms. Improving education is the direction to begin."[24] In 1910 he estimated that male literacy in Taishan was 90 percent, an impressive statistic that nonetheless left room for improving the educational standards of women as well as for reforming teaching methods.[25]

The magazine's editors also had explicit ideas about the new forms of government that should be established. According to "The Four Major Organizations That Ought to Be Established After the Revolution in Xinning," it was not possible to build without first tearing down. The essay's author then suggested that government should consist of four offices: one to supplement the executive branch, one to supervise the executive branch, one for self-defense, and one to reform a finance department that had yet to be established.[26] Staff writers eagerly pointed out the ills of state and society in Taishan and sketched out solutions in such articles as "Discussing That Self-government Should Eliminate Gambling" and "Inferring Reasons Why Hospitals Should Be Connected With Districts."[27] They suggested guidelines for improving elementary school curriculums and debated "The Harm of Believing in Geomancy."[28]

In order to produce the magazine that would propagate these ideals and ambitions, especially to Taishan's absent but financially important expatriate members, the members of the Xinning Magazine Society had to learn a host of new skills and technologies to collect, write, and edit news and articles, print the text, and set up a business office capable of managing overseas subscriptions and advertising accounts. The initial corps of writers and editors included chief editor Tan, the two Lius, and Zhao, as well as approximately sixteen news writers and two consultants, Zhang Shipeng of Panyu and Pan Huichou of Nanhai.[29]

The product of all these efforts was rather modest in appearance, measuring only thirteen centimeters in width by nineteen centimeters in height (or five inches by seven and a quarter) and bound in a plain paper cover adorned simply with the title *Xinning Magazine*, the date, and the society's addresses written in both Chinese and English. Publication occurred every ten days, on the fifth, fifteenth, and twenty-fifth of each month and each issue ranged between 70 and 120 pages in length. The typeface was large and square and arranged in vertical columns from right to left. This format remained unchanged until 1940. Up to that time, the physical process of publishing *Xinning Magazine* was probably quite similar to that used to print Chinese newspapers in New York, as described by Leong Gor Yun in 1936:

> Since it is impossible to construct a linotype for the Chinese ideographs without simplification, all the newspapers are set by hand. . . . The type cases . . . are arranged by families or root characters so that typesetting is a tedious and difficult job requiring a good memory and strong legs. An average compositor can set six hundred and fifty words an hour—if he can read the roughly scribbled copy. To Americans it is amazing to see the compositors run up and down between the type-cases picking up characters practically without looking.[30]

The content of *Xinning Magazine* was designed to inform and inspire readers to become active on behalf of reform. Each issue contained seven main sections. The first consisted of expository essays (*lunshuo*) examining current issues in Taishan and suggesting reforms. The second section, titled law and government (*fazheng*), was intended to help readers "distinguish between the beneficial and the destructive in order to indicate what should be encouraged and what done away with," with the goal of establishing local self-government and implementing constitutional rule. The third section focused on education (*jiaoyu*) and its dissemination. Industry and Taishan's economic development (*gongye*) came next in order of importance, followed by public documents (*gongdu*) published to educate readers about the rules and principles of government and Western-style incorporated businesses. Sections six and seven consisted of international news (*zhongwai yaowen*) and county news (*benxian xinwen*). A section added later consisted of miscellaneous articles, including literary works, contributed by readers (*zazu*).[31]

The editorial staff came by their materials in various ways. Some articles, especially essays, flowed from their own pens. Readers were encouraged to contribute news and their own writings to any of the sections. Amateur authors could receive two dollars for every thousand words written in the form of essays, poems, or songs or for pieces not published for payment elsewhere.[32] Articles were sometimes reprinted from other newspapers, especially those in Hong Kong.[33] Reports were submitted from various different villages, and reporters covered the activities of a county government that changed with each switch in provincial authority from one political faction to warlord rule and finally to single-party domination by the Guomindang.

The Audience Overseas

During its first years, the publishers and editors of *Xinning Magazine* did not treat overseas Taishanese readers as a special constituency. Initially they assumed that expatriate Taishanese were simply another group of Taishanese, equally responsible as those at home for the well-being and future of their home county and country. In the following description of Taishan, editor Liu Xiaoyun depicted overseas Taishanese as active participants in local affairs and even indicated that they were the county's main claim to national fame:

Our Xinning is a county that borders the ocean. Since the founding of the Ming, it has not had an important place in our country's history. But ever since it became legal to go abroad, not inconsiderable numbers of people have been going overseas to the extent that when speaking of this, some say that everywhere the sun rises and sets, the footsteps of Taishanese can be found. Much has been written about this, including details that are normally ignored. Thus the record of the activities of Taishanese are happily consumed by the people at home. Local brethren traveling abroad are the ones who send back money and start up various businesses. One also constantly bumps into them on the street.[34]

The Xinning Magazine Society did not feel the need to cater to overseas interests, for its members assumed commitment and responsibility on the part of *all* Taishanese, regardless of whether they lived in Taishan or had gone abroad. As a matter of course, all Taishanese were presumed to be concerned about Taishan and thus to support the magazine's goals: "To publicize what is good and to detest what is evil, to encourage the beneficial and get rid of the harmful, to improve society and encourage general circumstances are the goals of this society. In general, these are responsibilities of all our county's people."[35]

According to the editors of *Xinning Magazine*, this duty to nation and to native place included supporting the magazine: "This magazine is an organ for public opinion throughout the country. It is the responsibility of all those who count as people of this county to maintain it."[36]

Although initially *Xinning Magazine* did not seem to specifically target them, Taishanese abroad were among the most enthusiastic readers during the magazine's first year: "Each time a new issue appeared, [people] competed to tell others about it, overseas brothers in particular welcomed it, and within the space of a month it was popular on all five continents."[37] This popularity abroad was evident by issue no. 17 of the first year of publication. In this issue, the editors thanked the magazine's main supporters and listed comments and contributions deserving of particular attention. All on this list were in the United States, including Huang Jin of San Francisco who not only bought a subscription but also purchased $200–300 worth of advertising space. Next noted was the *Zhongxi Daily Newspaper* (*Zhongxi ribao*) also of San Francisco, which posted advertisements for *Xinning Magazine*. Also thanked were the Heshenglong Store of Boston for agreeing to distribute the magazine and Lei Wei of Portland for agreeing to sell $500–600 worth of stock. The Ningyang Benevolent Association of San Francisco also received thanks for supporting the endeavor.[38]

The preponderance of overseas readers affected the business organization of the Xinning Magazine Society in several critical ways. By 1910 the business center of *Xinning Magazine* had relocated to Hong Kong and managed distribution, advertising, subscription fees, and stocks, while staff in Taishan wrote and produced the magazine.[39] The first Hong Kong branch office was located at the Lishenghe *jinshanzhuang* at 32 Wing Lok Street in Hong Kong.[40] In 1915, when a change to weekly publication was considered, the plan was rejected because a ten-day schedule was better suited to mailing the magazine overseas.[41] Readers were encouraged to order their magazines through the Hong Kong office and then remit payments through the post office.[42] The society's Hong Kong office was responsible for all business matters, and payment was requested in Hong Kong currency.[43]

Like newspapers sold in Guangzhou, *Xinning Magazine* was distributed by vendors rather than post offices.[44] With so many overseas readers, however, distributors were scattered around the globe as well as within the county at Taishan City, in the main market towns of 25 districts, and at Guangzhou, Jiangmen, and Shanghai.[45] By 1919 *Xinning Magazine*'s web of overseas distributors had expanded to include 24 points of distribution within Taishan and Guangzhou, as well as several distributors in San Francisco and Boston. In 1927 and 1928 readers could find the magazine in places as disparate as Pittsburgh, Saigon, Los Angeles, Newark, San Diego, Caracas, Portland, Washington, D.C., Chicago, Philadelphia, New York City, Boston, Baltimore, Seattle, Vancouver, Toronto, Victoria, Calgary, Winnipeg, Montreal, Houston, Havana, Hawaii, Luzon, Rangoon, Singapore, Melbourne, Sydney, Hobart, Detroit, and Rabaul in Papua New Guinea.[46]

Despite its large overseas audience, the magazine's content focused on Taishan and China. The editorial office remained in Taishan City at the Front Street office. Readers were encouraged to contribute political commentary, editorials on current events, education, industry, education and technology, and literary pieces; the only condition for acceptance was that each contribution "use this county as its scope and must agree with the goals of this society."[47] When *Xinning Magazine* switched to the Western calendar in 1912, it did so not because many readers lived in Western countries but because China's new Republican government under President Yuan Shikai had made the same change.[48]

Qiaokan *as Village Rags: The Needs of Overseas Taishanese*

Despite the early political ideas that inspired its founding, *Xinning Magazine* lost its overt political orientation within a few years. This occurred in part because the original founders were co-opted into Taishan's new government, formed both before and after the fall of the Qing:

> Every time there are new projects, the idea is always first expressed in the magazine, and so our countymen accept it peacefully and cooperate with the new government [projects] carried out at that time, such as reforming prisons, planning and sponsoring self-government, establishing a police force, advocating schools for girls. At the time, the gentry still did not understand [these reforms], but the scholars and merchants of our county viewed them as being a matter of course. Whatever was needed was made available. With barely a difference of opinion, great capital was also accumulated in a short while. This then, was the strength of the magazine's promoters. Moreover, at the time I then became head of the Education Committee, Tan Yuzhi managed the sponsoring of education, Lei Yuquan became responsible for the police, and Li Daochao then was put in charge of encouraging industry. New control of the government was entirely in the hands of the same people.[49]

The drain of personnel into government service led to a decline in the reformist quality of pieces appearing in *Xinning Magazine*. After 1913, editorial pieces lost their activist edge and became more reflective, addressing topics such as "The Pessimism of Xinning Society," "The Sorrowful History of Last Year," and "Reflections on the Past Five Years."[50] Not until after the Guomindang consolidated control of China and began co-opting *qiaokan* as a means of courting overseas Chinese support would *Xinning Magazine* once again become overtly politicized. For much of the 1910s and 1920s, however, it remained more closely akin to a village newspaper, containing no visions of a reinvigorated Taishan but full of news and gossip about local events of interest to Taishanese around the globe.

County news and advertisements portrayed in countless variation the problems and small triumphs of life in Taishan's emigrant villages. Articles acquired a chatty tone: "Is This Man This Woman's Previous Husband?," "Resolving the Struggle for Students Between Private Academies," and "Resolving the Court Case of the Cai and Lee Clans' Struggle over Land." Through the wealth of commonplace detail and slightly salacious stories produced by *Xinning Magazine*, overseas Taishanese, many of whom were hardworking family men forced by circumstance to live lonely bachelor lives, gained access to the tempo of daily life in the home villages they had left behind.[51]

The following report is a typical example. The article, "Adopted Son Becomes Family Bandit," describes the dilemma of Chen Apei, long-term merchant in Southeast Asia but originally of Duhu District in the southeastern corner of Taishan. Chen and his wife, Woman Hu, had no descendants, for Chen was over 50 when he returned to China and Woman Hu was too old to bear children. So they adopted a son and called him Laitian. Laitian behaved well until they found him a wife in the daughter of Huang Mouzhuan of Wuhe District. After the marriage, his vicious tendencies asserted themselves; he began to gamble and then started stealing his wife's clothes and jewelry to sell to support his habit. At the time of the report, he had run off to Doushan and had not been heard of since.[52]

Two aspects of this article are deserving of comment. First, like most articles in *Xinning Magazine* and other *qiaokan*, it mentioned many specific details in the form of names, places, marital status, emigrant status (overseas experiences, work status, years spent abroad, financial situation upon return, and host community), as well as evaluations of personal character. *Qiaokan* provided precise details in each story that would recall to overseas Taishanese the specifics of life at home. The second notable feature of *qiaokan* articles is that they very often depicted problems distinctive to emigrant villages. In the case of Hu and his wife, the trouble was childlessness stemming from Hu's long absences overseas. Through such stories, Taishanese living abroad could know that their particular concerns and troubles were not theirs alone and that their hardships were shared with other expatriates and with Taishanese at home.

Xinning Magazine also kept overseas Taishanese informed of the latest changes in a society undergoing rapid change. Overseas Taishanese could sense the encroachment of Western ideas and values in the article "Modern Girl Runs Away Right Before Marriage," which told the story of Lanjuan, daughter of Tan Guangmou of Tangkou Village on the east side of Taishan City, who ran away before being married to the son of Huang Shi'en of nearby Nansheng Village. Tan Lanjuan had been educated in Taishan City before being matched by her mother and a matchmaker at the age of 28 to a man she had never before seen. Despite her objections that she could never love someone she had not met, her mother continued with the wedding preparations, and Tan ran away.[53] Taishanese abroad were also kept abreast of more notable tragic events. In 1917 a new section, "World of Bandits," provided a steady flow of information about the victims of and damage from bandit attacks, which had become endemic with the advent of warlord rule in Guangdong.[54] Drug smuggling and drug use also received frequent coverage, as did the occasional devastations of flood and famine.

Qiaokan restored a vital component of community to transnational Taishanese by providing a forum in which they could exchange news and information in a way that had once occurred in marketplaces. With the physical dispersion of Taishanese it was no longer possible to share gossip and prices in face-to-face encounters. The articles in *qiaokan*, and perhaps more important, their advertising sections, acted as transnational marketplaces for publicizing the availability of goods and services as well as making public announcements. The advertisements and announcements that appear in the back pages of *Xinning Magazine* provide a glimpse of the functions and concerns of a transnational society at work in the pre-electronic age.

The advertising sections suggest the workings of a vibrant transnational commercial economy. Side by side with an announcement for the money house Guang Feng Tai of Doushan, Taishan, appears an ad for a medicinal backache paste that was distributed from Taishan to New York to Sydney, Australia. Shareholders in the Huashang Gongyi Company, located in Rangoon, Burma, sought the whereabouts of a partner from Kaiping who had absconded to the United States with company funds. The Bank of Canton in Hong Kong appealed to Taishanese abroad by stressing management by Chinese merchants who would nonetheless operate according to English business guidelines.[55] A reader in the Philippines, absent from Taishan for fourteen years, announced the death of his mother and wife in Taishan and his desire to split the family property with his brothers.[56] As early as 1911, *Xinning Magazine* also offered readers advice on the best means of sending and receiving international mail.[57]

Not surprisingly, the advertising sections also reveal the needs of a community whose members were continually in transit. By the 1920s, ads for shipping companies appeared in the front of every issue, informing Taishanese of arrival and departure dates three months in the future, ticket prices for four classes of travel, and the medical examinations to be passed before passengers could board.[58] Hotels in Hong Kong, such as the New Taishan and the American, specifically solicited travelers between Taishan and the United States. The latter hotel marketed itself as "the returning expatriate's good opportunity."[59] The Eastern Ocean Shipping Company (Dongyang lunchuan gongsi), run by Liu Canchen at 234 Des Voeux Rd., Hong Kong, offered to assist people traveling from their villages to the United States by handling "paperwork" and conducting eye tests.[60]

These advertisements make clear the importance of overseas remittances to emigrant communities. About 70 percent of the advertisements in *Xinning Magazine* publicized businesses that handled overseas money: receiving remittances and redirecting them to villages not served by regular postal routes, guaranteeing safe delivery of such funds, managing lump sums for the dependents of overseas Taishanese, offering interest on savings accounts, issuing allowances to family members, and supervising the finances of younger brothers or children sent to school in Hong Kong. The businesses engaged in these kinds of service ranged from the newly established Western-style banks such as the Bank of Canton, the Kangning Bank, and the Bank of Taishan to the more traditional and specialized such as the Baochang Money Shop of Duhu St., Taishan City, and the Five Continents Receiving Company (Wuzhou huidiao youxian gongsi) at 38 Bonham Strand East in Hong Kong, to a sideline service of firms such as the Changsheng Gold Shop of 52 Wing Lok St. in Hong Kong or the Wansheng Firm, which sold oil, sugar, and sundries and received letters and foreign funds.[61] Almost all of these firms were based in Taishan, Guangzhou, or Hong Kong, but profited from business conducted with customers sending back from Southeast Asia, Australia, Cuba, Mexico, and North America.

The advertisements reveal some of the problems that long-term separations created for family units. Husbands and wives with little time together in which to try to conceive children became ready consumers of fertility drugs. Many advertisements for such medications appeared in *qiaokan*, suggesting the importance of producing children to Taishanese as well as the serious dangers to patrilineage posed by emigration. The Joint Medicine Firm (Xiehe yaohang) advertised fertility pills for husbands and "mothers of the nation" with the exhortation, "Give birth to heroes for heaven and earth, produce descendants for the ancestors." During the 1930s, the back covers of *Xinning Magazine* featured ads by the Hall of Heavenly Longevity Medicine Firm (Tienshou tang yaohang) for male and female fertility pills. Accompanying the slogan, "Cures women's menstrual illnesses and miscarriages; the first in curing male infertility" appear a variety of images: a winsome bride flirting with the reader with her eyes, a young couple playing with their three children, an elderly grandfather benevolently watching his daughter-in-law dandle two children on her knees. Another ad features the picture of a smiling young boy set into a larger picture of a grim old man. Perhaps more to the point was an illustration featuring a man on horseback shooting an arrow at the bull's-eye of a target from which a baby boy drops straight into the outstretched arms of an eager young mother.[62]

Qiaokan helped to breach separations in other ways. Matters that before 1850 would have been conveyed to friends and relatives in person were, in a transnational society, posted in *qiaokan* as an effective means of covering the distances that separated families and fellow villagers. Some announced matters as simple as a change of address. Taishanese long absent overseas, such as Xie Baijin, a knife sharpener working in Southeast Asia, posted notices informing interested parties that property he still owned in Taishan was not for sale and that anybody making purchases from his unscrupulous relatives would eventually lose their money. Other overseas Taishanese, like Mai Dungu of Shen Village, relinquished responsibility for the debts of gambling, opium-imbibing sons, or younger brothers and warned that anyone tempted to lend money to such wastrels would probably lose it. Chen Yuanxi of Chenhua Village informed readers that he had been cleared by a court in Guangzhou of charges of rape. Taishan residents sought out long-lost relatives who had gone overseas. Wu Mingxin of Fulin Village advertised in 1919 for the whereabouts of his eldest son, Wu Renzhun, who had gone to Southeast Asia more than 30 years earlier.[63]

Willing readers overseas were drawn to the many connections and contacts offered by *Xinning Magazine*. Unlike most newspapers published in the

United States, which required the backing of some financially well-off political supporter, it seemed able to survive as a business.[64] By 1911, stockholders were already being paid dividends.[65] Within its first decade, circulation grew rapidly from not more than 1,000 in 1910 to more than 4,000 by 1917.[66] This success gave the magazine society cause to raise advertising prices. Thereafter, *Xinning Magazine* was continuously able to charge 20 to 30 percent more than other *qiaokan* for advertising space.[67]

Conceptualizing Transnational Communities

The success of *Xinning Magazine* as a conduit for transnational, native-place-oriented communications set a precedent for other groups. Through the printing press and postal service it pioneered a process by which other county, village, or clan organizations could maintain contact with overseas members. Taishanese as far flung as Havana, Melbourne, Rangoon, New York City, and Minneapolis could share with readers in Taishan City or Baisha the story of Woman Xi of Xi Village who ran off with her hairdresser to Guangzhou. All around the world they could breathe a communal sigh and shake their heads about the weakness of women and the wickedness of big cities. Together they could worry about the bandits pouring over the northwestern border from Xinhui and donate money for the relief of flood victims in Haiyan. With the guidance of notices and editorials posted in their county's magazine they could contribute to the building of schools, roads, and hospitals that would lead to a better life for all in Taishan. A host of other *qiaokan* soon attempted to duplicate *Xinning Magazine*'s success.

These imitators never attained the readership or longevity of *Xinning Magazine* but are of interest because they represent the different ways that community and common interest across a transnational landscape were defined. Organizations based in Taishan employed a varying admixture of kinship, shared surname, village, district, and county or counties in order to demarcate a realm of concerns shared with Taishanese living overseas.

The *Four Counties Magazine*, for example, was established in 1916, and as suggested by its title, it targeted a community composed of the four counties of Enping, Xinhui, Kaiping, and Taishan. As noted by its editors, only magazines could surmount geographic separation and effectively carry the same set of ideas and information to all the places inhabited by émigrés from the Four Counties:

> If you wish to follow the Pacific coast, the Indian Ocean coast, the western ocean coast, and honestly and soul-searchingly inform the home villages of our overseas brothers and sisters, footsteps are not sufficient to get to each place and communicate with all. Through [this magazine] we will change corrupt practices and expunge the decadent practices of declining regimes. Communications within the country [will be] inculcated abroad, [a service] that is fitting for the magazine shared by the Four Counties.[68]

The founders of the *Four Counties Magazine* conflated the interests of Enping, Xinhui, Kaiping, and Taishan in reasoning that their history, customs, and social practices were very much the same:

> The dialect and customs in the Four Counties share great similarities and small differences. Socially speaking, they have long shared the feeling of mutual sufferings, as well as [habitually] traveling abroad to work. At the far edges of the sky and corners of the earth, every place has people from the Four Counties. The closest are in the many islands of Southeast Asia, Annam, Singapore, and India. The farthest are in North and South America and Australia. [This] is just as if they were the colonies of people from the Four Counties. Keeping in mind this [shared tradition of travels] and observing that the Four Counties are contiguous with each other, [one realizes that] the people also feel close to each other, that there is mutual affection and love and already those that are abroad and at home are as one. This magazine embodies the emotions of this [dispersed] society's love in carrying out the business of improving society.[69]

Although the *Four Counties Magazine* might be construed as competition for *Xinning Magazine*, in reality they shared compatible goals and comparable concerns for the fate of the nation. Both advocated mobilizing the masses as the best means of transforming local state and society.

> It is certain that effecting a nation's rise or fall is a responsibility which everyone shares. Only then will there be beneficial results. Thus, how can it be that commoners have responsibility and we still say that this is protecting the nation? Honestly speaking, because out of hundreds of societies there is not a single person who doesn't see this as a task that should be done. The people's morality, the people's intelligence, and the people's labor

will be exerted, the three will grow in the same direction, and thus the attitudes of the people to the country will swell. Then the ability of the people
directed to the nation will overflow, and within the space of one turn there
is nothing under heaven that cannot be done.[70]

Much as Chinese were accepting of the native-place loyalties of sojourners in
their midst, it was also recognized that the interests of the more broadly
defined community of the Four Counties did not necessarily conflict with
those of Taishan. The former simply represented a more inclusive concep-
tion of common interests than the latter. Because one was superimposed on
the other, like concentric circles, each could coexist with the other. As building blocks in the national entity that was China, they were simply different-
sized bricks.[71]

> Everything has at its center ethics and the people. And the people have an
> intimate relationship to individuals, possibly because groups of people
> become a family, grouped families become a clan, grouped clans become a
> society, several societies become a nation. This is what a nation is. Count-
> less small organizations make up one big organization. For this reason,
> those wishing to love the larger nation and protect the larger nation must
> start from small organizations. This is how the *Four Counties Magazine*
> came to be.[72]

Both *qiaokan* endeavored to help China "return to the people's natural principles"[73] and thereby rescue their country from a crisis described as "wind
and rain as dark as night, [when] the slumbering lion sleeps a long time,
wolves devour and whales consume."[74] The *Four Counties Magazine* resem-
bled *Xinning Magazine* in practice as well as in intent. Revenues came from
subscription fees, advertising income, and stocks. It also had offices in
Taishan and Hong Kong and distribution points throughout the United
States, Canada, Mexico, South America, Indonesia, the Four Counties, the
Philippines, and Vietnam. Content was similar, with the added attraction of
a local news section for each of the Four Counties rather than one for just
Taishan. Even some of the advertisements posted were exactly the same.

Throughout the 1920s and 1930s, many other *qiaokan* followed in the
footsteps of the *Four Counties Magazine* but veered more sharply from the
model set by *Xinning Magazine*. Apart from the *Taishan Overseas Chinese
Magazine* (*Taishan huaqiao zazhi*), most served transnational communities

numerically much smaller than that defined by the county unit of Taishan. Village, district, and clan organizations began publishing *qiaokan* for more exclusive audiences. The *Guanghai Monthly* (1927), *Haiyan Magazine* (1936–37), and *Wartime Shen Village* (*Zhanshi shencun*) (1937, 1939, 1940) were published by village or district organizations, and clan associations produced the *Huang Clan Monthly* (1926–27) and the *Lin Clan Magazine* (no date). Some *qiaokan* targeted surname groups from particular districts, such as the *Duanfen Monthly* (1920, 1923, 1936, 1949) for members of the Mei clan from the central district of Duanfen. Other *qiaokan* targeted combined surname groups. As previously mentioned, *Longgang Magazine* (1937–38) served readers surnamed Liu, Guan, Zhang, and Zhao. The district or single clan *qiaokan* were frequently associated with specific projects, such as the *Six Villages Taihe Hospital Report* (*Liucun Taihe yiyuan*) (1941–45) or the *Taishan Teachers' College Seasonal* (*Taishi jikan*) (1933).

Like *Xinning Magazine*, many of these smaller *qiaokan* were established in order to generate support for local schools. Unlike *Xinning Magazine*, however, smaller *qiaokan* solicited financial contributions directly from readers and funneled both earnings and donations to particular projects. Education was a major priority with clan leaders, and clan organizations provided considerable sums of money to send children to school. Income from clan lands enabled poorer children to attend elementary school and sponsored more promising students to enter schools abroad or in Guangzhou. In 1928, for example, the Li clan contributed 7,000 yuan of their 11,000 yuan income to the Li clan middle school in Taishan City. In 1928 the Huang Clan Education Committee and the Huang Clan shouldered most of the 13,400 yuan costs for sending about a thousand students to the Juzheng Middle School.[75] But before children could attend schools, the facilities had to be built. Yu Renqiu notes that of the 1,122 schools in Taishan in 1931, 1,113, or 99.2 percent, were private institutions. Of those, most were clan schools.[76] One of the main ways that clans and villages raised funds for such schools was by publicizing their local needs in the *qiaokan*.

Unlike *Xinning Magazine*, district and clan *qiaokan* often could not, and did not expect to, sustain themselves as simple businesses. In serving a more exclusively defined community, however, they could make greater claims upon the loyalties, and wallets, of their readers. Clan or district leaders would develop plans to build a school and then involve overseas kin or fellow provincials in the project. Very often the editors and publishers of *qiaokan* established to construct schools were also principals and teachers. For example, most of the members of the Fushan Monthly Society were involved in secondary or university education.[77] They published in the belief that overseas Taishanese would respond with loyalty and concern for their cause.

The *Nanshe Monthly*, first published in 1920, illustrates something of the relationship between Taishanese overseas and those who published *qiaokan*: "To the various brothers living temporarily overseas, the Nanshe [society] is also willing to report honestly in order to connect to the feelings of their thinking of the village because you empathize with the Nanshe society."[78] The concerns of overseas Taishanese for their homes were addressed through the news and local gossip in the magazines. *Qiaokan* offered themselves as a conduit through which expatriates could express their feelings for home.

The line between subscriptions and donations thus became blurred. For example, the *Yingchuan Monthly* declared its goals to be the promotion of the Chen clan's industry, education, and defense as well as the encouragement of common sense.[79] In support of the magazine's efforts, readers were asked to make contributions at set levels or higher in return for which they would receive twelve issues of the magazine.[80] The names of all donors would eventually be published in the magazine, and each reader who contributed more than twenty yuan received the additional honor of a six-inch photograph next to his or her name in print.[81]

Other *qiaokan* that used similar means to raise funds for schools included the *Wenjiang Monthly* (1924) for the Huang clan, the *Kanghe Monthly* (1926) serving Chens, the *Dongkeng Monthly* (1927) for those surnamed Li, and the *Xicun Monthly* (1930) for members of the Kuang clan.[82] The closer relationship of the publishers of clan *qiaokan* to their readers allowed them greater scope in making demands of overseas Taishanese. The *Kanghe Monthly* editors chided their audience for being insufficiently supportive: "This periodical's objective has been to be a gift to readers. This past year donations have decreased and finances are insufficient. . . . We honestly feel this cannot continue for long and so specially publish the following rules for readers." The rules consisted of minimum amounts that could be donated in order to receive a year's subscription: three yuan if ordering from within China or four yuan if subscribing from Hong Kong or overseas.[83] As an additional inducement to be generous, donors of twenty yuan or more were honored with four-inch photographs, and donors of 30–50 yuan were awarded six-inch photographs published in two issues.

Editors at the *Fushan Monthly* demanded not just money but also personal sacrifice from their readers. Established in 1935 for Zhao clan members living in the Fushi district of central Taishan, the *Fushan Monthly* exhorted its overseas readers to be loyal to Fushi:

> It is simply that in these times of poor industrial and business conditions our brothers traveling abroad have not resolved the problem of paying for their own clothing, food, and lodging. Under these circumstances, although there is the worry of not being able to provide for oneself, if by cutting down on food and clothing one dollar or dime can be sent back, even as mere bundles of armpit hair can be collected to make a complete pelt, (such) money is enough to demonstrate the honest spirit of their love and support, and accumulate into a lot of help. Publishing a monthly newspaper is truly a sorely needed plan for the saving of our village today, and donating money to the newspaper is also the responsibility of those overseas who cherish our village's preservation.[84]

In addition to asking readers to reduce their consumption of food and clothing, the Fushan Monthly Society also asked that contributors of articles forgo their payments of ten to 60 cents. Their stinginess and high demands did not seem to disturb readers, for in spite of slow economic conditions during the Great Depression, overseas Chen clan members did indeed find the dollars and dimes and occasionally even more to give to the *Fushan Monthly*. In October 1936, the society thanked eleven readers for donating a total of 428 French francs to the construction of a public park.[85] One reader in Mexico found giving money insufficient to express his gratitude to the editors: "The sphere of journalism is the leader for humankind. The gentlemen who produce the *Fushan Monthly* have ambitions in this direction and the project has now been established for a year already. . . . The overseas brothers from our village who have received this gift are not inconsiderable in number."[86] Yet another reader wrote that the recent flurry of publications from his hometown of Fushi was as welcome as "the sprouting of bamboo shoots after a spring rain."[87]

Money-raising *qiaokan* like the *Yingchuan Monthly* and the *Kanghe*

Monthly proliferated during the 1920s and 1930s. Despite the often self-serving and mercenary messages that they conveyed, during the Republican era overseas Taishanese were overwhelmingly responsive to the demands on their loyalties and for their money. As described in Chapter 2, overseas earnings also funded projects of substantial benefit to county, village, and clan communities. After supporting their families, building houses, and buying land, investment in education received the most attention, and Taishan enjoyed a boom in the construction of schools. By 1932, Taishan had 268 elementary schools and 1,010 lower-level elementary schools.[88] Taishan was among the most well endowed with middle schools and middle-school teachers in southern Guangdong. This expenditure resulted in high rates of school attendance as well as a greater number of children being educated. In 1932, Taishan had a 75 percent school attendance rate, male and female children included.[89] Overseas money enabled Taishan to educate far more of its children than its more commercially developed neighbors could.

Prosperity and progress in Taishan also assumed the form of its own railroad. As merchants and laborers traveled more often to Taishan City, the town grew into a miniature metropolis with several hundred businesses, paved roads, electric street lights, a movie theater, telephone lines, public bus services, and Western store fronts.[90]

Fertile Soil for Native-Place Loyalties

The strength of overseas Taishanese loyalty to Taishan, as expressed through the money and aid that they sent back, must be considered in light of conditions in their places of resettlement. American Taishanese maintained strong loyalties to Taishan in the face of widespread institutional, social, and economic discrimination in the United States and Canada. In 1882, after an inflammatory and highly racist campaign by white, working-class organizations, the U.S. Congress passed the first of many immigration laws that singled out Chinese as the only people to be named by race and class for exclusion from the United States. This law remained in force until 1943 and mandated that only specified, carefully defined, and verified classes of Chinese could enter the country: merchants, diplomats, students, teachers, tourists, and properly certified laborers. Chinese could not gain citizenship through naturalization if they chose to stay, nor could they marry outside their race. Most who managed to immigrate did so using fake names and statuses in order to gain access to the few narrow niches in the American economy allowed to Chinese—laundry work, restaurants, domestic service, and Chinatown stores by the turn of the century. Despite their restricted opportunities and confinement to urban ghettoes, Taishanese in North America could earn higher and more stable incomes by emigrating than by remaining in China. More would have resettled permanently if miscegenation laws and even greater restrictions on the entry of Chinese women had not made it so difficult to establish families.

Chinese in the United States were stuck between a rock and a hard place. On the one hand, pervasive and institutionalized racism made it difficult to establish permanent attachments to the United States. On the other, the native-place and kinship networks that provided the basis for mutual aid and protection necessary to survival in a hostile land only exacerbated their image as clannish and excessively loyal to China. To be sure, the Taishanese native-place organization, the Ningyang Association, and the various clan associations did offer services that reaffirmed ties to Taishan by organizing traditional religious festivals, providing funds for burial at home, and organizing fundraising drives for projects and disaster relief in Taishan.[91] However, the fervor with which Taishanese in North America supported such causes can be measured against the degree of alienation they experienced in both Canada and the United States.

Not until social and economic conditions and immigration laws began changing during World War II did Taishanese become more willing to relocate permanently to the United States. Until they could establish families and harbor realistic hopes that their children's lives might be better than theirs, Taishanese in America would remain loyal to Taishan because their hopes for a better future lay there. The limited scope of social, political, and economic mobility allowed to Taishanese all but forced them to channel their aspirations and interests toward their native place. As described in Chapter 2, the frustrations of their lives overseas led North American Chinese, only around 2 percent of all overseas Chinese, to send back just over 50 percent of all money remitted to China in 1930 and 1931.

Qiaokan provided faraway readers with a means of participating in a fuller life, albeit in Taishan. One reader, Mei Shiming, recalled that during the

1930s as he worked in the United States alone and away from his family, the magazine provided news of the events surrounding their lives in their home district of Duanfen, in the county of Taishan, and in the country of China.[92] For people living at the margins of society in the United States, unable to feel comfortable resettling permanently and also unable to return home because their families needed their overseas earnings, *qiaokan* like *Xinning Magazine* provided a window into a world where their participation in local society and government was warmly welcomed. Leong Gor Yun, a newspaper editor working in the United States, attributed great importance to newspapers in the lives of hardworking and hard-pressed Chinese men: "The influence of the Chinese press in Chinatown life . . . is incalculable. If it does nothing else, it speaks to the Chinese in a language he understands; it is his only medium for knowing what is happening in his world and the world at large. It gives him a perspective very much needed in a life as narrow as life in Chinatown."[93]

In return for their loyalty, overseas Taishanese received fulsome praise for their contributions to their native place. *Xinning Magazine* constantly reported events representing progress in Taishan, including the establishment of self-defense troops and self-government committees in villages and schools. Taishanese abroad received public honor and thanks for their contributions to the modernization of Taishan, with the publication of their names and amounts donated. In this way, expatriates not only were involved in the building, but also accrued a little social capital. Donor lists and the results of such donations constantly appeared in *Xinning Magazine* letting overseas Taishanese know that hard-earned and graciously donated funds were being well used by their compatriots at home. For example, in 1912 the self-government committee of the Tan Clan in Baishui thanked San Francisco donors for giving to the *fourth* round of fundraising, and in 1917 the self-defense troop of Sanhe published five pages of donor names from Hawaii, Boston, San Francisco, Portland, New York, Salt Lake City, Los Angeles, and Southeast Asia.[94]

Qiaokan provided effusive verbal rewards for overseas Taishanese seeking to exist beyond the daily humiliation, social frustration, and grinding drudgery of life in North America. By looking to Taishan, they could instead feel a tremendous sense of achievement.

As portrayed by *qiaokan*, the best things in life in *qiaoxiang* (the native-place community of overseas Chinese) stemmed from the success and generosity of those who remained loyal while overseas. Such depictions gave to expatriate Taishanese working in the narrow confines of Chinatowns overseas a sense of the ambitions and goals that those at home harbored for the progress of their native place. Although they could not directly benefit from these improvements, absentee Taishanese could enhance the lives of their relatives and kinsmen and thereby gain some vicarious enjoyment of the better future they could not hope for in the United States.

Repoliticizing Qiaokan: *The Rise of the Guomindang*

The loyalty of overseas Taishanese and their willingness to contribute financially to their home communities did not escape the notice of central government authorities. By the 1880s, the Qing had learned from its traveling emissaries that expatriate Chinese could be lucrative sources of money and support. Sun Yatsen found some of his most loyal followers while traveling abroad, and for their irreplaceable contributions to his eventual political success he called overseas Chinese "the mother of the Chinese Revolution." Up to 1929, fully one-quarter of the Guomindang's members lived abroad.[95] However, Sun died in 1925, and with his passing came dramatic changes in the political party to which he had recruited so many loyal supporters abroad. Under the leadership of Chiang Kai-shek, the Guomindang proceeded to unify China under the military rule of one party. After consolidating control of Guangdong and successfully completing the Northern Expedition, one of the projects to which it turned was courting overseas Chinese support. In 1927 this goal became official policy as the Guangdong Provincial Education Department issued a regulation that encouraged the raising of money among individuals outside of China.[96]

One strategy employed by the Guomindang to gain access to overseas capital was to establish and restructure government-run banks in an attempt to take over the remittance business. Before World War II, however, the efforts of the Bank of Canton and the Commercial Bank had little impact on the dominance of *jinshanzhuang* and their widespread network of mercantile partners in this area of financial service. Only after World War II, with the enforced inactivity of four years, did government institutions begin to gain control of the mechanisms that overseas Taishanese used to send money back and forth.

The Guomindang also attempted to court the support of overseas Chinese through publications. As suggested by Ge Gongzhen in his 1927 history of the Chinese newspaper industry, "If the government can create this kind of [overseas Chinese] newspaper, [it] can also maintain feelings for the fatherland and overseas Chinese, and can play a great role in the development of overseas Chinese industry."[97] The Guomindang proceeded to use magazines to publicize itself both through force and through co-optation.

With the permission of provincial authorities, the county branch of the Guomindang had the power to ban certain books and halt publication of magazines and newspapers that offended party sensibilities. For example, the *Taishan Daily Newspaper* was forced to shut down after only two or three months of publication because it insulted one high party official.[98] The publishing businesses that hoped to survive one-party rule were forced to acknowledge and at least superficially support China's new leaders.

After the Guomindang took control of county affairs in 1928, *Xinning Magazine* began incorporating party symbols into its layout. Sun Yatsen's speech on the Three Principles of the People appeared on the frontispiece, and the star from the Republican flag marked the beginning of each article. In 1932 a photograph of Sun Yatsen appeared with his speech on the first page. Over the course of the 1930s, content of the magazine also changed, with news of party activities and the increasing boldness of Japanese encroachments gradually replacing county affairs and gossip as the main focus.

After 1932, government and party activities slowly came to dominate the section on county news. News of the Guomindang included the development of "Methods for Encouraging Overseas Chinese to Return to China and Revive Industry," as well as accounts of party efforts to protect and care for their interests in "County Party Helps County Sojourners Retrieve Borrowed Funds."[99] Lin Yizhong of the government affairs committee asserted the desire of the Guomindang government to care for the sons and younger brothers that overseas Chinese sent back to study in China. The Guomindang did so, he said, because:

[Their] spirit of risk-taking struggle stirred people's admiration. And their ups and downs and vicissitudes are closely related to [affairs] within China.

[In matters] like the adjusting of finance and industrial investments, the benefits of overseas Chinese assistance have not been inconsiderable. Because the connection is so intimate, there is nothing about overseas Chinese that the government does not kindly protect.[100]

Xinning Magazine also publicized Guomindang support of overseas Taishanese by announcing measures taken to facilitate their return to China, such as improved methods for the inspection of travelers' luggage and crackdowns on thieves who preyed on recent arrivals.[101]

Embedded in Guomindang courtship of overseas Taishanese was the message that their loyalties and the financial contributions that they could make to China were essential to the well-being and survival of the nation. To be sure, money had always been an issue in the publishing of *qiaokan*. The founders of *Xinning Magazine* were originally members of the Anliang Bureau, which had been created to solicit money from overseas Taishanese. The magazine also constantly featured advertisements requesting donations as well as announcements thanking generous contributors. However, during the first years of the magazine's existence, appeals for involvement and sacrifice targeted all Taishanese. In 1912, *Xinning Magazine* had asked each of its readers, at home and abroad, to "sacrifice your lives to save the nation, cut down on your clothing and contribute your food, sacrifice your property to save the nation."[102] By the 1930s such appeals for public service focused only on those overseas and demanded aid primarily in the form of money.[103]

These mercenary attitudes to expatriates are illustrated most pointedly in the *Taishan Overseas Chinese Magazine*, which began publication in 1932. Editors claimed as their general objective the good of society, while the welfare of overseas brethren was their specific one.[104] The two were linked, they said, because:

The creativity and strength of overseas brethren in our China, and especially in our Taishan, is not only enough to attract the admiration and respect of people in society, it is also enough to influence the diminishing and growing, the vigor and weakness of society. Because of this, if the well-being of our overseas brothers increases day after day, then the well-being of society naturally will increase day after day.[105]

Overseas Chinese had become endowed with the power to make money and send it back, as well as the power to influence the very ebb and flow of society in China. Implicit in this statement is the suggestion that without over-seas Chinese support China would never be able to overcome its weakness and compete with modern nations.

Praise for overseas Taishanese mingled with explicit expectations of financial contributions:

> Our nation for the past few decades has depended upon our overseas Chinese in the attempt to reform. In reviving education, [we] depend upon our overseas brothers, in developing communications, [we] also depend upon our overseas brothers, in promoting the reclamation and cultivating of wasteland, [we] rely even more upon our overseas brothers. In addition, regardless of which cause we wish to establish, no matter which city we wish to reform, to the point that no matter what "spiritual building" or no matter what "material construction" [we attempt], there is no endeavor that does not rely directly or indirectly upon the economic strength of our brothers overseas.[106]

The exhortations to help the motherland were expressed in new terms that heightened the responsibilities of those overseas. In the first issues of *Xinning Magazine*, expatriate Taishanese were more neutrally described as "those who have gone overseas" (*chuyang zhi ren*) and as "Xinning people" (*Xinning ren*).[107] Other widely used phrases included "overseas countymen" (*haiwai yiren*), "overseas Xinning people" (*haiwai Ningren*), and "countymen sojourning overseas" (*luju haiwai yiren*). In the 1930s, however, words laden with even greater expectations of loyalty became commonplace. *Huaqiao*, the most well-known term, is perhaps still the most problematic. *Qiao* is the root of this word and is usually translated as "sojourn" or "sojourner."[108] After learning about the economic potential of Chinese overseas through the travels of emissaries, the Qing began applying the label *qiao* to overseas Chinese during the 1890s.[109] And so evolved the term *huaqiao*, usually translated as "overseas Chinese" but understood to mean Chinese who lived and worked abroad while remaining loyal and contributing patriots to China. Indiscriminately applied, *huaqiao* was a loaded term from the very start. By connoting loyalties to China's government on the part of Chinese overseas, who were often only interested in social stability and financial gain, it encouraged the belief of some host-society governments and people that Chinese were perpetual outsiders and therefore politically suspect.[110] The even more potent term *qiaobao*, here translated as overseas brothers or overseas brethren, also gained widespread usage. The phrase contains the character *bao*, which refers to the placenta or children of the same parents.[111] In combination with *qiao*, the word suggests that Taishanese abroad were not just sojourning Chinese but sojourners bound by blood to China.[112]

The heightened sense of connection between China, as represented by the Guomindang, and overseas Taishanese was needed to strengthen their sense of responsibility to the abstract entity that was the nation. Unlike clan, district, or village organizations, the Guomindang could not call upon the more immediate and more intimate bonds of extended family or native-place loyalties to persuade overseas Taishanese to contribute. Co-opting local publishing endeavors like *Xinning Magazine* and changing its content and language, however, did not sway many Taishanese overseas to the Guomindang cause. There were many reasons for Taishanese disenchantment with Chiang Kai-shek's branch of the Guomindang. After 1929, U.S. membership in the Guomindang plummeted from 12,210 to 3,000 in reaction to Chiang Kai-shek's purge of leftists from party ranks. A faction of conservatives also broke off after Chiang placed his political rival Hu Hanmin, a Guangdong native, under house arrest.[113] The most direct cause of conflict began in 1927 when the Ningyang Association started a boycott against *Young China*, the oldest and largest Guomindang operation in the United States, in retaliation for written attacks on the inactivity of Six Companies leaders. Not until the dispute ended in 1935, when the crippling number of Taishanese lost to their cause led the editors of *Young China* to issue a public apology, was the Guomindang able to attract Taishanese American supporters.[114] No longer forced to choose between loyalty to China and loyalty to Taishan, Taishanese flocked generously to the Guomindang cause, especially as it became clear that China faced the very real threat of disappearing through conquest by an expansionary Japan. In the belief that a strengthened China would generate greater respect for Chinese in the United States, Taishanese in America became ardent, and generous, nationalists. With China's autonomy and the hope of improving their own situation in the United States, Taishanese overseas began to give wholeheartedly to save their nation.[115]

Conclusion

The numerous *qiaokan* that appeared in the Republican era served a range of overlapping and not necessarily competing conceptions of transnational community. Their expressed content and goals and the ways in which readers responded illuminate the nature of the relationships that bound overseas Taishanese to Taishan. Bonds of kinship and native place, whether defined by village, district, county, province, nation, or some combination thereof, motivated overseas Taishanese to take an interest in local affairs and to contribute financially to scores of local welfare projects in the form of schools, hospitals, self-defense corps, and disaster relief. If roughly equated, the amounts given can be considered representative of the strength of the transnational bond. After the needs of immediate family members were filled, expatriates tended to give first to village and clan before contributing to district and county. Except during the war against Japan, China the nation took a backseat to more local constructions of identity and common interest.

Working with the strength of these preexisting loyalties and commitments, *qiaokan* served as effective communicators of local native-place and clan needs. They gave to expatriate Taishanese working in the narrow confines of Chinatowns overseas a sense of the ambitions and goals that those at home harbored for the improvement of their native place. They became involved in improving living conditions in their home communities and received public recognition for their contributions. *Qiaokan* gave to overseas Taishanese the sense of broader horizons and held out the promise that even though they could not personally benefit, their families, kinsmen, and fellow county-people would enjoy better lives through their hard work. The seductiveness of this self-sacrificing vision did much to distract Taishanese in America from investing their energies in new lives overseas.

Heroic Returns:
The Railroad Empire
of Chen Yixi, 1904–1939

Of the hundreds of thousands of Taishanese men who journeyed to North America, it was arguably Chen Yixi who came closest to attaining the heroic stature attributed to *huaqiao* in the pages of *qiaokan*. He possessed talent, determination, and luck enough to succeed amidst the fervent racism of foreigners and yet returned to invest his money and knowledge in his native place. Chen Yixi used the capital and skills he had acquired abroad in an ambitious attempt to improve life and opportunities in Taishan while magnifying his own fortune and stature. This wealthy Seattle merchant, labor contractor, and railroad engineer conceived and partially fulfilled a plan to rescue Taishan from its agricultural stagnation and transform it into a thriving commercial metropole serving all of Southeast Asia, northern and southern China, and the eastern coast of what is now known as the Pacific Rim. From his 40-year sojourn on Gold Mountain, Chen brought back not only capital and technical expertise but also considerable knowledge of the industrial processes fueling the economic development of the United States. He had made his fortune as Seattle grew from a coastal port serving Alaska and the Puget Sound region to an international entrepot with direct connections by rail and steam to Japan, China, and the entire southwestern and eastern portions of the United States. After attaining as much wealth and power as was permitted to a foreign-born Chinese man in the United States, Chen

Yixi returned to Taishan to set about building a railroad and a port that could forge a similar economic miracle in Taishan.

For his ambition, the strength of his loyalty to Taishan, and his business savvy and powerful convictions Chen's statue stands in the town square of the county seat. He came closest to fulfilling Taishan's hopes that migration might be its salvation by bringing back from Gold Mountain a dream of modernizing the county in a way that would enrich both Taishan and himself for decades, if not centuries, to come.

Although the Xinning Railroad could bring considerable advantages to the county, many of Chen Yixi's contemporaries were unappreciative and unsupportive of his schemes. Among Chinese there was a growing awareness that railroads were one essential key to modernity, and thus prosperity and national strength. However, local and provincial leaders at almost every level of society and government gave little help to a project that required tremendous resources and cooperation in order to become profitable. William Cronon, author of a compelling study of America's most famous railroad metropolis, Chicago, sums up the difficulties in this way:

> Unlike their predecessors, the corporations that ran railroads generally owned the entire operation: lands, rails, locomotives, cars, and stations, not to mention the labor and fuel that kept everything moving. . . . Although such extensive ownership rights conferred great power, with them came truly daunting levels of risk and responsibility as well. Running a railroad meant trying to achieve unprecedented levels of coordination among engineering technologies, management structures, labor practices, freight rates, resource flows, and—not least—natural environments, all spread over thousands of square miles of land.[1]

The Xinning Railroad would operate on a far smaller scale and never covered more than a few hundred square miles of land. Events reveal that even Chen Yixi himself did not understand the deep pockets and control of natural terrain, machinery, engineering technology, personnel, and government bureaucracy needed to complete his planned transformation of the geographic and economic landscape of Taishan.

In this chapter, I describe the rise and fall of Chen Yixi's dreams of a railroad empire centered on Taishan. Despite the strength of his beliefs in the power of railroads to bring prosperity, and the considerable success of fellow "empire builders" in the United States, Chen Yixi's hopes for the Xinning Railroad were doomed to failure for complex reasons. Chen learned about railroad technology and the lasting benefits of becoming a communications node during the decades he spent in the Pacific Northwest. In an America flush with the successes of robber barons who developed the United States while enriching themselves, Chen acquired an abiding faith in the economic miracles that came of technological improvements and capitalist reorganization of natural resources. Chen would soon find, however, that business principles and ideas that flourished in the United States did not fare so well when transplanted to China. Although the Xinning Railroad was exactly the kind of modernizing effort and enterprise expected of overseas Taishanese by *qiaokan*, political and financial institutions were ill equipped and ultimately unwilling to offer Chen Yixi the advantages and support he needed to complete such an all-encompassing transformation. Chen's failure to forge this economic miracle in Taishan suggests that in the end, migration and transnationality could bring but limited benefits to Taishan.

Tales of American Successes

In many ways, Chen embodied the archetypal American rags-to-riches immigrant success story. He was born in the mid-1840s to an impoverished family living in Langmei Village in the Doushan District of Taishan.[2] After a childhood spent helping his father eke out a living by herding cows and peddling pottery on the street, his big break came when he was around fifteen. A kinsman just returned from the United States, Chen Xidao, noticed the young man's cleverness and enterprising spirit and offered to take him to Gold Mountain. By 1862, Chen was in the United States.

More quickly and to a greater degree than most other Chinese at the time, he made the most of his opportunities by learning to speak English and attending engineering classes. By 1873 he had already became a junior partner in the Huachang Company (Wah Chong) of Port Gamble, Washington, the largest labor recruiting firm in the Pacific Northwest, which provided manpower for the developing regional industries of logging, canning, mining, and railroads. He also turned his hand to a variety of other endeavors, including the import-export trade and assisting railroad engineers. Chen's ready immersion into life in the United States is reflected in the fact that he brought over a wife from Taishan who gave birth to a son in 1875, reportedly the first Chinese baby born in the Pacific Northwest.[3]

As Chen prospered and flourished in the Puget Sound region, he became part of a circle of prominent local business leaders concerned with the economic growth of the Pacific Northwest and the recently founded city of Seattle in particular. In recognition of his business acumen and enterprising spirit, the mayor-to-be of Seattle, Henry Yesler, personally invited Chen to relocate from Port Gamble to the growing city. There he founded his own business, the Guangde firm (Quong Tuck Company), which dealt in general merchandise and acted as a labor contractor and general agent for all the Pacific steamship companies. The last undertaking was of great significance, for it enabled Chen Yixi to monitor the pulse of a developing intimacy between China and Seattle that grew from the beginning of direct traffic between the two in 1874.

Chen made the most of his connections to both the United States, his adoptive home, and China, the home of his birth. His flexibility would prove to be his greatest resource both in business and in times of personal danger. Chen built his personal fortune by managing and coordinating trade and the movement of people between China and the Pacific Northwest. The extensive network so established provided protection in times of crisis as well as in prosperity. In the winter of 1885 and 1886, Chen faced a danger that he survived and even triumphed over by drawing on both Chinese and American aid. In the wake of the massacre and physical expulsion of Chinese from Rock Springs, Montana, violent anti-Chinese sentiment spread, and calls for the expulsion of Chinese soon engulfed the Puget Sound region. In the face of organized intimidation and mob violence, Chen handled the threat to his family and substantial property holdings by refusing to be summarily driven from the area. He made repeated appeals to the San Francisco–based Chinese consul for intervention. Under the protection of powerful friends such as Mayor Yesler, he managed to remain in Seattle despite rioting mobs. After the area calmed down, Chen acted on the advice of his friend and local attorney Thomas Burke to ask the Chinese consulate to successfully claim restitution of some $700,000 for himself and other local Chinese. Seattle is one of only a handful of places in which nineteenth-century Chinese were able to claim damages after being driven out by discontented mobs. Chen's triumph over anti-Chinese elements stemmed from his astute use of the Chinese government's developing foreign diplomacy as well as his friendships with prominent, non-Chinese local business leaders. As a labor contractor, Chen developed close working relationships with other successful immigrants such as the banker Jacob Furth and Thomas Burke, the most prominent attorney in Seattle. Many of Seattle's leading businessmen had welcomed and even embraced Chen's presence in their city as a notable force in the growth of the local economy. It was a camaraderie born out of recognition that regardless of race or country of origin those who contributed most to the building of Seattle were almost all immigrants who by dint of hard work and determination overcame humble origins to become influential men of business.

Thomas Burke, a "diminutive and clever Irishman," had arrived in Seattle in 1875 with but ten dollars in his pocket. He soon amassed a small fortune through real estate deals and set himself up as a lawyer in partnership with John J. McGilvra, whose daughter, Caroline, he eventually married. He rose to become one of the most powerful men in Seattle, reputed to have "virtually hand-picked the state's congressional delegation and [to have] friends and associates in almost every public office."[4] In Chen Yixi, Burke recognized a kindred "can-do" spirit that formed the basis for many fruitful business and personal associations. When Burke built his block-long Burke Building, it was Chen who supplied the labor and imported the Chinese artifacts used to decorate it. Through open-minded men like Burke and Furth, Chen Yixi gained considerable insight into the sweeping changes that capitalism and industry were bringing to the vast vistas of the developing American West.

Between the Civil War and 1900, steam and electricity replaced human muscle in newly invented machines that transformed everything from the production of food and textiles to how people traveled and kept track of time. It was the age of the "empire builders," who colluded with the government and the courts to attain incredible wealth based on the promise and widespread belief that as they prospered so too would the rest of America through their development of the continent's vast resources of land and minerals. As the continent became unified under an expanding network of roads, railroad tracks, and canals, men such as Andrew Carnegie, James Mellon, and John D. Rockefeller became multi-millionaires as the administrators of new corporations that drew on the back-breaking—and often unhealthful—labor of millions of poorly paid immigrants from Europe and Asia to build empires of steel, finance, railroads, telephones and telegraphs, farming machines, oil and textiles. It was, in the words of Howard Zinn, "the greatest march of economic growth in human history."[5]

From his base in Seattle, Chen Yixi personally experienced the tremendous wealth, fascination with economic development, and valorization of these masters of industry through his involvement with the Great Northern Railroad and "empire builder" James J. Hill.

Hill arrived in Seattle in 1893 to a hero's welcome for having chosen Seattle as the western terminus of the Great Northern Railroad and for making it the primary node on trade routes connecting the Pacific Northwest to the East Coast, the Midwest, and the Southwest. Only two decades earlier, Seattle residents had witnessed what they thought would be the economic demise of their home: Tacoma's selection by the Northern Pacific Railroad Company as its western headquarters. Seattle businessmen feared that their city would become a commercial backwater, unable to compete without access to a major rail line. Such faith was placed in railroads that they planned to build their own under the leadership of Thomas Burke. But their inability to borrow sufficient capital from eastern banks doomed this effort to failure. Seattle managed to survive, nonetheless, by developing a healthy coastal maritime trade in logs, lumber, coal, livestock, and food products with ports on the Puget Sound basin, British Columbia, and the fjords and harbors of southeastern Alaska. Despite the soundness of this ship-based commercial economy, however, residents of Seattle continued to believe that railroads would ultimately determine the future of their city and the Pacific Northwest.

Under these circumstances, James J. Hill brought the Great Northern Railroad to Seattle, attracted by the possibilities of its readily expanded hinterland trade and its proximity to Asia. Thomas Burke became the Great Northern's West Coast counsel and tenaciously employed all the strategies and personal influence at his disposal to ensure that Hill did indeed choose Seattle as the Great Northern's western terminus. Burke was certain enough of the railroad's benefits to the city to convince local government to grant Hill a monopoly on the railroad lines within Washington and control of the waterfront, thereby ensuring Hill a lion's share of any future trade that might develop with Asia.

By 1896, Seattle had joined a network of railway lines controlled by Hill and became connected to the East Coast, the Midwest, and the entire American Southwest. The city became a central way station in a healthy trade connecting the East Coast of the United States to Japan, Shanghai, and Hong Kong. At first, local lumber and salmon constituted most of the cargo. However, Hill worked assiduously to cultivate profits for Seattle, and for himself, by encouraging the development of two-way traffic that complemented the export of rails, cotton, and grain to Japan with imports of tea and silk. In 1896, Hill signed an agreement with the Nippon Yushen Kaisha of Tokyo, and on August 31 of that year the *Miike Maru* arrived in Seattle, initiating a trans-Pacific shipping trade that would route millions of dollars in products through Seattle on the way to the East Coast or East Asia. Other steamship companies soon set up shop. In 1900 the China Mutual Steam Navigation Company began a line, as did Kosmos of Hamburg in 1901. Commerce with Asia increased dramatically. Between 1895 and 1896, trade to Japan more than doubled and tripled once again over the next year. By 1899, it was worth $8,052,857. By 1904, imports of tea, raw silk, curios, camphor, matting, and braid were valued at $6,625,964. Exports included lumber, flour, raw cotton, machinery, and heavy hardware. Between 1896 and the beginning of the twentieth century, Seattle's commerce expanded eightfold, and by 1916, the city had become the leading port on the Pacific Coast in dollar value of its imports and exports.[6]

Through Thomas Burke, Chen's Quong Tuck Company began acting as the railroad's main labor contractor and later become general agent for all transcontinental railroad lines ending in Seattle.[7] As Seattle grew into a main communications node in the developing trade between all of the North American continent and East Asia, James J. Hill grew rich, as did Chen Yixi.[8] Chen participated firsthand in the economic boom that resulted from the railroad and shipping empire that Hill constructed. Most striking about this success for Chen was that "unlike other port cities, Seattle accomplished this feat in the absence of a major industrial base."[9] From the vantage point of his own mercantile establishment located at 208–210 Washington Street, Chen applied the possibilities of Hill's strategies for the development and enrichment of Seattle to rural Taishan. Chen even delivered lectures on the subject to other Chinese American men casually passing time in the store. Hill and Burke themselves encouraged Chen's obsession by arranging for him to tour some of the main railway lines linked to the Great Northern. This vision of commercial prosperity and local ascendancy won by simply linking maritime shipping routes to extensive rail lines was one that Chen would carry back to Taishan.

Chen realized the tremendous power of railroads to end the isolation imposed by geography on Taishan, where rivers and hills hindered travel to the rest of Guangdong and especially to the prosperous Pearl River Delta. He saw that railroads brought "sudden sweeping changes to the landscapes and communities through which they passed."[10] Before railroads, travelers and transporters contended with roads and waterways that could be mired in mud, dried to a trickle, or covered in ice, depending on the season. In contrast, trains and tracks could defy most of the obstacles that weather could throw in the way of people seeking to journey from one town to another—often at a lower cost and certainly in a shorter amount of time. As they had done for the city of Seattle, railroads could transform an otherwise undistinguished coastal area into a lucrative entrepot through which trade goods could be routed. As a thriving nexus for coastal and regional commerce, Taishan's fortune could be made.

Using Western Learning to Strengthen China

Chen Yixi was already in his sixties at the time that he began this ambitious project. His decision to leave Seattle and return to Taishan was perhaps spurred in part by the limitations of life in the United States. Unlike his friend, Thomas Burke, Chen Yixi would never be able to acquire American citizenship, cast votes, help pick judges, or influence the state legislature, much less marry the daughter of an already influential man. Although Chen and Burke had moved to Seattle around the same time, the range of possibilities open to the Chinese immigrant remained limited to trading and labor recruiting, whereas the white immigrant could tie his ambitions and horizons to the wealthiest and politically most powerful men in the state and the region. By the turn of the century, Chen Yixi had accomplished all that was permitted to men of his race and could but sit by as his white counterparts, his colleagues in helping to build Seattle, attained ever higher levels of wealth and influence.

With the limitations of life in the United States and the inspiring examples of James J. Hill and Seattle's growth before him, Chen was swift to act on his own chance for empire when highly charged nationalist concerns for railroad autonomy rocked China in the years between 1903 and 1906. After decades of national decline and international humiliation, Chinese from all walks of life united in the growing fear that China would disappear altogether as foreign powers gained control of its strategically important railroad lines. Foreign domination of China's railroads had begun with concessions granted in the Treaty of Shimonoseki, signed after China's unexpected defeat by Japan in 1895. Of primary concern were the military uses to which railroads could be put by foreign powers. The Railroad Rights Recovery movement spurred gentry and merchants from all parts of China to transcend their regional loyalties to agitate for the cause of China as a sovereign nation. In 1904, local leaders from Guangdong, Hubei, and Hunan began to call on the Qing to retrieve the nation's railroad rights, protect the roads, and arrange for self-management of railroad lines. They specifically demanded the recovery of the Guangzhou-Hankou concession, which had been given to the American China Development Company and had later been taken over by Belgian interests without the consultation of Chinese authorities. As a bargaining tool against the Belgians, the Ministry of Foreign Affairs successfully used a clause in the original contract to revoke the American concession in November 1908. The Qing had never planned to build the line themselves, but public opinion enthusiastically endorsed the government's move and insisted that Chinese finance and build the railroad. Local gentry and merchant leaders joined with educated elites to sound the call for China to recover control of its railroads.[11] In partial response, the Qing attempted to win back some measure of autonomy by giving private Chinese companies charters to construct and manage certain railroad lines in November 1903. The court hoped by these means to build a Chinese-controlled network of rail lines piece by piece.[12]

Another series of events that spurred Chen to action began with Congress's decision in 1904 to renew the Exclusion acts in perpetuity. This deeply humiliating move led Chinese merchants in the United States as well as in Shanghai and Guangzhou to protest American discrimination against Chinese by leading a boycott of American goods. The merchants hoped to use peaceful means to demonstrate their opposition to Exclusion, if not to persuade Congress to revoke some of the more onerous terms of the laws. For a few months the movement enjoyed considerable local support among shopkeepers and consumers, but that support dissipated under government crackdowns driven by the need to maintain good foreign relations with the United States.

In this climate of heightened nationalist fervor, overseas Chinese were among the most enthusiastic of patriots to flock to the cause of recovering China's railroad rights by planning and investing in private railway lines. Enthusiasm for railroad investments was generally high, as demonstrated by the rush of people who bought stock to pay for the building of the Guangdong portion of the Guangzhou-Hankou line. According to the March 16, 1906, edition of the *North China Herald*: "Not only are the moneyed classes rushing for the shares but the poorest of the poor and even those who are supposed to have no cash to spare and hardly enough to keep body and soul together are buying up one or more shares. The accounts are very graphic, detailing as they do nuns, chair coolies, and even blind musicians" (p. 582).

The first attempt to build a private line was headed up by Zhang Yu'nan, another overseas Chinese merchant active in Malaysia and Indonesia, in his native province of Fujian. In 1903, Zhang solicited support from the powerful Qing general Yuan Shikai to build a railroad between Shantou and Chaozhou and hired Yale-trained engineer Zhan Tianyou (Jeme T'ien-yow) as the chief engineer. He raised money by selling 10,000 shares for a capital investment worth Ch.$2,000,000. Zhang and some friends put up half the funds, and the rest came from Chinese in Southeast Asia. Zhang encountered many difficulties during the course of building the railroad. Preparations for construction began in March 1904, and by August 1905 land, equipment, and building materials were ready. Actual building took place between September 1905 and October 1907 and cost Ch.$1,123,000. Only 24 miles of track were laid, with six stations. Zhang had to go back to Southeast Asia three times to solicit more money for the project. In the end, financial pressures led Zhang to contemplate transforming the venture into a joint Sino-Japanese company. Students and residents of Shantou caught wind of the plans and protested to the Ministry of Commerce, which ordered Zhang to redeem the Japanese shares. Without access to more capital, Zhang was unable to continue building, and "this line remained an orphan railway leading nowhere until it was finally demolished in 1939."[13]

Chen Yixi became the second overseas Chinese to charter a private railway line when he returned to Taishan in 1904. He embarked on his new career as industrialist and instigator of economic change in Taishan with great vigor and enthusiasm. He set out his plans in stages; the first consisted of a line connecting Taishan to the nearby port of Jiangmen, where one could catch a boat to Hong Kong. Beyond these humble beginnings, however, he hoped eventually to lay tracks that would connect Taishan with Foshan, Guangzhou, Hong Kong, the rest of China, Southeast Asia, and eventually Europe. He would build a port in Taishan and through this communications network transform Taishan into a major trading center controlled by Chinese; he saw it taking the place of the English colony, Hong Kong. In Chen's vision, Taishan would become China's Seattle and dominate trade along China's southern coast as the central nexus of both rail and steamship lines.

Building the Dream

Nationalism proved to be an encouraging early ally as Chen Yixi set about raising capital for the realization of this dream. Rather than turning to banks or to Congress, as American industrialists Hill and Rockefeller did, Chen and a fellow Taishanese, Yu Shi, embarked on lecture tours of North America and Southeast Asia under the slogan "Expand communications, build railroads" to convince fellow Chinese to invest in the endeavor.[14] Before his audiences Chen argued that railroads were essential to China's survival and asserted that Chinese had to reclaim control of their railroads in order to prevent the breakdowns in trade and communications that might occur if foreign nations decided to attack China. He added the promise that his railroad would be wholly Chinese, and that he would build the railroad using only Chinese capital, labor, and technological expertise, thereby severing dependence on foreign aid in any form.[15] Nationalism and self-sufficiency proved to be an attractive combination, and Chen and Yu quickly accumulated Ch.$2,758,412 for the first stage of the project.[16] Two-thirds of the capital came from Chinese Americans; merchants from Hong Kong, Singapore, and Taishan supplied the rest. Although predominantly Taishanese, investments came from concerned Chinese from many different parts of China. Unfortunately for Chen Yixi, convincing other Chinese to invest in the idea of a Chinese-owned and -built railroad was the easiest part of building the Xinning Railroad. As soon as he began trying to turn this dream into a reality, obstacles never faced by the likes of James J. Hill piled up fast at his door. Hill and other American "empire builders" of his ilk enjoyed widespread acceptance of the benefits that industrialization, and railroads in particular, could provide. When Hill proposed ending the Great Northern Railroad line at Seattle, local business leaders and public servants were so eager to ensure that he succeed that they caved in to almost every demand for monopoly rights and special concessions that he made to maximize profits for his company and for himself. Another example of general support for railroad construction was the federal government's considerable aid to the Union Pacific and Central Pacific Railroads in building a transcontinental railroad. After spending $200,000 in bribes in Washington, D.C., the Central Pacific received 9 million acres of free land and US$24 million in bonds. The Union Pacific gained 12 million acres of free land and US$27 million in government bonds in return for shares sold cheaply to U.S. congressmen.[17]

In contrast, bribes paid by Chen Yixi gained him nothing more than permission to build and run his railroad. Although he succeeded in raising funds, Chen had to build among Taishanese who initially regarded the Xinning Railroad as an innovation that would bring uncertain advantages at the cost of irrevocably harming the natural landscape. As a harbinger of such unwelcome changes, Chen found himself in the position of supplicant rather than benefactor when he began to build in Taishan. And, as a beggar asking for alms rather than a king dispensing favors, Chen was forced to make compromises that would ultimately doom his project to failure.

Before he could even begin construction, Chen had to pay provincial governor Cen Chunxuan a reported Ch.$300,000 for permission to begin building.[18] Problems with government officials occurred so frequently that Chen, without the aid of a Taishanese Thomas Burke, eventually decided to purchase an official position for himself for better protection.

Other problems soon followed. While still in the midst of planning, he learned that the powerful Zhen clan objected to the proposed path linking Huancheng, the county seat of nearby Xinhui, to Xinchang port, the commercial center of the Four Counties. The Zhens feared that the railroad would disrupt their favorable *fengshui* or geomancy. Chen was forced to reroute the line through Gongyi. Such twists and turns occurred many times, as villagers from other areas refused to sell land to the railroad company in the belief that the train would harm the luck of their villages.

Chen's promise to use only Chinese labor and technical staff also complicated the building of the railroad. He himself possessed the greatest engineering expertise available for the project. Unfortunately, this proved to be insufficient for all the challenges faced by the Xinning Railroad. The greatest obstacle was constructing a crossing for the railroad over the Niuwan River in southern Xinhui. Although the river was only about 100 meters wide, it was very deep and required the building of a bridge that was beyond the technical expertise of Chen to engineer. Unwilling to call upon foreign expertise, Chen was forced to find an alternative method of getting trains across the river. He decided to use a ferry system and bought a boat from Hong Kong, 350 meters in length. It was fitted with three tracks on deck, enough to carry fifteen train cars transferred from a specially constructed dock. This stopgap measure resolved the problem of crossing the river but added time and uncertainty to the trip because it was not easy to align the ship's deck to the level of the dock.[19]

Despite these difficulties, Chen managed to complete a line linking the central district of Doushan to the town of Gongyi at the northern border of Taishan in 1909. The train began service while Chen, in the face of continuing adversity, attempted to expand the line.

The unforeseen obstacles in building the first stage of the railroad had added unanticipated costs. Chen found himself short of funds in 1910 when he began trying to build the all-important link between Gongyi and the closest major port of Jiangmen. He could not borrow from Chinese sources of capital because Chinese banks were unstable, and his original overseas backers had given almost all they could.[20] The limits of overseas Chinese capital foreshadowed the problems that Chen would encounter when he attempted to expand his railroad to the lengths needed to transform Taishan into a major communications node. To continue expanding the railroad and effect Taishan's economic transformation, Chen was forced to relinquish his original goal of building the railroad without Western assistance by turning to foreign banks for loans. He did so after receiving permission from the provincial governor, Zhang Mingqi. However, this difficult encounter with fiscal realities caused Chen to lose much of his public reputation. *Xinning*

Magazine and San Francisco's *Zhongxi ribao* criticized him for years afterward for failing to keep his promise to use only Chinese capital.[21]

By 1913, *Xinning Magazine* routinely accused Chen of causing the financial difficulties of the Xinning Railroad through misappropriation of company funds and poor planning.[22] In hindsight, however, the personal sacrifices that Chen made for the railroad suggest that his determination to finish the project was far more powerful than greed in the way that he ran the railroad company. Chen Yixi worked as both general manager and head engineer for a nominal salary of Ch.$80 per month.[23] In 1910 he sold one of his own buildings in Seattle and reinvested the funds in the Xinning Railroad.

Chen persevered against worsening odds and oversaw the completion of the railroad's second section in 1911. The track linking Jiangmen to Gongyi, Taishan City, and Doushan was complete and ready for passenger and freight traffic. In 1917, Chen managed to add a trunk line connecting Taishan City to Baisha in the northwestern corner of the county. That same year he obtained permission from Sun Yatsen to develop a commercial port at the southeastern coastal town of Tonggu. In recognition of Chen's accomplishments and his visionary plan for railroads in Taishan's development, the Seattle Chamber of Commerce elected him an honorary member of their organization, although Chen would remain generally vilified by his fellow Taishanese for the rest of his life.

Despite an optimistic and energetically pursued belief that he could transform Taishan into the Seattle of China's southern coast, the Baisha trunk line was the last stage of the hoped-for communications miracle that Chen completed. In its entirety, the Xinning Railroad extended 137 kilometers and contributed substantially to the convenience of travel within the area. It connected the central terminus of Taishan City south to the town of Doushan in central Taishan, west to the town of Baisha, north to Gongyi, then on to Jiangmen at the edge of the Pearl River Delta. The powerful iron horse replaced foot traffic as the main means of travel to all these places. By cutting straight through the Hongling Mountains and bridging Taishan's many rivers, the train reduced the time needed for travel from Doushan to Jiangmen from a walk of at least one day to a ride of a little over two hours. Large goods, such as the heavy trunks brought back by Gold Mountain guests, no longer required the services of three or four porters to move.[24] The train also facilitated the import of products to feed the remittance-fueled consumption of Taishanese, including fruits, vegetables, and palm leaf from Xinhui, wood from the North River district of Guangdong, and handicrafts from Foshan and Guangzhou.[25] However, the railroad never linked Taishan to Guangzhou, much less the rest of China or even the unbuilt port at Tonggu.

Despite the demonstrated usefulness of the railroad in shortening travel times and lowering the costs of shipping goods, it contributed little to the realization of Chen's long-range plans for Taishan's prosperity. The company's income derived primarily from passenger traffic, which exceeded freight by a ratio of about four to one.[26] Taishan's limited economic prospects and the confined area served by the railroad did not give rise to a more substantial, and more profitable, business in transporting more commercial goods. After running at a loss during its first few years, the company grossed about Ch.$1,000,000 annually in the late 1910s. During the 1920s, however, the company fell on hard times; a combination of high operating costs and interference from local authorities made it difficult to keep the company out of debt, much less finance the communications empire planned by Chen. Even if the company had generated sufficient revenues to finance the expansion Chen Yixi dreamed of, there is some doubt whether Taishan could have duplicated Seattle's success because, unlike the Puget Sound region, which produced large quantities of lumber and salmon for export, Taishan did not have any natural resources or manufacturing centers that produced goods requiring transport.

The corners cut by Chen during construction also made it difficult to run the railroad efficiently. Many of the smaller stations had been cheaply built and lacked the barriers needed to ensure that all passengers had purchased tickets.[27] Staff employees tended to abuse the privilege of allowing a "limited number" of relatives to ride free of charge. It was also impossible to control the costs of operation. Despite the nationalist fervor that inspired its creation, the Xinning Railroad Company was forced to purchase trains, cars, machinery, and even coal on foreign markets. The company was thus vulnerable to wide price fluctuations. Between 1916 and 1918, the price of foreign coal rose so rapidly that coal expenditures tripled.[28] Additional expenses included the cost of combating bandit raids. The railroad carried many cash-laden Gold Mountain guests returned from overseas who were attractive vic-

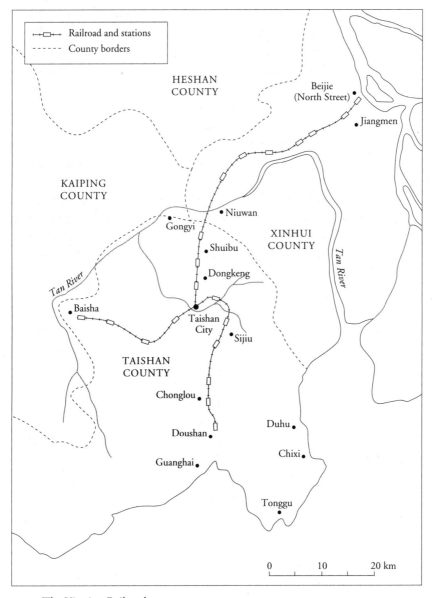

The Xinning Railroad

SOURCE: Zheng, *Taishan qiaoxiang yu Xinning nelu* and *Guangdong sheng xiantu ji* (Collected county maps of Guangdong Province). Guangzhou: Guangdong sheng ditu chubanshe, 1990.

tims for local thieves. The hiring of guards to protect paying customers constituted a heavy drain on running expenses. Amidst all the troubles faced by the Xinning Railroad, however, the worst were not bandits, unpredictable foreign markets, or unticketed passengers, but military representatives of the government who used their positions to exploit rather than encourage ambitious returnees like Chen Yixi.

As mentioned earlier, Chen was forced to pay bribes in order to receive permission to build. After the railroad started running, extortion became a constant problem. The worst freeloaders were military personnel who were entitled to pay reduced fares but used force of arms to claim the right to ride without paying at all. Corruption assumed more systematic forms as well. In 1918, 428 of 1,377 employees on the payroll were military men who received some 31 percent of the total personnel budget of 4,335 yuan. With the local consolidation of the Guomindang's power in preparation for the Northern Expedition, extractions became worse. In 1925 the general commander of Guangdong's military forces, Xu Chongzhi, extorted a Ch.$10,000 "loan" from the company to pay for military provisions. The troop leader stationed in Jiangmen made similar demands of Ch.$5,000 to Ch.$7,500 each month. Between 1925 and 1926, the company came to owe the government over Ch.$1,400,000.

Chen Yixi persisted in trying to develop the full potential of the railroad despite low earnings and the continued interference of local authorities. After completing the trunk line to Baisha in 1917, Chen turned to building a port at the southern town of Tonggu. To complete this next, crucial stage of his plan, however, Chen needed considerable sums of capital, namely a loan of 1 million U.S. dollars, payable at a rate of 8 percent interest.[29] During 1924 and 1925 he made repeated appeals to the Seattle Chamber of Commerce and wrote to a wide array of American businessmen and diplomats, including his old friend Thomas Burke; the U.S. consul general at Guangzhou, Douglas Jenkins; J. C. Herbeman of the Seattle China Club; the U.S. minister of the American legation in Beijing, a Mr. Schurman; vice-president of the Admiral Shipping Line, A. F. Haines; and even William Rockefeller. In a letter to Thomas Burke, Chen described the possibilities:[30]

> It is a finest harbor along the district of Sun Ning [Xinning] The water is deep enough for any kind of vessels. In fact it is the only harbor sheltered

from typhoons, and is the harbor where the fishing boats take refuge from the typhoons. It is near Macow [Macao] about 50 miles and Hong Kong is 78 miles. It is close to mainland, and do not need to build bridges across.[31]

Even as Chen busily looked to the future of the Xinning Railroad, dark clouds hovered over his project. His idealistic commitment to the economic transformation of Taishan was tragically cut short in 1926, when provincial authorities used a strike by technical staff to order a "reorganization" of the company as a ruse to seize control. Beginning in 1923, they had sought to acquire the railroad as a means of increasing state revenues. Every financial mishap and lapse in security became a reason to convert it to public management. The strike provided the final nail in Chen Yixi's coffin. On November 11, 1926, provincial authorities sent a five-member reorganization committee to assume "temporary" control for six months. Chen was not so easily ousted, and on February 21, 1927, the committee requested troop assistance from the Four Counties Occupational Forces to implement their takeover.[32] On April 21 of that year, Chen was forced to retire to Langmei Village, his dreams of transforming Taishan into a flourishing commercial center left unfulfilled. A little over a year later, in the summer of 1928, a severely depressed Chen fell ill and died. All that remained of his personal holdings were the Luhai Hotel in Hong Kong, stocks in the Bank of Canton, three houses in Langmei, and roughly twenty *mu* of land.[33]

In the meantime, the government extended its management of the company far beyond the originally designated six months; still, it remained unprofitable. Stockholder protests forced the reorganization committee to relinquish control to private hands in January 1929. Without Chen Yixi at its head, the railroad continued to fare poorly, and any hope of expansion was extinguished by the difficulty of simply staying in the black.[34] During the 1930s, passenger traffic decreased with the Great Depression, and in March 1935 the company was forced to cut fares.[35] Once again, provincial authorities, not financial insolvency, rang the railroad's final death knell. With the onset of war and the Japanese conquest of Guangzhou in October 1938, the government ordered the dismantling of all local railroads, including the Xinning Railroad, as a defensive measure. By February 1939, engines, cars, and ties had all been hidden or transported elsewhere. The railroad, which had once been valued at over HK$30,000,000, no longer existed and would never be rebuilt. All that was ever recovered of Chen's heavy investment of time, ambition, and hope was the 1942 sale of 23,782 railroad ties to the Guangxi-Guilin Railroad Company.[36]

Conclusion

In light of the grand possibilities that Chen Yixi envisioned for the Xinning Railroad and for Taishan, it seems entirely fitting that his likeness occupies a central space in Taishan City. His plan to transform Taishan into a major trading entrepot grew from the more than 40 years that he spent getting rich in the Pacific Northwest, where he gained intimate knowledge of the economic benefits a railroad could bring to a developing place. In projected scope and origin, the Xinning Railroad set Chen squarely in line with the heroically loyal and supremely talented *huaqiao* celebrated by the rhetoric of *qiaokan*, which opined that if Taishan were to prosper and attain modernity, it would be through the efforts of overseas Taishanese like Chen Yixi.

At an individual level, men like Chen could turn the broadened horizons of access to opportunities and resources in both China and the United States to considerable personal advantage. Chen Yixi became rich because he went to Gold Mountain and prospered. He survived potentially disastrous situations by using both Chinese and American connections to retain position and property in Seattle. But he was much less successful in using this combination for the betterment of Taishan.

When Chen returned to Taishan in 1904, he had acquired a wealth of personal experiences, technical expertise, and a vision for transforming Taishan's economic prospects permanently. If he had achieved his goals, today Taishan rather than Hong Kong would be the lucrative gateway to southern China.[37] Chen failed in this ambition for reasons that even the brightest and most determined of men could not have overcome.

Initial prospects for the railroad had seemed promising. In 1904, Chinese at home and abroad burned with nationalist fervor to reclaim China's railroad rights. Drawing upon this enthusiasm, Chen managed to raise enough capital from individual Chinese to begin construction. Soon thereafter, however, the project foundered, and for fairly fundamental reasons. The terrain and geography of Taishan rendered railroad construction expensive and ultimately unprofitable. Complications dogged each step of building a railroad that almost certainly could not attract enough business to justify its costs. Once built, the railroad served an area that could not produce sufficient food to feed its residents, much less excess goods for export. Even if Chen Yixi had been able to build his port and link the Xinning Railroad to Guangzhou, it is far from certain that profit-minded traders, farmers, and factory owners would have chosen to ship their goods through a place that had few products of its own or risk the tricky boat-to-rail transfer at Niuwan River.

The problems posed by nature never faced any real solution and were compounded by government interference, insufficient capital, corruption, and vulnerability to market forces, which drove up the cost of basic necessities. Chen received little of the help he needed to complete a project of such magnitude and scope. Local and provincial authorities not only failed to provide land and subsidies but also exploited and interfered with the fledgling railroad for personal profit. In short, Chen Yixi never stood a chance of becoming the James J. Hill of Taishan.

That a man of Chen Yixi's vision and talents and determination could not fulfill the mandate of *qiaokan* that overseas Chinese reform and develop their native place indicates that such longer-term benefits could not be achieved by living transnationally.[38] Overseas Taishanese could send back money and ostentatiously elevate the socioeconomic status of their families. Their donations could improve community life through the building of schools, guard towers, new walls, roads, movie theaters, and electricity plants and bring a flush of superficial prosperity to the now internationally connected county seat. However, all their money, good will, and considerable talents could not transform Taishan's fundamental dependence on agriculture. To this day, Taishan remains a land of farmers tilling rocky soil; young men still have to leave if they wish to become rich. For Taishanese stuck in Taishan, the Gold Mountain dream remains on Gold Mountain.

SEVEN

Conclusion: Unraveling the Bonds of Native Place

For close to a century, Taishan County and its thousands of absentee native sons remained intimate partners in a slow waltz that eventually expanded the reaches of their community to the far corners of the world. Through migration, Taishan became a transnational community bound to the tides of social, technological, economic, and political change in all the places where Taishanese had settled. Sojourning overseas had become a way of life, and employment elsewhere, but especially on Gold Mountain, was an eagerly pursued alternative to remaining in Taishan. Despite long-term separations and geographic dispersion, Taishanese at home and abroad continued to work toward common interests that revolved around raising children, promoting ancestral honor and the future of the family line, managing business endeavors, evading immigration laws, modernizing local industry and commerce, constructing community projects such as schools, roads, and hospitals, and supporting the Chinese nation against Japan. This sharing of priorities and activities was most intense between the years 1882 and 1943, when the Exclusion laws legally defined Chinese as being unwelcome in the United States. At the same time, Chen Yixi's railroad operated as a powerful symbol of all the advantages that capital and technology from overseas could bring to Taishan. Taishanese viewed the monetary contributions of overseas Taishanese as necessary to their survival and the most reliable route to prosperity. They also believed that the financial and technological contributions of overseas Taishanese could industrialize and modernize the economy and society of Taishan, and thereby bring a prosperity that would render migration from the rural and rocky county unnecessary for future generations.

But these expectations for transnationality and émigrés were never fulfilled. A community so geographically dispersed was highly vulnerable to changing conditions of international diplomacy, communications, and immigration laws. The example of Mei Shiming and his octogenarian children illustrates both the strengths and weaknesses of trans-Pacific sojourning: family structures and loyalties could survive more than six decades of separation and yet be held hostage to a succession of externally generated, uncontrollable situations like the Exclusion laws, the Cold War, and the Cultural Revolution. In their pursuit of an international field of economic opportunity, migrants like Mei Shiming and their families became engulfed in worldwide processes of political and economic conflict and cooperation that were beyond their control.

In this turbulent landscape of enlarged horizons, Taishanese continued to pursue their own priorities. They proved to be extremely adept at adapting existing networks and practices of kinship and native place and surviving in an increasingly integrated, industrializing world economy. They managed to sustain and even enrich functioning family units and community identities while physically dispersing to establish outposts of social and economic activity overseas. Commitments to family, whether embodied by wives, children, parents, and siblings or as an ideal yet to be achieved, remained a fundamental goal for most of those who went abroad. Restrictive U.S. immigration laws prevented all but the wealthiest Gold Mountain guests from bringing families with them to the United States, thereby ensuring that the goal of returning to Taishan was a common one, even if only as a distant, all but unattainable dream cherished as a means of making difficult living conditions abroad more bearable.

Secondary loyalties to clan, village, and native place also motivated men overseas to remain connected to Taishan but did not bind them to return. The money they sent back made possible the construction of schools, public roads, a railroad, an electricity plant, a movie theater, guard towers, a telephone company, and printing shops during the Republican era. For both their real and potential contributions, overseas Taishanese were regarded as the force that would fuel the engine of industrialization in Taishan. They became *huaqiao* or *qiaobao*, local heroes with the perseverance and luck to go overseas, where with courage and determination they might acquire the ultimate means of expressing their loyalty to Taishan: foreign capital and technology, which would bring modernization to Taishan and help restore greatness to China. In such a society, it was only natural that Chen Yixi became the most lauded local hero. But overseas capital and technology, even when channeled through highly motivated native sons, could not transform Taishan's moribund agricultural economy into a dynamic industrial or even commercial one.

In this conclusion I explore the steady fragmentation of Taishan's Gold Mountain dream. The strength of feelings for family, clan, and native place could not always guarantee allegiances to the physical space of Taishan. Breakdowns in the global order, or even in the relationship between China and the United States, could completely disrupt communications between Gold Mountain guests and their families and make it impossible to exchange the money and letters that were the lifeblood of families split between Taishan and the United States. Moreover, under favorable legal conditions, families could be relocated and reestablished elsewhere, thereby extinguishing one of the most compelling reasons for émigrés to return to Taishan.

The first major rupture in Taishan's transnationality occurred with World War II. International conditions of war blocked all communication for more than three years and resulted in tremendous suffering in Taishan. Even after peace returned, Taishanese were unable to resume the earlier patterns of their transnational lives on a planet now split between the "free" and the communist worlds. The resulting changes in immigration laws and social attitudes in the United States effectively displaced family loyalties from the physical site of Taishan when tens of thousands of Taishanese gained the right to reunite with relatives on Gold Mountain. This fundamental shift in the legal terms of Taishanese migration produced permanent changes in the balance of Taishan's transnational community and demonstrated one of its great weaknesses: the basic inability to control faraway political and economic conditions. This vulnerability made the long-term viability of a Taishan-centered migrant community impossible to maintain, as tragically revealed in Taishan's experience of World War II.

World War II and Its Aftermath

The Japanese invasion of China brought other kinds of havoc to transnationality in Taishan besides the destruction of the Xinning Railroad. Worldwide war disrupted the well-worn paths of communication that had reliably served Taishanese for decades, with calamitous consequences for the once prosperous families of overseas Taishanese. Such families were highly dependent on a two-way flow of letters and money across the Pacific, a dependence that rendered them vulnerable to relations between national governments and the continued functioning of complicated systems of steamships, trains, ferries, and couriers. With the onslaught of global turmoil, long-distance communications fell into utter disarray.

After 1937, Japanese troop movements and occupation of limited areas of Guangdong disrupted but did not end regular travel between Taishan and the crucial nexus of Hong Kong.[1] Money and letters from the United States continued to arrive, rerouted through Macao, Jiangmen, and sometimes even Vietnam.[2] However, in December of 1941, Japan conquered Hong Kong, and all civilian contact between Taishan and the United States ended for the duration of the war. Gold Mountain families who depended on overseas remittances for 70–80 percent of their income were cut off from their main source of support. Many dependents of Gold Mountain guests had never learned to plant their own fields or to support themselves. Such families had lost the practical skills needed to survive during wartime. Even those who knew how to farm had rented their land to tenants. Their resources were ones that could not be eaten: education, houses, and gold jewelry. The lives of leisure they had once enjoyed as part of an ascendant middle class became a handicap under the straitened circumstances of war.

Matters worsened in 1942 as Japanese requisitions of agricultural products led to food shortages throughout Taishan. Hungry Taishanese began eating the seeds of bamboo trees that had withered in the summer heat.[3] A drought arrived in 1943, followed by famine. Mai Yizhao recalls that in order to survive, his Gold Mountain mother had to sell first her jewelry, then household goods, clothing, furniture, and finally the house. In 1943, Gold Mountain wives began selling their children as a last resort or placing them with people better prepared to feed them. After relinquishing their children, many of these women sold themselves or ran away to the nearby districts of Yangzhou and Yangjiang.[4] In Taishanese recollections of the Sino-Japanese war, it is the harrowing experiences of 1943 that frame the central tragedy.

Those dead or fled numbered more than 150,000, or one-fourth of the total population of that time. Even in the relatively sheltered and self-sufficient southern district of Haiyan, the Japanese requisitioning of food products exacerbated agricultural shortages. In Tan'an Village, the Huang clan fell from over 50 households before the war to only about seven or eight afterward.[5] Estimates of the losses in human life vary, but all paint similarly tragic pictures. According to the *Yuesheng Monthly*, Taishan's total population had fallen from more than 1 million to 744,840. More than 200,000 people died in the war, half of starvation and the other half as casualties of war.[6]

After Japan surrendered on August 15, 1945, Gold Mountain guests came pouring back into the county bearing savings accumulated over several years of enforced silence. In early 1947 the American President Steamship line reported that 10,000 Chinese had left the United States bound for China and that 5,000 more had ordered tickets for departures from San Francisco.[7] Droves of single Taishanese American men returned to get married.[8] In 1946 alone, remittances to Taishan amounted to Ch.$14,200,000.[9] The *Yuesheng Monthly* reported that between 1946 and 1947, US$20,200,000 entered Taishan; in 1945 the figure was US$100,000.[10]

Upon finally arriving in Taishan, both money and men often found houses empty of their expected occupants at their destinations. Wives and children had died or fled, and their homes had been sold to new owners. Instead of joyful reunions, the returned Gold Mountain guests had to set about tracking down their loved ones and recovering what they had lost.[11] They had to learn whether their families were still alive and where they had gone. The security and comfort once associated with returns to Taishan had been shattered by war. Gold Mountain guests had to be the ones to find, and if possible reconnect, the strands of family that had once bound them so tightly to Taishan.

World War II ushered in other less visible but far-reaching changes that would fundamentally alter the conditions of transnationality in Taishan. The new world order of the postwar era rejected the imperialist ideologies that had once driven colonial expansion. On a globe now divided between the "free" and communist worlds, the United States aspired to leadership of the democratic nations in part by assuming a newly welcoming attitude to immigrants. The changes that had the greatest impact on Taishanese were new immigration laws that prioritized family reunification.

Surprisingly, the easing of immigration conditions did not occur with the end of Exclusion. Congress had repealed the act in 1943 to give face to the United States' wartime ally, China, secure in the knowledge that the strict quotas imposed by the 1924 general immigration bill would continue to prevent most Chinese from entering the United States or gaining citizenship by naturalization. The first real improvement in immigration conditions for Taishanese reunification was the War Brides Act, passed on December 28, 1945. In recognition of the many military personnel who had traveled abroad risking their lives for their country, Congress decided to permit citizen members of the U.S. armed forces to bring foreign-born spouses, fiancées, and minor children to the United States. Thus, it became possible for an estimated 12,000–15,000 Chinese American men to reunite with their spouses.[12] For the first time, more women than men left Taishan for Gold Mountain. Of the 8,714 Chinese immigrating to the United States between 1946 and 1950, 5,132 were wives of Chinese American men. Of these women, 95 percent (4,875) were war brides.[13] With their arrival, 5,132 fewer Chinese American men would feel the need to return to China to visit their families or to find a wife. During the 1950s the outflow of women outnumbered that of men by a ratio of about three to one (see Table 12).

Unstable conditions in Taishan, both natural and manmade, also encouraged departure from the county. In June 1946 a massive typhoon accompanied by violent rains hit Taishan County. Another torrent arrived the following month. Mountain streams flooded, killing 26 people and injuring ten others. Reported damage included the collapse of 103 houses, damage to thirteen others, and the sinking of 37 boats.[14]

But losses from natural disasters could not begin to match the damage inflicted by a fiscally irresponsible government. To finance its losing battle against the Communists, the Guomindang printed billions of dollars in unbacked currency. China's economy soon dissipated in a whirlwind of inflation. Between February 11 and 13, 1947, the value of Hong Kong dollars rose dramatically, as did the cost of goods and services. One kilogram of rice cost as much as Ch.$1,200. Cigarettes sold for Ch.$1,050 to Ch.$4,000 per pack. In 1948 prices rose even higher. A meal in a teahouse cost each person Ch.$200,000 to Ch.$250,000. A plate of dim sum cost Ch.$150,000 to

TABLE 12

Gender Ratio of Emigrants from Taishan,
Pre-1919 to Post-1977

Year	Ratio of men to women
Pre-1919	440:100
1920–37	427:100
1938–49	657:100
1950–65	31.6:100
1965–76	50.0:100
Post-1977	56.8:100

SOURCE: Chen Yintao and Zhang Rong, *Guangdong sheng Taishan, Xunde nuxing renkou guoji qianyi ji qi yinxiang de bijiao yanjiu* [Comparative research into the international migration of women from the two counties of Taishan and Shunde, Guangdong Province, and their effects] in *Guangdong renkou wenti yanjiu* [Research on population questions in Guangdong] (January 1989), p. 104.

Ch.$300,000. Rice sold for over Ch.$800,000 per kilogram.[15] The runaway inflation led people in Guangdong to prefer Hong Kong dollars as a hedge. Of the estimated 15 million Hong Kong dollars in circulation after World War II, 2 million were thought to be in use in Guangdong.[16] By 1948 the Guomindang, once thought to be the only political party capable of leading China into a brighter future, had lost much of its support among Taishanese Americans. Matters only went from bad to worse, however, with the Guomindang's loss of the civil war. After October 1949, Taishan's fate would be in the uncertain hands of Mao Zedong and the terrifying ideology of communism.

These chaotic economic conditions and traumatic political changes discouraged many otherwise nostalgic Gold Mountain guests from retiring to Taishan. In conjunction with the right acquired by some military service personnel to bring spouses to the United States and establish families there, the failure of the Guomindang to establish stability and prosperity in postwar China simply made the United States a more attractive place to live and raise children.

The number of Chinese living in family units in the United States increased over the next few decades as a thawing of American attitudes toward immigrants from Asia, Eastern Europe, and Africa made it easier to flee Communist rule in China. A series of refugee acts permitted successive waves of complete households to emigrate during the late 1940s and early 1950s. While the Cold War inhibited contact between Taishan and Taishanese Americans, growing awareness of civil rights enabled Chinese to attend colleges and universities and enter the professional classes in such numbers that the Asian American "model minority" stereotype was born in 1966.[17] The year before, the slow reopening of the U.S. immigration gates had culminated in the Immigration Act of 1965, which eliminated racial categories and privileged family reunification for even the parents, siblings, and adult children of U.S. citizens. As putative leader of the "free" world during the Cold War, the U.S. government had portrayed itself as a "land of justice and equal opportunity," in part by passing antipoverty and civil rights programs but also by stripping racial discrimination from its immigration policies.[18] In 1965, Congress passed a new general immigration law that abolished "national origins" as the main consideration for entry to the United States and instead permitted the parents, spouses, and unmarried minor children of U.S. citizens and residents to enter without numerical limitations.

Unfortunately, Gold Mountain families that had been unable to take advantage of the War Brides Act did not benefit from the more generous terms of the 1965 law because they were unable to leave a China embroiled in the isolationist sentiments of the Cultural Revolution. Only after Nixon's historic visit to Beijing in 1972 could Chinese Americans once again visit China, and only after Mao died and an economically pragmatic Deng Xiaoping took the helm were greater numbers of Taishanese able to leave Taishan. As soon as government policies and international relations permitted, Taishanese began to pour out of Taishan.

After suffering the loss of houses and land under Communist land reform and surviving the violent persecution and absence of reason during the Cultural Revolution, Taishanese with the appropriate family connections leaped at the chance to leave Taishan for Gold Mountain. Between 1978 and 1985, an average of 8,118 people left Taishan each year—about 138,000 in all. In 1980 alone, 16.2 percent of the county's population departed for other countries.[19] Between 1978 and 1987, Taishanese outmigrants alone constituted at least one-quarter of the number leaving Guangdong.[20]

True to their Gold Mountain heritage, Taishanese went to North America at much higher rates than other Cantonese. During the 1980s, 73.6 percent went to the United States and 9.2 percent to Canada.[21] In contrast, only 43.5 percent of immigrants from Guangdong as a whole went to the United States, 10.7 percent to Canada, 14.1 percent to Thailand, and 6.6 percent to Australia.[22]

By 1986 there were 950,000 people remaining in the county, 460,000 of whom were related to someone overseas.[23] In the population census taken in 1988, the Taishan County Statistical Bureau found that there were more Taishanese living abroad than in Taishan.[24] The houses once so proudly built and inhabited by the favored families of Gold Mountain guests had emptied, their doors locked and permanently shuttered. Writing in 1993, the sociologist Graham Johnson, described the more than 10,000 people, including three party secretaries, who had departed Duanfen District in central Taishan since 1979. He noted that they "[left] behind splendid houses, familiarity, comfort, even a modicum of prestige, for an uncertain future in an alien environment."[25] Except for a few rare individuals who returned to retire, in the 1980s Taishanese Americans preferred the higher standard of living, greater political stability, and better economic opportunities in the United States.

A newer trend is for overseas Taishanese to return to Taishan to find spouses and then take them overseas to live. In 1982 alone there were 810 such couples. Between 1979 and 1984, 4,509 Taishanese married and left the country. Of those, 95 percent were women. In 1983 alone, over 45 percent of marriages to foreign residents or citizens were to Taishanese from the United States.[26]

This phenomenon reveals that even Taishanese men who continued to regard Taishan as the best place to find a bride did not choose to raise their families there. The family, the social and economic institution that had once provided Gold Mountain guests with the most compelling reason for traveling back and forth between Taishan and the United States, was now in the United States. With the disjunction of the family from the physical site of Taishan, transnationality would never attain the same level of intensity sustained during the era of Exclusion. The goal of returning to retire or to visit, the importance of letters and remittances, the expectations of Gold Mountain youths that they would someday join their fathers overseas, and the long-term separations all became things of the past. For reasons far beyond their ability to control, no longer would the lives of Taishanese in America be so tightly bound to people and events in Taishan.

As opportunities for Chinese in the United States expanded, Taishan lost its appeal as a native place that both needed and valorized overseas Taishanese contributions. The possibility of establishing families and raising children and the probability that those children would fare better than their parents led Taishanese to transfer their hopes for a better future to the United States. In short, they have stopped being guests and sojourners in the United States even as they have abandoned the vaunted *huaqiao* roles assigned to them in Republican-era *qiaokan*. The greater ease of immigrating and gaining citizenship in the United States allows them to channel their energies and ambitions into building lives abroad rather than vicariously enjoying Taishan's progress from afar. With the departure of most of the relatives of Gold Mountain guests eligible for entry to the United States, including men and women in their eighties, there is much less reason for Taishanese Americans to return to Taishan. The weakening of commitments to their native place is reflected in declining rates of return visits, remittances, and donations.

This loosening of ties has not passed unnoticed in Taishan. Taishanese realize that hopes and plans for the modernization of Taishan now lie firmly in the hands of those who reside in Taishan. The sign that welcomed returned émigrés to the "home of overseas Chinese," once so prominently displayed next to the main bus station that had been the central terminal for the Xinning Railroad, was dismantled in 1994. The statue of Chen Yixi still stands in that dusty town square, but the city's commercial center now centers on a new bus station built in 1996 just a few hundred meters to the north. Shared native place continues to provide the basis for business connections, and overseas Taishanese are still solicited for investments and fundraising drives. However, appeals for financial support are made with the understanding that to attract capital in large amounts proposed projects must seem capable of generating real profits. This trend reveals that

Taishanese American priorities have moved overseas along with their families. As those that remain in Taishan learn the limits of what they can gain as a transnational society, slowly but surely their ideas and expectations of attaining the good life in Taishan disentangle from pursuit of the Gold Mountain dream.

Notes

Chapter 1

1. Before 1914, Taishan County was known by the name of Xinning. In North America, these two names are more commonly pronounced in the Taishanese dialect as Toisan and Sunning. Taishan County is not to be confused with its better known namesake, Tai Shan, or Mt. Tai.

2. Zheng Dehua and Cheng Luoxi, *Taishan qiaoxiang yu Xinning tielu*, p. 34. Mei Yimin gives 1846 as Chen Yixi's date of birth, but because Zheng's work is better documented I rely on his date. See Mei Yimin, "Taishan yinjin qiaozhi," p. 18.

3. For a discussion of how nationalism and the rise of nation-states heightened antagonisms to two famously entrepreneurial and successful "outsider" groups, see Chirot and Reid, *Essential Outsiders*.

4. June Mei, "Economic Origins of Emigration," p. 465.

5. Maalki, "National Geographic," p. 27.

6. Wang Gungwu, "Migration and Its Enemies," p. 131.

7. See Park, "Human Migration and the Marginal Man"; and Handlin, *The Uprooted*. Anthropologist Renato Rosaldo suggests that American acculturation is better described as a process of "deculturation"; see Rosaldo, "Ideology, Place, and People," p. 81.

8. In 1870, the U.S. Congress passed the Nationality Act, which limited the

right to citizenship by naturalization to whites and blacks. This exclusion of Chinese was upheld in the 1875 circuit court case *In re Ah Yup*.

9. For examples of early approaches to Chinese American studies, see Coolidge, *Chinese Immigration*; Miller, *The Unwelcome Immigrant*; Sandmeyer, *The Anti-Chinese Movement in California*; Saxton, *The Indispensable Enemy*; Siu, *The Chinese Laundryman*; Lee, *The Chinese in the United States of America*; Sung, *Mountain of Gold*; Lyman, *Chinese Americans*; and Chinn, *Bridging the Pacific*. Siu and Lee were students of Park recruited specifically so that they could help him examine the "Oriental" problem in assimilation. Lee was Park's most enthusiastic Asian American disciple but reached beyond her mentor's ideas to conclude that full assimilation required the erasing of racial as well as cultural differences. See Henry Yu, "The 'Oriental Problem' in America."

10. Through the 1970s, exploring the experiences of Chinese Americans during the Exclusion era was complicated by deeply rooted legacies of shame and silence regarding a time when Chinese had to lie to enter the United States only to live and work as outcasts. It was a largely working-class population, separated even further from later, native-born generations by language, scarcity of written documents, and unwillingness to speak of earlier frauds and times of hardship. Beginning in the 1980s, scholars began breaching the silences that obscured experiences of Exclusion. They used government records such as immigration files, congressional reports, census materials, court transcripts, county deeds, leases, and mortgages; oral interviews; and Chinese-language materials, including personal and business letters, newspapers, poetry, and organization records; see Sucheng Chan, *This Bittersweet Soil*; Sucheng Chan, ed., *Entry Denied*; Yung, *Unbound Feet*; Nee and Nee, *Longtime Californ'*; Lai, Lim, and Yung, eds., *Island*; McClain, *In Search of Equality*; and Wong and Chan, eds., *Claiming America*.

11. A minority of scholars of Chinese America use Chinese-language materials to produce groundbreaking work that nonetheless has yet to provide analysis that transcends the nation-state. See Siu, *The Chinese Laundryman*; Lai, *A History Reclaimed*; Lai, *Cong huaqiao dao huaren*; Hom, *Songs of Gold Mountain*; Renqiu Yu, *To Save China*; Haiming Liu, "The Trans-Pacific Family"; Armentrout-Ma, *Revolutionaries, Monarchists, and Chinatowns*; Henry Tsai, *China and the Overseas Chinese*.

12. See Thistlethwaite, "Migration from Europe Overseas." For other examples of this newer approach, see Morawska, *For Bread with Butter*; Yans-Mclaughlin, *Family and Community*; Kerby Miller, *Emigrants and Exiles*; Wyman, *Round-Trip to America*; Thomas and Znaniecki, *The Polish Peasant*.

13. Rouse, "Mexican Migration," p. 12.

14. Schiller, Basch, and Blanc-Szanton, eds., *Towards a Transnational*

Perspective on Migration, p. ix. Also see Basch, Schiller, and Blanc-Szanton, *Nations Unbound*.

15. On the deterritorialized nation-state, see ibid. On borderlands, see Anzualdua, *Borderlands*. On the transnational migrant circuit, see Rouse, "Mexican Migration." On the diaspora, see Gilroy, *The Black Atlantic*; Safran, "Diasporas in Modern Societies"; Cohen, *Global Diasporas*; and Tololyan, "The Nation-State and Its Others," and "Rethinking Diaspora(s)."

Despite the current popularity of using the conceptual lens of diaspora to analyze experiences of migration, I do not employ the term in this study of Taishanese migration. Although much of Cohen's definition of the term does apply to Taishan during the Exclusion era, it loses relevance for the years after World War II. Furthermore, because ethnic Chinese in their places of settlement have often faced repression and government suspicion of their political loyalties— and diaspora bears implications of continuing desires to return home— generalized use of the term diaspora seems to violate the rights of individual ethnic Chinese and Chinese communities overseas to define their own identities and ethnic sensibilities.

16. Rouse, "Mexican Migration," p. 14.

17. Practicality and the strength of the Gold Mountain dream determine this book's focus on Taishanese migration to the United States. Although migrants to Southeast Asia also played a major role in the economy and society of Taishan, it is difficult to research and coherently describe the activities of migrants in so many places. It is ideas and images of Gold Mountain that have featured most powerfully in the evolution of Taishan's transnational community, and a majority of Taishanese émigrés traveled there.

18. For a sampling, see Gupta and Ferguson, "Beyond 'Culture' "; Appadurai, "Disjuncture and Difference"; Ong and Nonini, eds., *Ungrounded Empires*.

19. According to James Lee, "as early as the second century B.C. rural society was geographically highly mobile"; he lists the seminomadic activities of herdsmen and slash-and-burn agriculturalists, mobile merchants, itinerant craftsmen, vagabonds, and migrant laborers. See Lee, "Migration and Expansion in Chinese History," p. 39.

20. Native-place-based cooperation included highly organized native-place associations (*huiguan*); dominance of a particular trade, service, or artisanal product; and a sense of mutual responsibility toward others from the same native place. Other words that have meanings that resonate with *guxiang* are *jiguan*, *sangzi*, *lao-jia*, and *yuanji*. See Goodman, *Native Place*, p. 4.

21. See, e.g., Skinner, "Mobility Strategies," pp. 335, 351. Also see Mann, "The Ningpo *Pang*"; Strand, *Rickshaw Beijing*, p. 31; Rowe, *Hankow*, pp. 226, 229, 229–

30; Honig, *Sisters and Strangers*; Perry, *Shanghai on Strike*; Leong, *Migration and Ethnicity*; and Goodman, *Native Place*.

22. Wang Sing-wu, *The Organization of Chinese Emigration*, pp. 311–14.

23. Yen Ching-hwang, *Coolies and Mandarins*; Irick, *Ch'ing Policy*; Fitzgerald, *China and the Overseas Chinese*; Wang Gungwu, *Community and Nation*; Wang Gungwu, *China and the Overseas Chinese*; Wang Gungwu, *The Chinese Minority in Southeast Asia*; Wang Gungwu and Cushman, eds., *Changing Identities*; Skinner, *Chinese Society in Thailand*; Skinner, *Leadership and Power*; Wickberg, "The Chinese Mestizo"; Wickberg, *The Chinese in Philippine Life*; Wickberg, "The Chinese in Philippine Economy and Society"; Suryadinata, ed., *Ethnic Chinese*; Reid, ed., *Sojourners and Settlers*.

The wealth of experiences and particularizing details has made it difficult for any scholar to write a competent overall treatment of Chinese overseas, although a few have produced comparative studies of Chinese in Southeast Asia. See Heidhues, *Southeast Asia's Chinese Minorities*; Purcell, *The Chinese in Southeast Asia*; Lynn Pan, *Sons of the Yellow Emperor*; and Lynn Pan, gen. ed., *Encyclopedia of the Chinese Overseas*.

Chinese-language scholarship tends to be more emphatic about the continuing loyalty and major contributions of Chinese overseas to China. See Zhu Shijia, ed., *Meiguo pohai Huagong*; Chen Hansheng, ed., *Huagong chuguo shiliao*. Liu Boji's two-volume *Meiguo huaqiao shi*; Yang Guobiao, Liu Hanbiao, and Yang Anyao, *Meiguo huaqiao shi*; Lin Jinzhi, *Jindai huaqiao touzi guonei qiye shi yanjiu*; Lin Jinzhi, *Jindai huaqiao touzi guonei qiye shi ziliao xuanji: Fujianshuan*; Lin Jinzhi, *Jindai huaqiao touzi guonei qiye gailun*; Lin Jinzhi, "Haiwai huaren zai Zhongguo dalu touzi"; Lin Jinzhi, *Jindai huaqiao touzi guonei qiye shi ziliao xuanji: Guangdong zhuan*; Lin Jinzhi, *Huaqiao huaren yu Zhongguo geming he jianshe*; occasional publications by the Institute of Southeast Asian Studies at Zhongshan University such as *Huaqiao yanjiu* and *Huaqiao shi lunwen ziliao suoyin*; and by the Overseas Chinese Research Center in Jinan University, *Huaqiao lunwenji*.

24. Contrast, for example, Chirot and Reid, eds., *Essential Outsiders*, with Seagrave, *Lords of the Rim*, or the various essays collected in *The Living Tree*. In particular, the idea of *guanxi* capitalism has generated considerable excitement. Also characterized as Confucian, *guanxi* capitalism refers to the successful use of particularistic ties of kinship and friendship in the highly visible recent successes of multinational corporations run by ethnic Chinese families based primarily in Southeast Asia and Hong Kong.

25. Chen, *Emigrant Communities in South China*; Woon, *Social Organization in South China*; Watson, *Emigration and the Chinese Lineage*; Zheng and Cheng,

Taishan qiaoxiang yu Xinning tielu. For a study of non-Chinese migration that raises many similar issues, see Brettell, *Men Who Migrate*.

26. Wang Gungwu, "Sojourning," pp. 1–3.

27. For a discussion of the strategies adapted by modern nation-states to maintain sovereignty over the increasing flows of people, capital, and resources around the world, see Ong, *Flexible Citizenship*, chap. 8.

Chapter 2

1. The Chinese text reads *"relie huanyin ning dao Taishan qiaoxiang lai,"* and translates to "You are warmly welcomed to Taishan, home of overseas Chinese." The sign was dismantled in 1994.

2. K. Y. Chan, "The Role of Migration," p. 42.

3. Mei Yimin, "Taishan yinjin qiaozhi," p. 17. K. Y. Chan cites an estimate of 1.135 million but does not give her reference; see "The Role of Migration," p. 42. Also see Huang Zhongyan, *Qiaoxiang shehui de lishi*, p. 23. Nine hundred thousand lived in Taishan, but 1.1 million lived overseas. Liang Yan estimated that in 1986, 460,00 of 950,000 Taishanese were related to people overseas; see Liang Yan, "Guangdong sheng Taishan qiaoxiang," p. 165. In 1984, residential population was recorded at 940,000, overseas population in the five continents at 700,000 plus 300,000 in Hong Kong and Macao; see *Taishan dilizhi*, p. 1. According to an official of the Baisha Overseas Chinese Affairs Office, these figures were produced by asking residents of Taishan how many relatives they had overseas.

4. Tan Xin, ed., *Siyi Fengguang*, p. 49.

5. *Xinning xiangtu dili*, p. 15. The abbreviated terms *ning* and *tai* are also used to refer to the county. Native-place associations serving Taishanese were called Ningyang.

6. *Xinning xianzhi*, p. 8:6b.

7. Graham Johnson describes Duanfen District in the late twentieth century: "Its prospects for growth and development were, until recently, hampered by inadequate communications." During the 1980s "the economy . . . remained agricultural and firmly based on grain production, (but) its base has diversified. Cash crops, such as fruit and sugarcane and the raising of poultry, have become widespread. Duanfen has prospered since reform, but its incorporation into the world-wide system has not occurred on the same scale as other units in central and eastern portions of the Pearl River Delta"; see Johnson, "Family Strategies," p. 112.

8. See Sucheta Mazumdar's lively account of Guangzhou and its merchants' ready adaptations to the demands of developing commerce with Spanish,

Portuguese, Dutch, English, and American traders, *Sugar and Society in China*, chap. 2.

9. The Four Counties are known in Chinese as Siyi, or Szeyup in Cantonese.

10. The districts of Sanba (meaning three-eight) and Sijiu (four-nine) are named for the days of the ten-day cycle that they hosted markets.

11. *Taishan xian huaqiao zhi*, p. 9.

12. Xavier died on Shangchuan Island in 1552. His body remains in the church that he constructed there.

13. *Taishan dilizhi*, p. 35.

14. See Naquin and Rawski, *Chinese Society in the Eighteenth Century*, p. 168.

15. See Zheng and Cheng, *Taishan qiaoxiang yu Xinning tielu*, p. 86.

16. Huang Jianyun, *Taishan gujin gailan*, vol. 1, p. 217.

17. *Taishan xianzhi*, pp. 16a–17b.

18. *Taishan dilizhi*, p. 30; Huang Jianyun, *Taishan gujin gailan*, vol. 1, p. 196. Of this, paddy fields took up 1,168,700 *mu* (70.4 percent), nonirrigated farmland 490,300 *mu* (29.6 percent), and gardening land 32,200 *mu* (1.9 percent).

19. Wakeman, *Strangers at the Gate*, p. 179. This figure is much lower than the estimated national average of 2.19 *mu* per person.

20. Murray with Qin Baoqi, *The Origins of the Tiandihui*, p. 7.

21. Zheng and Cheng, *Taishan qiaoxiang yu Xinning tielu*, p. 2.

22. *Taishan xianzhi*, pp. 8:12b–15a.

23. Huang Jianyun, *Taishan gujin gailan*, p. 217. The Chinese is *di guang ren xi, wu chan fengfu, zhanluan bu ji*.

24. Ibid., p. 213. In 1531, to attract settlers to an area devastated by pirate raids, the government gave people a three-year tax break.

25. Li Yiji, *Haiyan xiangtushi*, p. 138.

26. *Taishan dilizhi*, pp. 21–22. In 1512 Taishan had 7,741 households and 25,497 people. During the Ming and through the fourteenth year of the Shunzhi reign (1657), Taishan's population never exceeded its 1512 peak of 25,497. Because censuses were taken irregularly, I can locate population counts only for 1512, 1657, 1839, 1921, and 1938. In addition, during the Qing, overburdened organs of local government produced fairly unreliable estimates of population. In 1921 the estimated population was 800,000 exclusive of Chixi; in 1928 it was 984,491 including Chixi; in 1938 it was 885,300 (also taken from provincial statistics); and in 1941 it was 1,029,352.

27. *Taishan dilizhi*, p. 43.

28. K. Y. Chan, "The Role of Migration," p. 47. Chan cites the deputy head of the Taishan County Overseas Chinese Affairs Office.

29. Declining ratios of man to land forced many people all over China to pick

up and move during the eighteenth century and led to all sorts of problems for provincial authorities. "Shack people" began farming hilly land along the Zhejiang and Anhui border, and unemployed single men displaced from their villages in Guangdong and Fujian then joined the Heaven and Earth secret society (Tiandihui). See Osborne, "The Local Politics of Land Reclamation"; and Murray, "Migration, Protection, and Racketeering," pp. 177–89.

30. Zheng and Cheng, *Taishan qiaoxiang yu Xinning tielu*, p. 86.

31. Cited in Chen Qian, "Taishan xianqiao," p. 128, based on materials taken from London archives and written up in the 1948 issue of the Malaysian Taishan Benevolent Association Unified Memorial Special Edition (*Malaiya Taishan huiguan lianhe jinian tekan*). Also see *Taishan xian huaqiao zhi*, p. 261.

32. *Taishan xian huaqiao zhi*, p. 260. Mei was listed as a donor on the commemorative stone carvings of several organizations.

33. Cheng and Liu, with Zheng, "Chinese Emigration," p. 62.

34. Wakeman, *Strangers at the Gate*, pp. 98–100; and Jung-fang Tsai, *Hong Kong in Chinese History*, p. 21.

35. Wakeman, *Strangers at the Gate*, p. 136. During the nineteenth century, three main triads were at work in southern China: the Heaven and Earth Society (Tiandihui), the Triple Dot Society (Sandianhui), and the Three Unities Society (Sanhehui).

36. See Murray, "Migration, Protection, and Racketeering," p. 177.

37. Wakeman, *Strangers at the Gate*, pp. 118, 136.

38. Ibid., p. 145.

39. Ibid., pp. 149–50.

40. *Taishan xian huaqiao zhi*, p. 262.

41. Zheng and Cheng, *Taishan qiaoxiang yu Xinning tielu*, p. 7; and Huang Jianyun, *Taishan gujin gailan*, vol. 1, p. 16.

42. Sow-theng Leong, *Migration and Ethnicity*, p. 74.

43. Myron Cohen, "The Hakka or 'Guest People,'" p. 50.

44. Sow-theng Leong, *Migration and Ethnicity*, p. 62.

45. *Taishan xianzhi* 21, pp. 11a–14b.

46. Huang Jianyun, *Taishan gujin gailan*, vol. 1, p. 214. Also see *Chixi xianzhi*.

47. *Taishan xian huaqiao zhi*, pp. 321–22.

48. June Mei, "Economic Origins of Emigration," p. 476.

49. *Taishan xian huaqiao zhi*, pp. 262–63. Also known as Lei Yamei, Louie prospered as the owner of gold mines in Wei Zhou and tin mines in Australia. He became the first importer of Chinese tea to Australia, co-wrote a book in 1878 protesting government maltreatment of Chinese, and later became an owner of the Australian Commercial Bank (Aozhou shangye yinhang).

50. In 1868, coolie brokers active in Taishan included Luo Yuanying, Chen Chengjiu, Gu Yaxing, Cheng Fulong, Mei Guanyao, and Zhang Yaliang, among others; *Taishan xian huaqiao zhi*, p. 339. June Mei notes that most men from the Four Counties did not go abroad as coolies and that most ended up in the desirable destinations of North America or Australia; see June Mei, "Economic Origins of Emigration," p. 483.

51. See Hsu, "What Is Special About Taishan?" pp. 12–14.

52. Southern California Chinese American Oral History Project (hereafter cited as SCCAOHP), sponsored by the UCLA Asian American Studies Center and the Chinese Historical Society of Southern California, interview 153, p. 9. The interviews were conducted between 1978 and 1982.

53. Restrictive immigration laws caused the number of Taishanese in the United States to decline from the 1890s through the 1920s, when a second generation of Chinese Americans began to be born. In 1942, however, Taishanese in the United States numbered only about 13,500, or 46 percent of the total population of 27,500. Hoy, *The Chinese Six Companies*, p. 17.

54. Mo, *Aiguo huaqiao Chen Yixi*, p. 16.

55. Lai, "Historical Development," pp. 14–15.

56. Ibid., p. 16. Taishanese surnamed Yu formed a surname group with those from Kaiping and Enping and did not participate in the Ningyang Benevolent Association.

57. Chen Lanbin, "ShiMei jilue," pp. 59a–60b. Membership in the other organizations was estimated as follows: the Sanyi Benevolent Association, serving people from the Pearl River Delta counties Nanhai, Panyu, and Shunde, had 12,000 members; the Yanghe, serving those from Zhongshan, Dongguan, and Zhuhai, had 13,000; the Gangzhou, serving those from Xinhui and Heshan, had 16,000; the Renhe, serving Hakka, had 4,000, and the Hehe, serving those surnamed Yu [Yee] including members from Taishan, had 40,000.

58. Li Gui, *Huanyou diqiu xinlu*, vol. 3, pp. 28a–b. Li Gui had participated in the World's Fair.

59. *Taishan County Government Report* (1931), cited in Mo, "Aiquo huaqiao Chen Yixi zhuanlue," p. 16. According to Zheng, "Shijiu shiji mo Taishan qiao-xiang," p. 65, if this figure is added to the numbers of Taishanese reported to be in Southeast Asia, then in 1901 more than 200,000 Taishanese were living overseas. Zheng cites *Guangdong sheng Xinning tieluzhi* (gazetteer of the Xinning Railroad in Guangdong Province) (1914), p. 2, for these figures.

60. Huang Jianyun, *Taishan gujin gailan*, vol. 1, p. 214; and *Taishan xianzhi* 8, p. 6b. Huang cites the 1921 *Chixi xianzhi* estimate that by 1901 more than 200,000 Taishanese had gone overseas.

61. *Taishan xianzhi* 8, p. 6b.

62. According to a survey conducted by C. F. Remer of American banks in Hong Kong in 1930–31, just over 50 percent (HK$136.8 million) of all remittances sent to China through Hong Kong (HK$272.7 million) came from the United States and Canada. Considering that an April 3, 1926, article in the *Times* (*Shibao*) recorded that U.S. and Canadian Chinese accounted for just 1.7 percent of Chinese overseas (162,000 out of 9,634,000), the amounts of money sent back by American Chinese are indeed staggering. Another matter to consider is that over half of Chinese in the United States were from Taishan. See Remer, *Foreign Investments in China*, p. 183.

63. Chinn, with Lai and Choy, *A History of the Chinese in California*, p. 18. Over the same time period, records indicate that 24,041 Chinese returned from the United States.

64. According to Charles Denby, former U.S. minister to China (1885–98), tickets from Hong Kong or Macao to the United States cost $55, although the actual expense of travel was only five dollars. Denby, *China and Her People*, vol. 2, p. 110.

65. The earliest ships on this line were paddle steamers that were replaced by screw steamships "as the demands of the traffic required." In 1902 the Pacific Mail Steamship Company built new steam liners with 18,000 horsepower and 18,000 tons displacement. In 1903–4, the company purchased even larger ships in the form of the *Mongolia* and the *Manchuria* with displacements of 27,000 tons each. Wright and Cartwright, *Twentieth-Century Impressions of Hongkong*, p. 203.

66. Robert Lee, "The Origins of Chinese Immigration to the U.S.," pp. 188–89. Lee cites ads that appeared in the *China Mail*, May 30, 1853, and the *California China Mail and Flying Dragon*, March 1, 1967.

67. *Taishan xian huaqiao zhi*, pp. 41, 339.

68. Wright and Cartwright, *Twentieth-Century Impressions of Hongkong*, pp. 200–207.

69. *Xinning Magazine*, no. 9 (1916), p. 57.

70. *Angel Island Immigration Station*, pp. 29–30. This passenger added, "I heard very few Chinese came as first class. Four hundred dollars was quite a bit of money in those days."

71. Ibid., p. 30.

72. Siu, *The Chinese Laundryman*, p. 107.

73. Jung-fang Tsai, *Hong Kong in Chinese History*, p. 2. Exports from the United States included flour, dried fish, and other commodities. Trade between the two countries increased from US$11.4 million in 1867 to $26.8 million in 1872.

74. *Jinshanzhuang* can be compared to *nanbei hang* (north-south firms; *Nam*

Pak Hong in Cantonese), which began by specializing in the transport of goods between northern and southern China. They later expanded operations to encompass Europe, America, and the northern and southern hemispheres. During the 1850s, *nanbei hang* began charging a 2 percent commission for selling goods for customers. Hence their nickname, *jiuba hang* (nine-eight firms; *Kau Pat Hong* in Cantonese). See "The Nam Pak Hong (Nanbei hang) Commercial Association of Hong Kong," p. 218.

75. Liu Zuoren claims that *jinshanzhuang* started between 1881 and 1890, but *Xinning Magazine* ads for these businesses date such services back to the 1850s; see Liu Zuoren, *Jinshanzhuang de yanjiu*, p. 21. In 1916, Shengyuan Yinhao with branches in Taicheng and in Hong Kong (at 109 Wing Lok St. under the management of Liu Kong'an) claimed a history of more than 60 years, which would date *jinshanzhuang* remittance services back to the early 1850s; see *Xinning Magazine*, no. 9 (1916), announcements in back. Changsheng Goldshop in Hong Kong at 52 Wing Lok St. advertised itself as having been in operation as a receiving company for more than 60 years, or since the 1870s. During that time it also offered currency exchange, savings accounts, and security boxes; see *Xinning Magazine*, no. 25 (1934), second page of the announcement section. According to Elizabeth Sinn, "California traders" were represented on the board as early as 1869; see Sinn, *Power and Charity*, p. 273.

Liu's article contains other inaccuracies. He describes the largest Chinese American import-export business as having 48 branches in the 1950s and operating under the name the Zhongxing Company. The only business chain of this magnitude was the National Dollar Stores, founded and operated by Joe Shoong. However, the National Dollar Stores sold primarily domestically manufactured products rather than products imported from Hong Kong or China. See Liu Zuoren, *Jinshanzhuang de yanjiu*, p. 21.

76. *Anglo-Chinese Directory of Hong Kong*, pp. 90–94. The directory also lists 3 firms doing business with Peru; 3 with Havana; 8 with Japan; 20 with the Philippines; 26 with Annam, Tonkin, and Saigon (present-day Vietnam); 10 with the Straits Settlements (present-day Malaysia); 26 with Singapore; 10 with Penang; 13 with Java, Sourabaya, and Sandakan (present-day Indonesia); 2 with India, and 1 with Spain (pp. 94–99). See also the *Chinese Commercial Directory*, pp. 392–446, which lists 46 businesses serving Singapore, 6 in Singapore and Annam, another 6 in Singapore and Swatow, 6 in Penang, 11 in Java (Indonesia), 15 in Japan, 23 in Manila, 21 in Annam, 16 in the Straits Settlement (Malaysia), 15 in Bangkok, 2 in Holland, 4 in Havana, and 3 in Calcutta. In the 1920s, 380 *jinshanzhuang* were run by Cantonese; see Lin Jiajin et al., *Jindai Guangdong qiaohui yanjiu*, pp. 55–56.

77. These foodstuffs were preserved and prepared for shipping by companies

like Zhangguang Yuan (Cheung Kwong Yuen), founded by Pun Wan Nam (Pan Wannan) in 1887. By 1917, Zhangguang Yuan was "one of the most important canning export houses of south China"; see Jung-fang Tsai, *Hong Kong in Chinese History*, pp. 30–31. Also see Feldwick, ed., *Present Day Impressions of the Far East*, p. 588; Wright and Cartwright, *Twentieth-Century Impressions of Hongkong*, p. 248; and Cheng Tzu-ts'an, *Xianggang Zhonghua shangye jiaotong renming zhinanlu*, p. 491.

78. On food exports, see Spier, "Food Habits of 19th Century California Chinese," pp. 126–36; Feldwick, ed., *Present Day Impressions of the Far East*, p. 558; and Jung-fang Tsai, *Hong Kong in Chinese History*, pp. 26–27.

79. SCCAOHP, interview 19, p. 15.

80. *Xinning Magazine*, no. 15 (1919), and no. 17 (1927).

81. Wright and Cartwright, *Twentieth-Century Impressions of Hongkong*, pp. 133, 285–86. China complied with foreign pressure in 1896 and established a postal service modeled on Western lines. Before that time, indigenous postal services consisting of the Imperial Government Courier Service and "native posting agencies" adequately served the needs of Chinese. Of the two, Wright and Cartwright considered the latter "[f]ar more obstructive to rapid progress. . . . These, also, have had a long life, but, unlike [the Imperial Government Courier Service], they are wholly independent. . . . Their innumerable ramifications—fast couriers, or rapid 'post-boats,' as the style of country decides—extend to all connections which, with their slow ways, have for centuries answered the requirements of busy and thrifty communities." The object of Wright and Cartwright's worries was a class of businesses that included a *jinshanzhuang*: "These posting agencies are essentially shop associations, for the most part engaged also in other trades. The transmission of parcels, bank drafts, and *sycee* [cash] is the most lucrative part of their postal operations." The Imperial Postal Service wisely decided to supervise rather than displace these systems when it came into existence in 1896.

82. During the last half of the nineteenth century, the Qing legalized the use of foreign silver coins, and so Mexican silver dollars came into common usage and remained popular through the 1930s. Cantonese resisted Qing attempts to issue paper currency near the end of the Guangxu reign (1875–1907), as they did after 1911 when the Republican government in Beijing issued new currency though the Communications Bank. In Guangdong, people clung to the two-tiered system of silver and copper coins. This was the currency in use in Taishan. However, by the 1920s and 1930s, it was not uncommon for people to have U.S. dollars as well as Hong Kong bills lying around the house. Li Yiji, *Haiyan xiangtushi*, p. 37.

83. At least this was the opinion of Liu Zuoren, who headed up the research branch of the Guangdong Provincial Bank during the 1930s.

84. Liu Zuoren, *Jinshanzhuang de yanjiu*, p. 21. Another nineteenth-century method was to convey the remittance money in the form of marketable goods bought and sold at each end of the journey. During the 1920s and 1930s, both government officials and private merchants attempted to develop Western-style banks and postal systems to wrest the remittance business from *jinshanzhuang*. These challengers arose in the form of foreign banks, Chinese government banks (for example, the Bank of Canton, the Communications Bank, and the Bank of China) and the Chinese postal service. See Lin Jiajin et al., "*Jindai Guangdong qiaohui yanjiu*," p. 48.

85. An example of business connections based on kinship or acquaintanceship can be found in the firm of Lisheng He in Hong Kong. In 1919 the new proprietor, Tan Wenbing, notified customers that with the death of his older cousin, Tan Wenyue, he would be taking over as manager but that the business would continue as before. He pointed out that Tan Wenyue's son, Ziju, would be going to Hong Kong to help out. Tan asked his customers, whom he addressed as "brother, kinsmen, and friend" who already had accounts to write to him and explain their accounts; *Xinning Magazine*, no. 15 (1919), announcement section.

86. Businesses offering remittance services to Southeast Asia were called *minxinju*. Other names included *pixinju*, *piju*, *huidiaoju*, and *xinju*.

87. The Chens of Huaying Chang were of the Liangxing branch of the Chen clan living in Damei Village. A minority of partners were relatives from the Zeng clan of nearby Shangge Village. Interview with village elders of Damei Village, July 31, 1995.

88. Huaying Chang account books (Hong Kong: Special Collections, University of Hong Kong, unpublished materials, 1899–1937), record of individual accounts (*geke fuji*).

89. Huaying Chang account books (1919), accounts for transactions within China (*neibu gehao laiwang shu*).

90. *Xinning Magazine*, no. 25 (1917), announcement section.

91. Ibid., no. 15 (1919), announcement section.

92. Ibid., no. 27 (1935), pp. 71–72.

93. Ibid., no. 15 (1919), p. 55.

94. Liu Zuoren, *Jinshanzhuang de yanjiu*, p. 22.

95. For example, the firm of Cheng Chang, based in Seattle, sent nineteen such packets to Huaying Chang in 1919. The number of individual remittances enclosed ranged from two to twenty. The large mailings occurred right before Chinese New Year. Huaying Chang account books (1919), record of individual accounts.

96. By the twentieth century, *jinshanzhuang* ran something along the following lines. The largest *jinshanzhuang* employed as many as ten people, but most had only four or five employees. Most were partnerships, not stock companies. Staff included a manager, as well as an accountant and three or four service people. Liu Zuoren, *Jinshanzhuang de yanjiu*, p. 21.

97. *Xinning Magazine*, no. 6 (1935), pp. 64–65.

98. Ibid., no. 24 (1932), front-page advertisements. One *li* was equal to one one-thousandth of a tael of silver.

99. Huaying Chang account books (1919), transactions with the interior. The dollar amounts used throughout the account of Chen Kongzhao probably refer to Hong Kong dollars.

100. Huaying Chang account books (1905, 1915, 1925, 1929, 1935), record of individual accounts.

101. Liu Zuoren, *Jinshanzhuang de yanjiu*, p. 22; and interview with Jiang Yongkang. Jiang started running a *jinshanzhuang* after World War II.

102. This practice was known as *zhengpi huigang*.

103. As will be discussed in the following chapter, U.S. immigration laws attempted to exclude all Chinese laborers from the United States. Chinese had to demonstrate that they were members of a class eligible to immigrate: merchant, merchant family, student, diplomat, U.S. citizen or child of a U.S. citizen. The immigration bureau suspected almost all Chinese of lying about the basis for their right to enter the United States and required them to undergo arduous interviews upon arrival before being allowed to land.

104. *Xinning Magazine*, no. 4 (1912). Liu Zanchen also offered to inspect old immigration papers (*jiu zhi*) and tell people whether they were still valid (possibly with an eye to selling the proof of identity to somebody else wishing to go to the United States).

105. Liu Zuoren, *Jinshanzhuang de yanjiu*, p. 21.

106. "Interviews with Detainees at Angel Island Project," interview with Jeong Foo Louie conducted August 29, 1976.

107. *Taishan xian huaqiao zhi*, p. 341. The rest of its business was in medicines, dried seafood, dried goods, and currency exchange, and acting as a postal agency.

108. Lin Jiajin et al., "*Jindai Guangdong qiaohui yanjiu*," p. 54. After World War II the two banks began working together. The occupation of Hong Kong by the Japanese completely disrupted the activities of *jinshanzhuang*. This lapse enabled the two banks to win a larger share of the remittance business. In 1927 the Guangdong Postal Service entered the fray by working with banks and money shops in order to establish the range of foreign and local services needed to handle

remittances from beginning to end. In 1937 alone, the postal service handled Ch.$777,700 (p. 50).

109. SCCAOHP, interview 20, pp. 7, 21.

110. *Xinning Magazine*, no. 16 (1931), p. 3.

111. Liu Zuoren, *Jinshanzhuang de yanjiu*, p. 21.

112. Yao, *Guangdong sheng de huaqiao huikuan*, p. 42.

113. Lau, "Educational Development in Taishan County," p. 91 n. 70.

114. At least in Kaiping, investment from overseas Chinese reached its peak in 1928–31, partly because of favorable exchange rates. The world depression that followed, however, caused many to return to China during 1933–34. See Woon, *Social Organization in South China*, p. 92.

115. Renqiu Yu, "Chinese American Contributions to Education," p. 48.

116. Pan, *Ningyang cundu*, p. 66a.

117. *Taishan xianzhi* 8, p. 6b.

118. Zheng, *Shijiu shiji mo Taishan qiaoxiang*, 67, 69. Zheng cites figures from Zhao Tianyi, *Diaocha Guangzhou fu Xinning xian shiye qingxing baogao* [Report on an investigation into industry and commerce in Xinning County, Guangzhou] regarding sugar and peanut oil production.

119. *Taishan xianzhi* 8 p. 6b.

120. SCCAOHP, interview 163, p. 3.

121. Renqiu Yu, "Chinese American Contributions," p. 48.

122. Chen and Zhang, "Guangdong sheng Taishan," pp. 92–93. Even after the upheavals of the Cultural Revolution, remittances constituted 55 percent of the earnings of overseas relatives in 1978.

123. SCCAOHP, interview 81, p. 7.

124. Ibid., interview 156, p. 7.

125. *Xinning Magazine*, no. 11 (1935), p. 28. The criminal was found to be Mei Ren of the same village. Wealthy overseas Chinese households kept their wealth in the form of U.S. dollars, cashier's checks, Hong Kong dollars, silver dollars, and gold jewelry.

126. Cheng and Liu, with Zheng, "Chinese Emigration," p. 66.

127. Siu, *The Chinese Laundryman*, p. 186. Siu states that the Gold Mountain guests moved to the city were those who were "dissatisfied with the backwardness of the village."

128. Woon, p. 91. In emigrant areas, land tenancy actually decreased with the flurry of land purchases. Tenancy rates in Siyi were significantly lower than the average tenancy rates in the rest of Guangdong.

129. Quoted in Siu, *The Chinese Laundryman*, p. 115.

130. The legend continues to survive in the minds of Fujianese illegal

immigrants who pay up to US$40,000 to come to the United States only to spend years working in sweatshop conditions trying to pay off their debts.

131. SCCAOHP, interview 126, p. 1.

132. Ibid., interview 125, p. 2.

133. *Xinning Magazine*, no. 31 (1934), p. 23. Contrast this success with David Kulp's accounts of Phenix Village, to which only one-tenth of emigrants returned successfully: "Many of them, while in foreign lands, are barely able to send back enough money to keep their families alive. Not a few persons are forced to live from hand to mouth, finally broken in productive efficiency, a charge upon their families, or dying miserable deaths away from home with none to burn the candles." Kulp, *Country Life in South China*, p. 53.

134. Lau, "Educational Development in Taishan County," p. 48.

135. Ibid., p. 37.

136. *Taishan xian huaqiao zhi*, p. 119.

137. Huang Jianyun, ed., *Taishan gujin gailan*, vol. 1, p. 18.

138. Lau, "Educational Development in Taishan County," p. 67.

139. Ibid., p. 202. The county with the next highest budget was Zhongshan (1,142,020 yuan), then Panyu (839,587 yuan), followed by Nanhai (855,229 yuan). The counties of Shunde and Dongguan spent only about half as much as Taishan (685,347 and 692,080 yuan respectively). Of the other Four Counties, the highest spender was Xinhui (184,913 yuan).

140. As will be discussed in the conclusion, this railroad was a costly failure, for Chen Yixi never raised enough money to connect it to either the Guangzhou-Hankou or the Guangzhou-Kowloon line. Chen's ambition of transforming Taishan into a communications center that could supplant Hong Kong was never realized.

141. Zheng, "Shijiu shiji mo Taishan qiaoxiang," p. 66.

142. Mei Yimin, "Taishan yinjin qiaozhi," pp. 19–20.

143. Huang Jianyun, ed., *Taishan gujin gailan*, vol. 1, p. 19.

144. Ibid., p. 18.

145. Mei Yimin, "Taishan yinjin qiaozhi," p. 21.

146. Huang Jianyun, ed., *Taishan gujin gailan*, vol. 1, pp. 17–18.

147. Mei Yimin, "Taishan yinjin qiaozhi," p. 21.

148. Ibid., p. 21.

149. See *Taishan fengcai*, pp. 148–53 for examples of Taishan English. See *Taishan fangyan* for pronunciations. There is, for example, a complete range of assimilated English terms related to the playing of volleyball.

150. *Taishan huaqiao zazhi*, no. 31 (1934), p. 5.

151. Cheng and Liu, with Zheng, "Chinese Emigration," p. 71.

152. Cited in Lau, "Educational Development in Taishan County," p. 62.

153. Ibid., pp. 61–62.

154. *Xinning Magazine*, no. 19 (1922), pp. 8–11.

155. SCCAOHP, interview 157, p. 31.

156. *Xinning Magazine*, no. 24 (1921), pp. 13–14.

157. Ibid., p. 21.

158. Ibid., no. 23 (1934), p. 30.

159. Ibid., no. 34 (1934), p. 61.

160. Ibid., no. 23 (1934), pp. 32–33.

161. Control of Guangdong changed hands several times after 1911, with various political factions competing for military supremacy. Within Taishan, attempts to develop local institutions of self-government never really took root.

162. See SCCAOHP, interview 160, pp. 160–63.

163. *Xinning Magazine*, no. 17 (1934), p. 5. The internal reasons are listed as taxes and overproduction.

164. SCCAOHP, interview 81, p. 7.

165. Ibid., interview 74, p. 6 of the English translation.

166. *Xinning Magazine*, no. 11 (1935), p. 14. For provincial relief measures, see Lin Yizhong, *Guangdong jiuji shiye huiguo huaqiao jishi muci*, p. 10. From 1931 until the date of publication, the provincial government attempted to provide temporary food and lodging for returned overseas Chinese. It tried to find employment for the able in factories and in road-building and placed the sick and elderly in homes and hospitals. Long-term plans for local economic revival included the development of mining, preparing fallow lands for cultivation, and developing new industries.

167. At its peak, Xinchang City had more than twenty banking businesses. After 1932, bad business conditions caused five to close down altogether and nine to cease paying out money from savings accounts. Only six were able to carry on business; *Xinning Magazine*, no. 31 (1934), pp. 43–44. Of 369 businesses in the city, 72 failed; *Xinning Magazine*, no. 34 (1934), p. 54.

168. SCCAOHP, interview 81, p. 1, and interview 17, p. 3.

169. Ibid., interview 126, p. 1.

170. *Angel Island Immigration Station*, p. 22.

171. Cited in Siu, *The Chinese Laundryman*, p. 114. The man added, "If I had known beforehand that this is the way I would have to toil, I would never have come here. I would rather have stayed with the family and be poor."

172. Ibid., p. 113.

173. Renqiu Yu, *To Save China*, pp. 26, 28.

Chapter 3

1. Charles McClain points out that this was the first time in U.S. history that a law presumed guilt rather than innocence. In requiring Chinese to carry certificates of legal entry, Congress institutionalized the assumption that Chinese had entered illegally and needed to prove otherwise. See McClain, *In Search of Equality*, p. 203.

2. In this chapter, I will try to speak as specifically as possible to the immigration experiences of Taishanese. However, my findings are limited by existing resources. Most documents and secondary literature distinguish Chinese by race, not by the more detailed, and often more accurate, categories of county or dialect group. When available and so labeled, I have used materials pertaining to Taishanese, such as immigration case files and interviews from the Southern California Chinese American Oral History Project. When I speak of Chinese in general rather than Taishanese specifically, it is because there is no specific information available about Taishanese. However, the reader should note that between 60 and 80 percent of Chinese Americans were from Taishan and that many of the experiences of Taishanese are relevant to those of Chinese from other counties.

3. Chen Lanbin, "ShiMei jilue," folio 12, pp. 59b–60a; and Li Gui, *Huanyou diqiu xinlu* 3: 28a. Also see Gibson, *The Chinese in America*, p. 21, for comparable estimates of the population of Chinese from the Four Counties.

4. Hoy, *The Chinese Six Companies*, p. 8.

5. For a detailed description of Chinese economic activities in California during the nineteenth century, see Ping Chiu's extremely useful monograph, *Chinese Labor in California, 1850–1880*.

6. Sucheng Chan's award-winning *This Bittersweet Soil* discusses the tremendous contributions of Chinese to the foundations of California's agricultural economy.

7. Saxton, *The Indispensable Enemy*, p. 7.

8. Sucheng Chan, "The Economic Life of the Chinese in California," p. 112.

9. Chinn, with Lai and Choy, *A History of the Chinese in California*, p. 49.

10. Ibid., p. 63.

11. Queues were the pigtails that Chinese men were forced to wear as symbols of their loyalty to the Qing. Cutting one's queue, which many men did after the 1911 revolution, was a dramatic gesture of resistance to the Qing and was punishable by death. Any Chinese man who hoped to return to China had to retain his queue.

12. See McClain, *In Search of Equality*, pp. 65–69, 73–79, for Chinese court

challenges to laws that targeted Chinese for economic discrimination. According to McClain, the judicial rulings in these cases helped to define the rights of equal protection and due process guaranteed in the Fourteenth Amendment.

13. The first laws passed closed the shrimp season for May, June, July, and August in hopes of forcing Chinese-run shrimp camps to close. In 1905 more legislation banned the export of dried shrimps and shrimp shells from California. After the Exclusion law was renewed in 1892, Chinese abalone fishermen were forbidden to operate their junks in "foreign waters."

14. Sucheng Chan also notes that this time period coincides with the decline of artisan manufacturing in general, so it was not only Chinese who disappeared from small-scale manufacturing. Chan, "The Economic Life of the Chinese in California," pp. 115–16.

15. Ibid., p. 116. Chan cites figures from the fourteenth census of the United States conducted in 1920.

16. Southern California Chinese American Oral History Project (hereafter SCCAOHP), interview 81, p. 7, and interview 156, p. 7.

17. Siu, *The Chinese Laundryman*, p. 85.

18. Maurice Freedman discusses similar patterns of emigration through clan contacts from the New Territories of Hong Kong to Chinese restaurants in Great Britain during the 1960s. Every aspect of the flow of labor was controlled by the original pioneers, who effectively recruited, financed, and conveyed any needed labor. See "Emigration from the New Territories," p. 225.

19. Siu, *The Chinese Laundryman*, pp. 77, 91–92.

20. Ibid., pp. 92–94; and Renqiu Yu, *To Save China*, pp. 10–11.

21. Renqiu Yu, *To Save China*, pp. 12–13.

22. Charles McClain notes that it was to the great misfortune of Chinese that California's constitutional movement coincided with the rise to prominence of Denis Kearny's Workingmen's Party, which attracted support by blaming Chinese for white working-class ills. See *In Search of Equality*, p. 79.

23. Davis, *History of Political Conventions*, p. 265.

24. *New York Tribune*, May 1, 1869.

25. *The Argonaut*, December 29, 1877.

26. See Choy, Dong, and Hom, eds., *The Coming Man*, for an account of the pervasiveness of images of Chinese coolies in the culture of nineteenth-century America.

27. Sandmeyer, *The Anti-Chinese Movement in California*, p. 25. Sandmeyer quotes from the *Congressional Record*, 44th Congress, 1st session, 2850–57.

28. Historian Andrew Gyory argues that it was national politicians, and not Californian representatives or labor organizers, that spearheaded the racist

platform of Chinese exclusion and turned it into national law; see Gyory, *Closing the Gate*. His arguments contrast with the work of earlier scholars who emphasized the role of California politicians and labor organizers in fueling a sense of crisis stemming from Chinese immigration; see Sandmeyer, *The Anti-Chinese Movement in California*; and Saxton, *The Indispensable Enemy*.

29. For a more detailed discussion of how the anti-Chinese movement fit into national political strategies and thought during the 1870s, see Saxton, *The Indispensable Enemy*. Miller's *The Unwelcome Immigrant* provides an intellectual history of evolving stereotypes and perceptions of Chinese during this period.

30. Chinn, with Lai and Choy, *A History of the Chinese in California*, p. 26.

31. The Chinese American community did not accept the Exclusion laws passively. The Chinese consulate funded a test case to challenge the sudden cancellation of Certificates of Return. Unfortunately, in 1889 the Supreme Court in the case of *Chae Chan Ping v. the United States* supported the right of the U.S. government to revoke Certificates of Return despite previous treaty agreements. McClain and McClain, "The Chinese Contribution," p. 18.

32. The Chinese Six Companies spearheaded attempts to challenge the constitutionality of this measure and on the advice of reputable legal counsel ordered thousands of Chinese to refrain from registering in the belief that the law would be struck down as unconstitutional. The Six Companies collected US$60,000 to pay for legal counsel for the test case of *Fong Yue Ting v. United States*. Three laborers without certificates questioned the right of the U.S. government to deport them. At least one of the laborers had tried to get a Certificate of Residence but was refused by the collector of customs on the grounds that he had insufficient proof of his legal entry to the United States. The case went to the Supreme Court, which found that despite treaties between the two nations, "a sovereign state has plenary and unconfined power over immigration" and that the power to deport or expel is the same as exclusion. Cited in McClain and McClain, "The Chinese Contribution," pp. 18–19.

33. See the Geary Act passed May 5, 1892 (25 Stat. 25) and the McCreary Act passed November 3, 1893 (28 Stat. 7).

34. U.S. Department of Commerce and Labor, *Annual Report 1905*, p. 80, notes that the term "laborer" for "twenty-five years . . . has been construed by judicial and executive authority to represent all Chinese persons who were not specifically enumerated in the treaty of 1880 as entitled to come to this county." In 1909, the immigration service noted the problems with defining Chinese social classes so simplistically. "There is no reason why there should be any more objection to the entry to this country of a real physician or chemist of the Chinese race than to the entry of a merchant"; *Annual Report 1909*, p. 129.

35. This act also dramatically decreased immigration from Eastern Europe. For the first time, the immigration bureau distinguished between immigrant aliens (those eligible for citizenship), and nonimmigrant aliens (those ineligible for citizenship).

36. World War II changed the relationship between China and the United States, and the U.S. government took small steps to acknowledge the service of Chinese to the war effort. In a gesture of goodwill, the Exclusion acts were finally repealed on December 13, 1943 (57 Stat. 600–601). However, because the 1924 Immigration Act was still enforced, and the Chinese quota remained at 105, immigrating to the United States remained difficult for Chinese until 1965. Chinese did become eligible to naturalize but many were daunted by the many requirements demanded. Chinese alone were still defined by race and not by country of birth. Chinese were considered anybody at least 50 percent Chinese by descent. Chinese wives and children of American citizens were chargeable to the Chinese quota of 105, unlike European wives and children. Only after World War II did Chinese dependents of U.S. citizens become nonquota immigrants, on August 9, 1946 (60 Stat. 464; 64 Stat. 6).

37. Chinese court challenges during the nineteenth century also helped to define the extent of equal protection and due process guaranteed by this amendment. See McClain, *In Search of Equality*, pp. 83–132.

38. U.S. Department of Commerce and Labor, *Annual Report 1926*, p. 8.

39. Estimates range on the higher side of 90 percent, but because no official statistics exist, it is possible only to cite people's guesses. In 1909, the immigration bureau cited the reports of one Commissioner North of San Francisco: "Thousands of Chinese persons have been declared by the courts and other appropriate authorities to be natives of the United States during the past fifteen years. Of this number I verily believe nearly 90 percent are fraud; but their cases have been adjudicated, and there is no gainsaying their present citizenship"; see U.S. Department of Commerce and Labor, *Annual Report 1909*, pp. 129–30. The SCCAOHP also offers some estimates of the number of illegal entries; see the following files: interview 126, p. 2 (95 percent); interview 45, p. 9 (estimated ten out of eleven); interview 12, pp. 12–15 (estimated 90 percent).

Another indication of the number using paper identities can be found in the records of *jinshanzhuang*. In 1941 the Gold Mountain firm Wah Ying Cheong recorded helping eleven customers set sail for the United States. Of the eleven, eight did so using paper identities. Wah Ying Cheong, customers' travel accounts (*geke xieli bu*), 1941.

40. Some Chinese, out on bail pending court decision on whether they were born in the United States, simply traded places with other Chinese men willing to

return to China at the government's expense. Immigration authorities noted, "This last abuse is due to the difficulty of distinguishing Chinese persons from one another." U.S. Treasury Department, Bureau of Immigration, *Annual Report 1903*, pp. 96–97.

41. U.S. Department of Commerce and Labor, *Annual Report 1907*, p. 107.

42. U.S. Department of Commerce and Labor, *Annual Report 1926*, p. 8.

43. U.S. Department of Commerce and Labor, *Annual Report 1903*, p. 96. Trying to exclude Chinese at immigration stations was but one aspect of the immigration service's attempts to control the number of Chinese in the United States. Deportation was another tool that the bureau wielded. Thus Chinese could not rest easy in the United States even after they had gained admission. According to the 1907 immigration bureau report, deportation was a weapon necessary to the enforcement of the Exclusion laws:

> Experiences demonstrated that to make the exclusion laws effective of their purpose some measure must be adopted by which the expulsion of those laborers who enter without inspection, or who gain regular admittance by fraud and perjury, could be accomplished; hence the registration acts and the provision therein for the deportation of all Chinese laborers found in the country not in possession of the certificates of residence prescribed. This is the part of the law that is most bitterly opposed, especially in the interior and eastern districts of the United States. Yet upon its rigid enforcement depends any reasonable amount of success in the continuance of the exclusion policy.

In 1907, 503 Chinese were arrested and 336 actually deported. Idem, *Annual Report 1907*, p. 90.

44. Chinese Exclusion Case Files #21685/1–16. Because so many Chinese immigrated under fraudulent identities and are still very protective of their status, I have given each person a pseudonym to protect their privacy.

45. U.S. Treasury Department, *Annual Report 1902*, p. 71. For a discussion of immigration officials and the institutionalization of their hostility to Chinese attempting to immigrate, see Erika Lee, "At America's Gates," chaps. 3 and 6.

46. *Angel Island Immigration Station*, p. 20. This passage is taken from the interview with Ira and Edwar Lee. Ira Lee was the son of Reverend Lee Hong, one of the founders of the Hip Wo Chinese School. Edwar Lee was a Methodist minister. Information courtesy of Him Mark Lai, written comments, October 10, 1997.

47. SCCAOHP, interview 156, p. 3.

48. U.S. Treasury Department, *Annual Report 1903*, pp. 98–99. This comment was made by the Chinese inspector at the Malone, New York, immigration station

in describing the many Chinese who crossed the Canadian border and then gained entry by claiming U.S. citizenship.

49. Ibid., p. 99.

50. U.S. Treasury Department, *Annual Report 1909*, p. 128.

51. U.S. Department of Commerce and Labor, *Annual Report 1912*, p. 57. This scheme was reportedly "backed by half a dozen wealthy Chinese of this city, and these men and this attorney are said to have divided many thousands of dollars between them as profits on the undertaking."

52. Ibid., p. 57.

53. U.S. Treasury Department, *Annual Report 1903*, p. 103.

54. SCCAOHP, interview 20, pp. 16–20.

55. This firm was known by the name Quong Fat Cheung in the United States.

56. Chinese Exclusion Case Files #13509/30. The costs were US $50 for merchant papers, which would allow the "investor" to apply for a permit to go abroad and return to the United States, and US$50 per son brought over.

57. U.S. Department of Commerce and Labor, *Annual Report 1911*, p. 136. Excerpted from a letter dated November 28, 1910, and translated by the immigration service. Lee Sing Ng seems to have helped people locate papers to document the status they wished to immigrate under. Specifically mentioned are student papers and arrangements for sneaking across the Mexican border. He also advised people about financing their trips and helped them find moneylenders willing to forgo half the debt in case people were not able to land in the United States.

58. Such witnesses could be bribed or carefully chosen for the regularity of their visits to Chinatown.

59. Native-born sons were known as *tusheng zi*, native-born grandsons as *tusheng sun*, and citizens' sons as *jimin zi*. These terms and their Chinese characters were provided by Him Mark Lai.

60. In this section, I use the term "paper son" to describe a multigenerational system in which men who came as the sons of U.S. citizens could themselves claim citizenship and bring over sons of their own. Paper sons also referred to men who immigrated as the sons of merchants. Merchant sons, however, could not bring over sons of their own unless they were able to demonstrate merchant status.

61. David R. Chan, "The Tragedy and Trauma of the Chinese Exclusion Laws," pp. 198–99.

62. U.S. Treasury Department, *Annual Report 1903*, p. 98. The report quotes from the "Report of Proceedings of Chinese-Exclusion Convention," p. 51. The convention was held in San Francisco, November 21–22, 1901.

63. U.S. Department of Commerce and Labor, *Annual Report 1904*, p. 147.

64. U.S. Treasury Department, *Annual Report 1903*, pp. 98–99.
65. U.S. Treasury Department, *Annual Report 1902*, p. 76.
66. U.S. Department of Commerce and Labor, *Annual Report 1909*, p. 126.
67. According to Him Mark Lai, the increase in Chinese immigrating in this category may be connected to a series of court decisions made during the 1920s that more clearly defined the rights of foreign-born offspring of U.S. citizens.
68. U.S. Department of Commerce and Labor, *Annual Report 1926*, p. 8.
69. *Angel Island Immigration Station*, p. 21.
70. A law effective February 10, 1855, through May 14, 1934, stipulated that a child born abroad of a father who was a citizen of the United States at the time acquired U.S. citizenship at birth if the father had lived in the United States before his or her birth. If the child was born after May 24, 1934, the U.S.-citizen father had to have lived in the United States for ten years before the birth. Mothers could not confer the same right of citizenship to children born overseas. Kung, *Chinese in American Life*, p. 97.
71. U.S. Department of Labor, *Annual Report 1928*, p. 16. The United States Supreme Court held in the case of *Chin Yow v. United States* that such persons were not citizens and must be classed as aliens unless their fathers had resided in the United States before their birth. The immigration service commented, "This decision is a most salutary one."
72. The immigration bureau recognized that thousands of Chinese who were born abroad and even less Americanized than those already present in the United States could enter and claim citizenship through their fathers. In 1915 the agency attempted to limit this category of immigrants by permitting only those who were dependents of their father's household to enter. Any Chinese male over the age of eighteen had to prove dependent status and any over the age of 21 was excluded altogether. Federal courts thwarted this effort by ruling the same year that age and timing should not dictate when the foreign-born offspring of native-born citizens could step forward and claim their citizenship. The next year, the bureau tried again to exclude foreign-born citizens of Chinese ancestry who had already reached adulthood by claiming that such immigrants showed no "spirit of American allegiance" in coming so late. Again, the courts ruled that these kinds of assumptions discriminated against Chinese.

Only with respect to third-generation foreign-born citizens was the bureau able to impose some limits. By an act of Congress, passed in 1907, foreign-born children of foreign-born fathers could not claim U.S. citizenship unless their fathers had resided in the United States before their birth. Not until 1925 did this statute undergo judicial scrutiny, when it was upheld by the Supreme Court.

My thanks to Him Mark Lai for bringing to my attention the work by

Wenhsien Chen, "Chinese Under Both Exclusion and Immigration Laws"; see pp. 287–94.

73. Chinese Exclusion Case Files #36330/5–9.

74. The Immigration and Naturalization Service began the Chinese Confession Program in 1956 in an attempt to identify paper sons and prevent more Chinese from immigrating fraudulently. The program held out the promise of legalized status for those who confessed. A main condition of the program, however, was that those who participated had to implicate all others involved in the same chain of immigration. Because preserving the secrecy of paper identities from government authorities had been so deeply ingrained in the community and because most Chinese Americans had learned not to trust state bureaucrats, the Confession Program was very controversial. It was also used, on rare occasions, to deport persons deemed to be communist or unwelcome in the United States. About 30,000 Chinese Americans had their status adjusted under the program, about one-quarter of the total population of 1950.

For further discussion of the confession program and its impact on Chinese Americans, see Ngai, "Legacies of Exclusion," pp. 3–35.

75. Chinese Exclusion Case Files #12907/5–1.

76. *Angel Island Immigration Station*, p. 21.

77. Ibid., 34.

78. Taishan County Museum. The books were described as donated by Chao Jing, Huang Zhang, and Huang Weichang but were undated.

79. "History of Chinese Detained on Angel Island."

80. *Angel Island Immigration Station*, pp. 21–22.

81. Ibid., p. 34.

82. Chinese Exclusion Case Files, #12907/5–1.

83. *Angel Island Immigration Station*, p. 21.

84. Roger Tom, interview.

85. Johnny Wong, interview.

86. Jiang Yongkang, interview.

87. Lai, Lim, and Yung, eds., *Island*, p. 75.

88. Wong Louie Sue, interview; "History of Chinese Detained on Angel Island," interviews with Jeong Foo Louie, August 29, 1976, and Johnny Wong, May 6, 1994.

89. Interviews with Wong Louie Sue and Johnny Wong, May 6, 1994. Because the papers had been purchased from a friend of his mother's, Johnny Wong worked for his paper family to repay the debt. Usually, however, paper families went their separate ways in America. Some did stay in touch to ensure the availability of corroborative testimony if needed in the future.

90. *Angel Island Immigration Station*, p. 47. Some Chinese Americans who availed themselves of the confession program chose to keep their fake names or incorporated their real names into fake names.

Chapter 4

1. *Xinning Magazine*, no. 31 (1934), pp. 52–53. The only explanation offered by this article for the misinterpretation of Zhen Cheng's twelve-year absence was that accepted by the village elders. Although the idea of a soul returning to reclaim its bones in order to appear in corporeal form would be unacceptable to most Western-educated readers, this story offers a striking example of the intersection between local belief systems and the long-term absences associated with Gold Mountain sojourns.

2. Nee and Nee, *Longtime Californ'*, p. 17.

3. Lucie Cheng, "Free, Indentured, Enslaved,"pp. 420–21.

4. Included in the Page Act was a requirement that female immigrants from China, Japan, and other Asian countries carry certification that they had not been transported to the United States for "immoral purposes."

5. Sucheng Chan, "The Exclusion of Chinese Women," p. 106, n. 39, citing the California State Legislature, "Chinese Immigration: Its Social, Moral, and Political Effect," *Report to the California State Senate of Its Special Committee on Chinese Immigration* (Sacramento: F. P. Thompson, Superintendent of State Printing, 1878), p. 154.

6. Ibid., pp. 107, 109.

7. U.S. Department of Commerce and Labor, *Annual Report 1906*, p. 91. The year covered by each report is the fiscal year, which begins on July 1 and ends on June 30 of the year named in the title.

8. U.S. Department of Commerce and Labor, *Annual Report 1911*, p. 139.

9. U.S. Department of Commerce and Labor, *Annual Report 1906*, p. 91. Furthermore, Chinese women who were considered prostitutes at time of entry or found to become such within three years could be deported as well (170 Fed. Rep., 566, and also 24 Op. Atty. Gen., 706). U.S. Department of Commerce and Labor, *Annual Report 1910*, p. 131.

10. Even attempts to satisfy Western marriage customs were viewed by the immigration service with skepticism:

One of the singular and unanticipated results of the increase of Chinese citizens of this country was shown by several appeals by the wives of such citizens against the excluding decisions of the officer in charge at San Francisco. The appellants were married at a consulate of the United States in China by a Methodist missionary to young Chinamen whom the courts had determined to be citizens by birth in this country. It was in evidence that the wives had never seen their husbands until brought to the consulate to be married to them and that the purpose of such marriage was to bring appellants to this country to enter houses of ill-fame.

U.S. Department of Commerce and Labor, *Annual Report 1905*, p. 87.

11. The first measure taken to alleviate the problem of family separation was the War Brides Act of December 28, 1945, which allowed the foreign-born spouses of U.S. armed forces members married during World War II to enter the United States. Public Law 213, passed on July 22, 1947, extended this right to alien spouses ineligible for citizenship if married to a U.S. citizen within 30 days of the passing of the War Brides Act. Approximately 6,000 Chinese women entered the United States during the three years that this act was effective.

12. "History of Chinese Detained on Angel Island," The interview of Mrs. Lee was conducted December 14, 1975.

13. U.S. Department of Commerce and Labor, *Annual Report 1907*, p. 102.

14. Hayner and Reynolds, "Chinese Family Life in America," p. 630.

15. Glenn, "Split Household," p. 38. Glenn does not specify whether this family was from Taishan.

16. Sandra Wong, "For the Sake of Kinship," pp. 63 and 82.

17. Lyman, *Chinese Americans*, p. 68.

18. According to one old-timer, a man had to be educated and have money in order to marry in the United States. SCCAOHP, interview 134, p. 14.

19. Marked preferences for marrying Chinese were apparent in other host countries as well. In Malaysia, which had no laws against miscegenation, the Islamic religion of Malaysian women deterred Chinese men who refused to convert. In contrast, assimilation occurred more easily and frequently in Thailand because Buddhist wives were more acceptable to Chinese men. As noted by Skinner, Chinese emigration to Thailand had occurred for centuries, but no Thai Chinese community existed beyond the third generation because of such intermarriages. Nonetheless, in a 1957 survey of 135 leaders of the Thai Chinese community, Skinner found that 87 percent of their wives were Chinese, with 56 percent having been born in China. Skinner, *Leadership and Power*, p. 53.

20. Schwartz, "Mate-Selection," p. 563. According to Schwartz, "there is a tendency in all categories for grooms to marry Chinese brides of like origin. In those cases, however, where this does not occur, "merchant-group" grooms tend to marry Chinese brides of unlike origin, while laundry-worker and restaurant-worker grooms tend more often to marry non-Chinese." After 1925 the incidence and proportion of out-marriages among Chinese declined steadily; see pp. 564 and 566.

21. Siu, *The Chinese Laundryman*, p. 123.

22. Glenn, "Split Household," p. 40.

23. SCCAOHP, interview 134, p. 2.

24. "History of Chinese Detained on Angel Island," August 29, 1976.

25. Interview with Judy Ng. In the seven interviews I conducted with elderly Taishanese women, Judy Ng was the only one to use the word "love" in reference to her relationship with her husband. The term "grass widow" referred to women who were divorced or living separately from their husbands. The term "grass widow" probably derives from the definition of grass as "pasture" (putting cows out to pasture—i.e., to feed on the grass). The phrase was applied to people, specifically lords or attendants at court, who were relieved of their duties and sent to the countryside. This usage seem to have arisen in the late sixteenth century. See the *Oxford English Dictionary*.

26. Interview with Mai Yizhao.

27. *Xinning xianzhi* 21, pp. 1a–14a. Of these women, several lived out their lives in poverty, some resorting to farming or weaving to support their choice of chastity. See 21, p. 12a (Woman Wu); 21, p. 12b (Woman Huang); 21, p. 12b (Woman Chen); 21, p. 13a (Woman Li). In contrast, the 1839 gazetteer, the last to be published before 1893, listed no such widows among its female exemplars.

28. *Angel Island Immigration Station*, Hilda Wong, May 8, 1976, pp. 139–41.

29. For an analysis of the ecological, aesthetic, and functional attributes of village structure in Taishan, see Hammond, "Xiqi Village, Guangdong," pp. 95–105.

30. Interviews with Johnny Wong, March 6 and 8, 1994.

31. Interview with Mai Yizhao.

32. Interview with Judy Ng.

33. *Xinning Magazine*, no. 31 (1934), p. 9. The Chinese term for a woman's unblemished reputation is *duli wu wenyan*.

34. Ibid., no. 6 (1935), p. 65. Loss of reputation could affect men as well as women. A returned laundry owner, upon hearing laughter outside his window, assumed that people were laughing at him because his wife was having an affair and so committed suicide. Ibid., no. 8 (1936), pp. 60–61.

35. Ibid., no. 24 (1921), p. 11.

36. Ibid., no. 17 (1935), p. 67. When his wife's family heard of the attack they gathered together various uncles and cousins to claim revenge. Chen apologized and acknowledged his fault in the matter.

37. Ibid., no. 12 (1923), p. 35.

38. *Zuoxin Seasonal*, September 1929, p. 29.

39. *Xinning Magazine*, no. 17 (1934), pp. 70–71.

40. Ibid., no. 9 (1935), pp. 77–78. Many other articles about villagers taking punitive action against adulterous couples were published. See *Xinning Magazine*, no. 8 (1935), pp. 38–39; no. 17 (1934), p. 72; and no. 31 (1934), pp. 55–56. In the last story, the wronged party, Fan Zhi, decided to remarry after his wife ran away with her lover so that he could still have children. He contacted a matchmaker who arranged for him to meet a prospect at a teahouse. The candidate turned out to be his former wife, now abandoned by her lover. With no way of escaping, Woman Zhu began telling Fan Zhi of the hardships she had suffered since leaving him and in the end he forgave her. The two reconciled.

41. *Xinning Magazine*, no. 31 (1934), pp. 74–76.

42. Interview with Mei Shiming.

43. Sandra Wong, "For the Sake of Kinship," p. 150.

44. Rose Hum Lee, *The Chinese in the United States of America*, chap. 10; Sung, *The Adjustment Experience*, p. 174; and Glenn, "Split Household," p. 37.

45. Glenn, "Split Household," pp. 38–39. Glenn is careful to note:

> The split household is not unique to the Chinese and, therefore, cannot be explained as a culturally preferred pattern. Sojourning occurs where there are (a) large differences in the level of economic development of receiving vs. sending regions, and (b) legal/administrative barriers to integration of the sending group. Three examples of the phenomenon are guest workers in Western Europe; gold-mine workers in South Africa; and Mexican Braceros in the American Southwest. . . . Although the persistence of sojourning for several generations makes the Chinese somewhat unusual, there is evidence that legal restrictions were critical to maintaining the pattern.

For an excellent study of a community characterized by sojourning economic patterns, see Caroline Brettell's study of Lanheses, Portugal, *Men Who Migrate*.

46. See Pearl Buck's bestselling *The Good Earth*, which won the Pulitzer Prize and became an MGM movie starring Paul Muni and Luise Rainer in 1937. Also see Fei, *Peasant Life in China*, and *Xiangtu Zhongguo*.

47. Glenn, "Split Household," pp. 38–39.

48. Cohen, *House Divided*, p. 59.

49. See Irene Taeuber's discussion of John Lossing Buck's survey of Chinese farm families in "The Families of Chinese Farmers," p. 71. The national average for family size was 5.2. I do not have figures specific to Taishan, but some research suggests that the average household size in areas with relatively high proportions of overseas Chinese households may have been larger than elsewhere. Dependence

on remittance income tended to delay household separations, thereby increasing the number of stem households. See Johnson, "Family Strategies," pp. 118–19.

50. Sung, *The Adjustment Experience*, p. 173.

51. Sandra Wong, "For the Sake of Kinship," pp. 56–57. Corporate property here refers to property jointly owned by lineage organizations. This chapter focuses on single-household families and their economic structures and functions. Although these nuclear and stem family units also owned property jointly, their modes of interaction and levels of commitment should not be confused with those of much larger lineages. For more on the role of clan and fictive kinship ties in transnational networks, see Chapter 5.

52. Cohen, *House Divided*, pp. 58–59. Cohen notes, "Some of the problems encountered in dealing with Chinese family units might be clarified if it is first understood that while the *chia* is a discrete kin group, it can display a great deal of variation in residential arrangements and in the economic ties among its members."

53. Loosely based on Cohen's usage, I distinguish between family and household. Family here refers to the economic family. Household refers to units composed of conjugal pairs with or without children. Thus a family might include several households—that of the family manager in addition to the households formed by his married sons. In other cases, such as that of nuclear families, the family is the same as the household.

54. Cohen, *House Divided*, p. 79.

55. Ibid., pp. 81–82.

56. Sandra Wong, "For the Sake of Kinship," p. 45.

57. Ibid., p. 37.

58. Ibid., p. 138. Wong commented on her subjects: "The informants expressed a strong sense of commitment to work hard and sacrifice in order to make lives easier for their children and/or parents. They seemed to live their lives for others, and being apart from family members or spouses is one of the accepted common sacrifices. A drive emanates from within them to not rest until all members who so desire are reunited or financially assisted in some way. It is only then that they feel successful and satisfied with their lives" (pp. 151–52).

59. According to a survey conducted by C. F. Remer of American banks in Hong Kong in 1930–31, just over 50 percent of all remittances sent to China through Hong Kong came from the United States and Canada. If an April 3, 1926, article in the *Times* was correct that U.S. and Canadian Chinese accounted for just 1.7 percent, or 162,000 out of 9,634,000, of Chinese overseas, the amounts of money sent back by American Chinese were indeed enormous. Another matter to

consider is that over half of Chinese in the United States were from Taishan. See Remer, *Foreign Investments in China*, p. 183.

60. See Table 2 in Chapter 2. From the late 1920s through 1978, remittances from abroad made up at least 50 percent of overseas Chinese families' incomes and allowed families to escape subsistence farming. Families with incomes over 3,000 yuan derived 68.3 percent of their income from overseas remittances, those with incomes between 400 and 2,999 yuan received 44.9 percent from abroad, and those earning below 400 yuan relied on overseas support for only 12.9 percent of their income. See *Shafu Monthly* and Liang, "Guangdongsheng Taishan qiaoxiang," pp. 167–69. According to Graham Johnson's research in Duanfen in the early 1990s, remittances from abroad were still the largest determinant of income disparities. See Johnson, "Family Strategies," p. 128.

61. Interview with Xiao Fangye.

62. Cited in Siu, *The Chinese Laundryman*, pp. 183–84.

63. SCCAOHP, interview 19, p. 4.

64. Interview with Mai Yizhao.

65. Cited in Siu, *The Chinese Laundryman*, pp. 181–82.

66. U.S. laws and immigration service policies made it easier for merchants to bring their wives and children to the United States. With U.S. citizenship, these children could travel relatively freely between the United States and China. Such families were more markedly transnational, for they were able to choose from educational, economic, and social opportunities available on both sides of the Pacific. In his detailed study of the family of Sam Chang, Haiming Liu describes a Chinese American household during the 1920s in which one son and three daughters enjoyed the benefits of educational and job opportunities in both the United States and China. Sam Chang, an asparagus farmer with merchant standing, first came to the United States to take over his father's herb business. Chang managed to teach his children both Chinese and English, thereby enabling them to function in either society. Sam's son, Tennyson, was educated at Nankai University in Tianjin, then acquired a bachelor's degree in political science at the University of Southern California before pursuing a master's degree at Columbia. His eldest daughter, Constance, went to junior high school in Los Angeles and received a high-school diploma from Nankai and a bachelor's degree from Yenjing University in Nanjing. She went on to obtain a master's degree in education from Columbia. The next child, Estelle, attended high school in China and then entered UCLA. See Haiming Liu, "The Trans-Pacific Family."

67. Sandra Wong, "For the Sake of Kinship," p. 51. Wong contends that female-managed households are a "bonafide form of household composition among Overseas Chinese, and its importance can no longer be overlooked."

Graham Johnson noted a continuing preponderance of female-headed households in the Duanfen District in Taishan. He also found that households are much less likely to divide in overseas Chinese-dominated areas, resulting in higher numbers of stem families and fewer nuclear households. There were greater numbers of single-person households and widows as well. Johnson, "Family Strategies," pp. 118, 128.

68. SCCAOHP, interview 84, p. 3. Although wives could acquire property, they seemed to have less power to dispose of it. Courts determined that property that had been sold in desperation by wives during World War II when remittances were cut off should be returned to their original owners. The courts handed down such decisions because women did not have the right to sell family land. When the wife of one Liu Yamao, who had just lost his job in Indonesia, sold their maid as a concubine, she was arrested for selling the property of her husband. *Xinning Magazine*, no. 34 (1934), pp. 30–31.

69. Xiao Dexing letters, letters to Chen Shi.

70. Glenn, "Split Household," p. 39.

71. Interview with Xiao Jinliu.

72. Sung, *The Adjustment Experience*, p. 178. Such experiences were not uncommon; Of the 40 people interviewed by Wong, 29 grew up with absent fathers. Of the 29 fathers, 21 had left to work overseas and regularly sent money home to support their families; three men had established new families with new wives or run off for some other reason; one man worked in another village and visited only on holidays; one father pretended to be the informant's uncle for immigration purposes; and three of the men had died before their children's eighth birthdays. The low rate of abandonment is probably not representative, because Wong only interviewed subjects in the United States. Most of her informants were able to immigrate because close relatives, husbands, parents, or siblings had paid for their passage. If she had interviewed women in Hong Kong and Taishan as well, it is likely that the rate of abandonment would have been reported to be significantly higher. See Sandra Wong, "For the Sake of Kinship," p. 50.

73. Interview with Xiao Bolian.

74. *Xinning Magazine*, no. 24 (1932), pp. 70–71.

75. Ibid., no. 8 (1935), p. 63.

76. Sandra Wong found that only three out of 40 informants' fathers abandoned their Chinese families for newly established ones in the United States.

77. Cohen notes, "Of course, it is probable that a great many, if not most, of the persons who went out looking for work were failures. Failure did not necessarily mean an inability to survive. The critical standard was whether survival was accompanied by remittances. Failure, indeed, might sometimes have the same

result as success—a return to the original *chia* household." Hence the greater numbers of Taishanese who made their way home during the Great Depression. Cohen, "Developmental Process in the Chinese Domestic Group," p. 35.

78. Glenn, "Split Household," p. 37.

79. June Mei, "Economic Origins of Emigration," p. 486. Mei cites U.S. Senate, Report No. 689 (Report of the Joint Special Committee to Investigate Chinese Immigration. (Washington, D.C.: U.S. Government Printing Office, 1877), p. 33. Mei's figure of 148,000 differs significantly from the 100,686 cited by Paul Siu for 1880. See Siu, *The Chinese Laundryman*, p. 250.

80. SCCAOHP, interview 69, p. 5. David Kulp estimates that in Phenix Village in eastern Guangdong only one-tenth of all emigrants ever returned. Kulp, *Country Life in South China*, vol. 1, p. 53.

81. Interview with Johnny Wong, March 6, 1993. When Wong went to the United States himself, he tracked down his grandfather in Chicago but was unable to confirm that his grandfather had taken a second wife.

82. *Xinning Magazine*, no. 24 (1935), p. 69. The Chinese term for eccentricity is *xiancheng wei qi*.

83. Interview with Wong In Oy, February 14, 1995. Also see interviews with Huang Meixian, Wu Yimin, and Judy Ng.

84. *Xinning Magazine*, no. 24 (1932), pp. 70–71. Mrs. Xu remarried even though her husband faithfully sent back large sums of money. The Xu clan was upset at her betrayal and set about trying to locate her. When they finally did, with the help of the Security Bureau in Taishan City, the ceremony had already been performed and the bridal gifts exchanged. In order to extricate her from the second marriage, the presents had to be returned. The Security Bureau determined that the matchmakers, Lin Mouye and his wife, were responsible for paying for the valuables, and the latter duly produced Ch.$300 to settle the affair.

85. Ibid., no. 17 (1934), p. 70.

86. Ibid., no. 11 (1935), p. 40.

87. According to Ann Waltner, "Adoption, as a legal fiction, is a way in which people can tamper with nature, making good a natural deficiency." *Getting an Heir*, p. 4.

88. See *Xinning xianzhi* 21, p. 12b on Woman Huang; 21, p. 12b on Woman Chen; 21, p. 12a on Woman Huang; 21, p. 11b on Woman Chen.

89. Siu, *The Chinese Laundryman*, pp. 157–63. Although the selling of daughters in times of trouble is better known, Chinese also sold sons. Poverty could produce terrible desperation, and male heirs of all ages could be purchased. If no nephews were available for adoption locally, Taishanese usually looked to their poorer neighboring counties for possibilities.

90. See Waltner, *Getting an Heir*, pp. 48–53.
91. Interview with Mai Yizhao.
92. Interview with Mrs. Wu, February 17, 1995.
93. *Xinning Magazine*, no. 17 (1934), p. 75.
94. Ibid., no. 6 (1935), p. 57.

Chapter 5

1. Murray, "Migration, Protection, and Racketeering," p. 179.
2. Lai, "Historical Development," p. 15. The Four Counties Association had formed in 1851, after itself separating from an organization founded and dominated by merchants from the Three Counties of Nanhai, Panyu, and Shunde.
3. See Chen Lanbin, "ShiMei jilue" pp. 59a–60b; and Li Gui, *Huanyou diqiu xinlu* 3, p. 28a–b. Taishanese played such a dominant role in the United States that the presidency of the Six Companies, or the Chinese Consolidated Benevolent Association, alternated every two years between a representative of the Ningyang Association and one of seven other associations.
4. Associations were not entirely benevolent in function and purpose. They were controlled by members of the merchant class who used their positions of authority, as well as the vulnerability of Chinese in the United States, to extract fees of varying kinds from association members. By the 1920s, lower-class Chinese consistently accused leaders of the Six Companies of ignoring their interests and well-being. The formation of the Chinese Hand Laundry Alliance in 1933 is one manifestation of this discontent. See Renqiu Yu, *To Save China*, chaps. 1, 2.
5. Goodman, *Native Place*, pp. 243–45. Some of the major disasters cited by Goodman are the flooding of three major Guangdong rivers in 1915 and an earthquake that hit Chaozhou prefecture and Mei County in January 1918.
6. Goodman notes the importance of actively maintaining a sense of community identity: "The existence of a positive Guangdong identity depended on its construction and vigilant defense by a wealthy Guangdong sojourner elite. In contrast, groups without influential elites lacked the wherewithal to establish and maintain their reputation and therefore lacked a key element in the formation of a positive sense of group identity." Goodman, *Native Place*, p. 107.

See also Benedict Anderson's illuminating comments about the role of "print capitalism" in making it "possible to 'think' the nation." According to Anderson, the printing press made possible newspapers, also described as "one-day best-sellers," which helped construct imagined national communities by involving thousands in "a mass ceremony" of shared reading: "It is performed in silent privacy, in the lair of the skull. Yet each communicant is well aware that the cere-mony he performs is being replicated simultaneously by thousands (or millions) of others of whose existence he is confident, yet of whose identity he has not the slightest notion." Anderson, *Imagined Communities*, pp. 22, 35.

7. Goodman noted the unifying possibilities of the business networks that connected Guangdong merchants in cities throughout China: "Although the grouping together of fellow provincials segmented cities internally, it also resulted in the transcendence of urban borders, integrating urban centers into larger interurban networks of fellow-provincials. Sojourning Guangdong merchants in Shanghai were in close touch with sojourning fellow-provincials in other ports where they maintained business interests." Goodman, *Native Place*, p. 12.

8. Liu Xiaoyun, "Plans to Completely Rebuild Taishan," *Xinning Magazine*, no. 12 (1912), p. 1. Liu notes that only a few men in each village could not read. Unfortunately, Liu does not specify what level of literacy he used to make this assessment. Although his estimate of the level of literacy may sound high, it is within the realm of possibility if one considers the large number of schools that had been built in Taishan with overseas money.

9. This last group had formed on the basis of the vows of brotherhood sworn by four legendary heroes, Liu Bei, Guan Yu, Zhang Fei, and Zhao Yun in *Romance of the Three Kingdoms*.

10. Before 1949, a variety of organizations published well over 100 *qiaokan* in Taishan. According to Huang Zhongji, who cites a draft of the 1986 *Taishan Gazetteer*, 115 *qiaokan* had been published. Of these, 15 were county publications, 16 village publications, 61 clan publications, and 23 school publications. Zheng Dehua and Wu Xingci, who surveyed the Taishan County Archives in 1981, counted 122, as does the Taishan County *Overseas Chinese Gazette*. See Hsu, "Living Abroad and Faring Well," appendixes; Huang Zhongji, "Taishan qiaokan shihua," p. 45; *Taishan xian huaqiao zhi*, pp. 207–15; and Zheng Dehua and Wu Xingzi, "Yipi you jiazhi de huaqiaoshi ziliao," pp. 454–88.

11. Hsieh, "The Ideas and Ideals of a Warlord," p. 203.

12. Goodman, *Native Place*, p. 196.

13. Lo and Lai, *Chinese Newspapers Published in North America*, pp. 6–7. Also see Lai, "Kuomintang in Chinese American Communities," p. 178. In order to convey the image of a newspaper printed by U.S. citizens supporting revolution in China, the publishers of *Young China* incorporated the image of an eagle into their masthead.

14. Liu Xiaoyun, "Preface to the *Xinning Magazine*," *Xinning Magazine*, no. 1 (1909), p. 3.

15. Zhao Gongchen, "Looking Back on the Tenth Anniversary of the Magazine," *Xinning Magazine*, no. 4 (1919), pp. 1–2.

16. *Xinning Magazine*, no. 16 (1910). The product of these endeavors, the Taishan Middle School, to this day remains the most highly regarded school in the county.

17. Apart from the opinions expressed in *Xinning Magazine*, little is known about Tan Yuzhi, Zhao Gongchen, Liu Richu, or Liu Xiaoyun. The magazine was their main legacy and provides the only record of their lives and activities.

18. The leaders of the Xinning Magazine Society were extremely grateful to Tan for his support: "Although in this matter there are goals as yet unattained, upon encountering Sir Tan Xiaofang of Hubei, who governed our county as a *jinshi*, an enterprising spirit, and a real go-getter, education expanded and it was the beginning of arriving at responsibility. Thus he agreed with the members of the Education Committee on every point. He heard word that they had organized a county newspaper and praised the project tremendously, repeatedly encouraging them. Then, in the spring of 1908, it was published." *Xinning Magazine*, no. 4 (1919), p. 2.

19. Of all China's *qiaokan*, *Xinning Magazine* is the only one to survive China's turbulent twentieth century, interrupted only by the Japanese occupation of Hong Kong (1941–45) and the Cultural Revolution (1965–75). After the death of Mao in 1976, it was the first *qiaokan* to resume publication with Deng Xiaoping's reforms in 1978.

20. Liu Xiaoyun, "Preface to the *Xinning Magazine*," no. 1 (1909), p. 5.

21. *Xinning Magazine*, no. 1 (1909), p. 17.

22. Goodman, *Native Place*, pp. 197–98.

23. Tan Shouzun, "Essay on the Founding of the *Xinning Magazine*," *Xinning Magazine*, no. 1 (1909), pp. 1–2. But while the activities of the Xinning Magazine Society met with Tan's approval, the magistrate held great contempt for "the gentry [who] have been shirking their responsibilities to their native place for a long time [and] the cunning ones who know only to exploit commoners and their families for profit."

24. Liu Xiaoyun, "Preface to the *Xinning Magazine*," no. 1 (1909), p. 5. Magistrate Tan shared this view. In 1909 he gave a talk to the Education Research Committee and commented, "To improve society today, we must start with education. If we wish to reorganize and improve education, we must start with improving the private academies." *Xinning Magazine*, no. 2 (1909), p. 16.

25. Liu Xiaoyun, "Plans to Completely Rebuild Taishan," p. 1.

26. *Xinning Magazine*, no. 31 (1911), pp. 1–3.

27. See "Xinning Ought to Encourage the Republic" by Wulai, *Xinning*

Magazine, no. 36 (1911), pp. 6–8; or "Xinning Amidst the Republic," *Xinning Magazine*, no. 1 (1913), pp. 1–5. See also *Xinning Magazine*, no. 2 (1913), p. 9; and *Xinning Magazine*, no. 16 (1913), p. 5.

28. *Xinning Magazine*, no. 20 (1911), p. 14, and no. 6 (1909), p. 1.

29. Zhao Gongchen, "Looking Back on the Tenth Anniversary of the Magazine," p. 2. The news writing staff included Lei Yuchuan, Ma Liqing, Li Daochao, Tan Weichen, Ma Huidong, Kuang Mingpu, Lei Yintang, Yu Youkui, Yu Zhongshan, Yu Kunji, Huang Shi'an, Kuang Zhuoqing, Huang Jingqiu, Li Xunzhi, Mei Jianxing, and Lin Jinyan, among others.

30. Leong Gor Yun, *Chinatown Inside Out*, p. 160. Some of the characters in *Xinning Magazine* are printed sideways or upside down, supporting Leong's account of Chinese printing. Leong Gor Yun was the pseudonym of famed Chinese American newspaper man Y. K. Chu, who edited the *Chinese Commercial Times* in New York during the 1930s. Chu wrote the book to expose the corruption of the Chinese Consolidated Benevolent Association, but because he feared that the powerful organization would boycott his newspaper he used a fake name.

31. Liu Xiaoyun, "Preface to the *Xinning Magazine*," pp. 3–6.

32. *Xinning Magazine*, no. 4 (1912), p. 72.

33. See, for example, *Xinning Magazine*, no. 28 (1910), pp. 10–20, or no. 17 (1910), pp. 5–13.

34. Liu Xiaoyun, "Preface to the *Xinning Magazine*," p. 5.

35. *Xinning Magazine*, no. 4 (1912), p. 72.

36. Ibid., no. 15 (1919), p. 54.

37. Zhao Gongchen, "Looking Back on the Tenth Anniversary of the Magazine," p. 2.

38. *Xinning Magazine*, no. 17 (1909), p. 7. In 1910, one American reader cabled a four-page response to the magazine. *Xinning Magazine*, no. 12 (1910), pp. 16–20.

39. *Xinning Magazine*, no. 24 (1910), p. 5.

40. Ibid., no. 22 (1912), p. 79. In 1935 the Hong Kong branch office moved to the Fu Yuan Bookstore, 245 Queen's Road, Central, second floor, when Lee Sang Wo closed down. See *Xinning Magazine*, no. 24 (1934) and no. 5 (1935).

41. *Xinning Magazine*, no issue no. (1915), p. 16.

42. Ibid., no. 25 (1940), p. 18.

43. Ibid., no. 31 (1917), p. 42. The society posted an announcement notifying readers that because currency remittance costs were so high the distributors were losing money. Readers were encouraged to pay new higher prices and notify the Hong Kong branch office if they were unwilling to continue subscribing at these prices. *Xinning Magazine*, no. 17 (1911), p. 14.

44. Lee and Nathan, "The Beginnings of Mass Culture," p. 368.

45. *Xinning Magazine*, no. 22 (1912), p. 79. According to Lee and Nathan, through new roads and railroads and a "growing and increasingly efficient Chinese Post Office and a spreading network of bookstores, and . . . traditional letter-carrying hongs (*min-hsin chu*), riverine paddle-boats and the like, the urban-centered press achieved wide distribution throughout the nation." See Lee and Nathan, "The Beginnings of Mass Culture," pp. 369–70.

46. *Xinning Magazine*, no. 15 (1919) and no. 27 (1927). In the announcements section of one issue the Xinning Magazine Society sought distributors in Sydney, Mexico City, Peru, Singapore, Thailand, Saigon, Tokyo, Beijing, and Shanghai to fulfill reader requests for local distributors. Interested businesses were asked to supply proof of their business status. *Xinning Magazine*, no. 24 (1921).

47. *Xinning Magazine*, no. 4 (1912), p. 72.

48. Ibid., no. 4 (1912), p. 74.

49. Ibid., no. 4 (1919), p. 3.

50. Ibid., no. 18 (1914), pp. 8–10; no. 2 (1915), pp. 1–6; no. 11 (1916), p. 1. Ge Gongzhen notes a similar change in Chinese magazines but sets the transition as pre– and post–World War I. Perhaps the real transition is the May Fourth Movement. Ge notes, "Before the European war, during the first years of the Republic, Chinese examined administration and made suggestions about how it should be divided. So, what each magazine discussed always emphasized government, focusing on standards of administration. After the European war, Chinese started gradually to explore the meaning of human lives, realizing that fate cannot be relied upon, sought a fundamental path to resolving." See Ge, *Zhongguo baoxue shi*, p. 188.

51. *Xinning Magazine*, no. 22 (1912); no. 13 (1917), pp. 20–21; no. 21 (1928), p. 22. Some of the reports on village matters contain far-fetched and even supernatural elements. The stories of Zhen Cheng in Chapter 4 and Woman Tan in Chapter 2 are examples. Although by present-day standards such details seem unrealistic, they do offer a sense of how village Chinese interpreted and recounted events of interest in their lives.

52. *Xinning Magazine*, no. 6 (1934), pp. 66–67.

53. Ibid., no. 25 (1932), p. 57.

54. Also see ibid., "The Robbing of a School in Nancun," no. 19 (1922); and "Courage of a Villager Who Shot to Death a Bandit," no. 22 (1912).

55. *Xinning Magazine*, no. 25 (1917), announcement section.

56. Ibid., no. 31 (1917), p. 43.

57. Ibid., no. 3 (1911), p. 71.

58. Ibid., no. 4 (1912), p. 85. This ad was posted by the Maoli Shipping

Company of Hong Kong for travel to Mexico. In 1916 the Pacific Steamship Company offered passage between Hong Kong and San Francisco but advised customers that they must first be checked for hookworm. A doctor from the company itself checked for glaucoma. See *Xinning Magazine*, no. 9 (1916), p. 57. Also see ad in issue no. 17 (1923), front page.

59. *Xinning Magazine*, no. 4 (1927), p. 91, and no. 25 (1940), announcement section.

60. Ibid., no. 4 (1912), announcement section.

61. Ibid., no. 24 (1932), announcement section; no. 15 (1919), announcement section. Like Taishanese laborers in the United States, who almost always used a local store or their clan association as a mailing address, Taishanese villagers could rarely receive mail at their own homes. Government-run postal networks were not extensive enough to serve most of rural China. Money shops or *jinshanzhuang* either dispatched a courier to take money and letters to their homes or sent word that money had arrived and waited for the designated recipients to pick it up.

62. *Xinning Magazine*, no. 11 (1934), p. 2; no. 33 (1932); no. 34 (1930); no. 2 (1934); no. 11 (1934); no. 12 (1923), announcement section.

63. *Xinning Magazine*, no. 24 (1917), announcement section; no. 24 (1921), announcement section; no. 24 (1932), p. 93; no. 24 (1921), announcement section; and no. 15 (1919), announcement section.

64. Lo and Lai, *Chinese Newspapers Published in North America*, p. 6. According to Lo and Lai, "The group connected with the party holding the political reins in China enjoyed an advantage in the local Chinese community, which helped bring in some subscriptions and advertisements. The newspapers speaking for the "out" groups had to depend more on the financial resources of a smaller circle of loyal supporters"; see p. 7.

65. *Xinning Magazine*, no. 17 (1911), p. 14. Leong Gor Yun noted that only one Chinese-language newspaper published in the United States broke even: "*The Journal* by its independence has acquired the largest circulation, and thus also the largest advertising revenue. It is the only one of the lot since the beginning of the Chinese-American press ever to make money, and only *The Nationalist Daily* in New York in boom days ever so much as broke even." But even so, circulation was not high: "Even the successful *Journal*, with advertising rates twice and three times those of its competitors, has an average circulation of only about 5,000 in peacetime, rising to about 10,000 on war in China or Tong war in America. With such small circulations, the universal price of 5 cents helps carry the papers." Leong Gor Yun, *Chinatown Inside Out*, pp. 158–59.

66. Karl Lo notes that Chinese-language newspaper circulation in the United States rose steadily from 1900 to 1950, so it is likely that *Xinning Magazine* circula-

tion increased over those decades. According to Lo's survey of the *Ayer Dictionary of Publications* (Philadelphia, 1900–1950), Chinese newspaper subscribers in the United States numbered fewer than 1,000 in the first decade of the twentieth century, between 3,000 and 4,000 in the 1910s, and 2,000 to 8,000 during the 1920s and 1930s. In 1938 and 1939, *Young China* passed the 10,000 subscriber mark. Other newspapers enjoyed especially high circulation during the war with Japan, which then fell off for unclear reasons during 1944. See Lo and Lai, "The Chinese Vernacular Presses," p. 172.

67. *Xinning Magazine*, no. 25 (1917), p. 53. The magazine society formulated plans to increase circulation to 4,000 in 1913. See *Xinning Magazine*, no. 31 (1913), p. 7. Despite these numbers it is still difficult to know how many people actually read the magazine because newspapers and magazines were commonly shared among several readers. Lee and Nathan estimate that during the Republican era an average of fifteen readers read each copy of every periodical issued; see "The Beginnings of Mass Culture," p. 372. Also see *Xinning Magazine*, no. 8 (1917); no. 7 (1931); no. 8 (1936); *Four Counties Magazine*, no. 1 (1916); and *Taishan Overseas Chinese Magazine*, no. 14 (1933).

68. *Four Counties Magazine*, no. 1 (1916), pp. 3–4.

69. Ibid., p. 3.

70. Ibid., p. 2.

71. Goodman notes the utility of native-place ties in allowing Chinese to form groups of varying size: "In practice the flexibility of the native-place tie provided both the convenience of local communities for day-to-day purposes and larger combinations with greater political clout when the issue was the nation." Goodman, *Native Place*, pp. 237–38.

72. *Four Counties Magazine*, no. 2 (1916), p. 3. The editors claimed that this principle was based on "Occidental ethics."

73. Ibid., no. 1 (1916), p. 3.

74. Ibid., p. 1.

75. Lau, "Educational Development in Taishan County," pp. 64–65.

76. Renqiu Yu, "Chinese American Contributions," p. 55. In 1929 the *Taishan Education Bi-monthly Report* (*Taishan jiaoyu banyue kan*) recorded the importance of schools to clan leaders: "The road of (establishing) a school is certainly the crown on a clan. (If) they want to honor the ancestors, (then) they cannot help but establish a school." Cited in Lau, "Educational Development in Taishan County," p. 62.

77. *Fushan Monthly*, no. 3 (1936), pp. 42–46. The head of the society was Zhao Jianping, the chief editor Zhao Xuanmin. It was put together in Fushi but published in Taicheng by the Tongwen Company. Of a total of 62 society

members, nineteen were in Fushi, thirteen elsewhere in Taishan, sixteen in Guangdong, six in China, and only seven lived outside China: one in Hong Kong, four in Southeast Asia, one in Rangoon, one in the United States, and one whose whereabouts was unknown.

78. *Nanshe Monthly*, no. 4 (1920), p. 1.

79. *Yingchuan Monthly*, no. 1 (1926), p. 2.

80. Subscribers to *Xinning Magazine* received a far better deal. In 1926 the minimum contribution required for twelve issues of the *Yingchuan Monthly* was three yuan. In 1928 *Xinning Magazine* charged readers only 3.80 yuan for a year's subscription of 35 issues. *Xinning Magazine*, no. 28 (1928), back page.

81. *Yingchuan Monthly*, no. 1 (1926), p. 4.

82. Renqiu Yu, "Chinese American Contributions," p. 71. Other strategies for raising funds included circulating money-collecting booklets with the cooperation of clan organizations in the United States and sending fund-raising representatives on a lecture circuit sponsored by the Ningyang Benevolent Association and the relevant clan organizations (see p. 60).

83. *Kanghe Monthly*, no. 3 (1930), p. 1.

84. *Fushan Monthly*, no. 2 (1935), p. 6.

85. See *Fushan Monthly*, no. 12 (1936), p. 35; no. 3 (1936), p. 47; no. 5 (1935), pp. 30–31. Despite the willingness of readers to donate funds, the magazine did not have a large enough readership to entice businesses to pay three yuan per issue for advertising. The cost for a year's subscription was 40 cents.

86. *Fushan Monthly*, no. 8 (1936), p. 6. This reader went on to claim, "I am the person who loves this monthly magazine the most, my love is so deep that it cannot feel the intimacy of its words" (p. 9).

87. *Fushan Monthly*, no. 2 (1935), p. 8.

88. Lau, "Educational Development in Taishan County," p. 67.

89. Ibid., pp. 202, 204–8, citing statistics from the 1934 and 1935 editions of *Guangdongsheng jiaoyu gaikuang* (General situation of education in Guangdong Province) published by the Guangdong Provincial Educational Bureau.

90. Zheng and Cheng, *Taishan qiaoxiang yu Xinning tielu*, pp. 84–85.

91. According to Bryna Goodman, *huiguan* within China demonstrated similar kinds of loyalties to native place: "The substantial involvement of native-place associations in native-place affairs meant that when the native place suffered, association directors and sojourners reached deeply into their pockets. Guangdong province was beset by both natural and militarily induced disasters throughout the early Republican period. . . . In the event of small and localized disasters, each Guangdong *huiguan* assisted its home area." See Goodman, *Native Place*, pp. 243–45.

92. Interview with Mei Shiming.
93. Leong Gor Yun, *Chinatown Inside Out*, p. 161.
94. *Xinning Magazine*, no. 22 (1912), p. 69, and no. 21 (1917), announcement section.
95. Lai, "The Kuomintang in Chinese American Communities," p. 194.
96. Renqiu Yu, "Chinese American Contributions," p. 58 n. 71. The Ningyang Association assumed a similar policy when in 1928 it stated one of its organizational goals to be the promotion of public welfare projects in Taishan.
97. Ge, *Zhongguo baoxue shi*, p. 267.
98. *Xinning Magazine*, no. 26 (1932), p. 10. In 1934 the county party received orders from the provincial office that several books were to be banned, including a selection of stories by Ding Ling, Lenin's *The Right of Nations to Self-Determination*, and Li Da's *Principles of Agricultural Problems. Xinning Magazine*, no. 24 (1934), pp. 64–65.
99. *Xinning Magazine*, no. 31 (1934), pp. 58–59; no. 14 (1931), p. 65.
100. Ibid., no. 31 (1934), pp. 11–12.
101. Ibid., no. 27 (1935), pp. 15–16.
102. Ibid., no. 10 (1912), p. 5.
103. By the 1940s, lower-class Chinese Americans resented being considered "*arding*—stupid folks easily manipulated by the elite and whose only role was to donate money." See Renqiu Yu, *To Save China*, p. 166.
104. *Taishan Overseas Chinese Magazine*, no. 1 (1932), p. 2.
105. Ibid., no. 11 (1932), p. 7.
106. Ibid., no. 1 (1932), p. 6.
107. *Xinning Magazine*, no. 1 (1909), p. 5.
108. *Qiao* also lent itself to more innocuous but highly useful purposes, including *qiaohui*, remittances from overseas Chinese; *qiaojuan*, the family members and dependents of overseas Chinese; and *guiqiao*, overseas Chinese who return from abroad to live in China. Perhaps the most complex concept associated with sojourning is that of *qiaoxiang*, which is most often commonly translated as "emigrant community." This awkward turn of phrase does little to capture the sense of belonging and nostalgia for home associated with the word in Chinese.
109. According to Dino Cinel, the Italian government had similar hopes for overseas Italians during the first decades of the twentieth century. See Cinel, *The National Integration of Italian Return Migration*, p. 4.
110. The situation became particularly uncomfortable for Chinese in Southeast Asia after World War II as newly established governments tried to gauge the political loyalties of Chinese "guests" who might adhere to the leadership of communist China.

111. *Far East Chinese-English Dictionary*, p. 1114.

112. The term *qiaobao* was first used in *Xinning Magazine* in 1916 but did not start appearing regularly until after 1932.

113. Lai, "Kuomintang in Chinese American Communities," p. 190.

114. Lai, *Cong huaqiao dao huaren*, pp. 225–27.

115. See "New York Overseas Chinese Start a Movement to Donate One Hundred Cars," *Xinning Magazine*, no. 15 (1939), p. 93; "Countymen in the United States Advocate Changing Funds to Buy Planes to Funds to Buy Food to Alleviate Crisis," no. 19 (1939), pp. 24–26; and "Chicago Countymen Again Donate Over $10,000 Chinese Dollars in Remittances to Save Refugees," no. 19 (1939), pp. 31–32.

Chapter 6

1. Cronon, *Nature's Metropolis*, pp. 80–81.

2. The year of Chen's birth was either 1844 or 1846. See Zheng and Cheng, *Taishan qiaoxiang yu Xinning tielu*, p. 34; and Mei Yimin, "Taishan yinjin qiaozhi qiaoli gaishu," p. 18.

3. McCunn, *Chinese American Portraits*, p. 47.

4. Ibid., p. 51; Berner, *Seattle 1900–1920*, p. 14; and Burke, *A History of the Port of Seattle*, p. 7.

5. Zinn, *A People's History*, p. 247; see also p. 251.

6. For accounts of Seattle's rise as a trading center, see Burke, *A History of the Port of Seattle*, p. 10; Berner, *Seattle 1900–1920*, pp. 10, 29–32. This success led Welford Beaton to title his history of Seattle *The City That Made Itself* (Seattle: Terminal Publishing Company, 1914).

7. Chin, *Golden Tassels*, p. 65.

8. Chen showed his commitment to the Seattle area by building the Canton Building in 1889. He was the first to rebuild after a devastating fire that year and chose the enduring medium of brick for his new property.

9. Berner, *Seattle 1900–1920*, p. 29.

10. Cronon, *Nature's Metropolis*, p. 72.

11. See Huenemann, *The Dragon and the Iron Horse*, p. 68.

12. By 1907, nineteen such lines would be chartered, providing the promise of railway links between Chengdu, Chongqing, and Hankow, from Beijing to Kalgan, Qunming to Luzhou, Hangzhou to Shanghai, Changzhou to Fuzhou, Shanghai to Suzhou, Guilin in Hunan to Nanning in Yunnan, Harbin to Qingshan, and, of course, Taishan to Jiangmen.

13. Of the nineteen railroad companies chartered by the Qing, only two man-

aged to raise the needed capital without government aid. It is no coincidence that these two companies were the only ones headed up and supported by overseas Chinese. See Lin Jinzhi, "Jiefangqian huaqiao zai Guangdong touzi," p. 46; and En-han Lee, *China's Quest for Railway Autonomy*, pp. 94–96.

14. The slogan in Chinese was *kaikuo jiaotong chuangjian tielu.*

15. In the first month of 1906, Chen reported to the court that he would build the railroad without foreign investment, without foreign capital, and without foreign labor in order to avoid giving control to outsiders. The company's regulations, formulated in April 1906, also list similar prohibitions against using foreign aid. See text of report reprinted in *Taishan wenshi* #9, p. 6, and text of company regulations, pp. 8–12. The Chinese is *bushou yanggu, bujie yangkuan, bugu yanggong, yi mian chuanli waiyi.*

16. Zheng and Cheng, *Taishan qiaoxiang yu Xinning tielu*, p. 38. The initial capitalization of the Xinning Railroad was only about $US1.4 million, a tiny sum compared to the $40 million in stock issued when Hill reorganized his Minneapolis and Saint Cloud lines for expansion toward the Pacific as the Great Northern Railway. See Malone, *James J. Hill*, pp. 128–29.

17. Zinn, *A People's History*, pp. 248–49.

18. Chen Bang, "Aiguo huashang Chen Yixi," p. 51.

19. Ibid., pp. 52–53.

20. The Qing government was about to collapse, and each of his overseas backers could commit only an additional 5,000 yuan, or US$2,500, to the project. Shares were five yuan, or US$2.50 in price, and purchased in blocks ranging from one to 1,000 in size.

21. Chen Bang, "Aiguo huashang Chen Yixi," p. 54.

22. See, for example, *Xinning Magazine*, no. 8 (1913), p. 7.

23. En-han Lee, *China's Quest for Railway Autonomy*, pp. 96–97.

24. Chen Bang, "Aiguo huashang Chen Yixi," p. 55.

25. Zheng and Cheng, *Taishan qiaoxiang yu Xinning tielu*, pp. 69–70.

26. Zheng and Cheng, *Taishan qiaoxiang yu Xinning tielu*, p. 68. What little freight the railroad carried were mostly imports, which exceeded exports by a ratio of 30 to one.

27. In 1934 the company announced an attempt to cut down on freeloaders by hiring special inspectors to check whether passengers had tickets. *Xinning Magazine*, no. 31 (1934): pp. 22–23.

28. Zheng and Cheng, *Taishan qiaoxiang yu Xinning tielu*, pp. 70–71.

29. Letter from Chen Yixi to Thomas Burke, February 23, 1925, reprinted in Zheng and Cheng, *Taishan qiaoxiang yu Xinning tielu*, pp. 186–87.

30. Letter from Chen Yixi to Thomas Burke, April 18, 1924, reprinted in

Zheng and Cheng, *Taishan qiaoxiang yu Xinning tielu*, pp. 184–85; also see letters from Chen Yixi to Douglas Jenkins, June 2, 1924; to J. C. Herbeman, June 2, 1924; and to Mr. Schurman, June 2, 1924, all in the Guangzhou Municipal Museum.

31. Zheng and Cheng, *Taishan qiaoxiang yu Xinning tielu*, pp. 70–71.

32. Ibid., p. 76.

33. Chen Bang, "Aiguo huashang Chen Yixi," p. 58. Despite its official record of running in the red for much of its history, the Xinning Railroad may have brought indirect benefits to Chen Yixi's fellow Chens of the Six Villages in the Doushan District of Taishan. The clan ran the *jinshanzhuang* enterprise, Huaying Chang, described in Chapter 2. According to the historian Ming K. Chan, who belongs to a different branch of the same Chen clan, the railroad enhanced the business's reputation for stability and reliability. Comments offered by Ming K. Chan at my 1999 presentation at the annual meeting of the Association for Asian Studies, "Trading with the Gold Mountain."

34. According to Cronon, railroads were a costly investment whether they made money or not:

> Fixed costs of running the railroad are high and remain the same, regardless of how much freight or passengers are carried. Even before any money can be charged or the trains start running, enormous capital outlay and time must be invested in order to assemble all the basic equipment and supplies—laying of track, buying of engines, training of engineers, coal supplies. Taxes and interest on borrowed bonds to pay for these initial costs remained a large part of the operating budget. Operating expenses also remained constant, regardless of volume of goods carried. . . . Ties rotted, bridges collapsed, and rails rusted no matter how few trains passed over them. Workers had to clear tracks of snow so that just one train could complete its journey. Even expenditures that one might think would vary most directly with volume of operation—fuel consumption, wear and tear on engines, and workers' wages—had quite a large component of fixed costs. A locomotive consumed a tenth of its daily fuel simply heating itself to the point that it could produce steam. Another fourth of its fuel consumption went toward moving its own weight. As a result, perhaps a third to half of all expenditure on locomotive fuel bore no relation whatsoever to how fully a train was loaded. Wages followed a similar pattern. A large portion of a railroad's employees, especially its managers, clerical staff, and maintenance workers, had to stay on the job even when little freight and few passengers were riding the rails. And a train needed the same number of engineers and conductors whatever the size of its load.

All of this meant that the trains had to keep running, whether full or empty, because they needed to earn as much as possible to cover operating costs. Cronon, *Nature's Metropolis*, pp. 84–85.

35. Third-class passage was reduced to 25 cents, second-class to 40 cents, and first-class to 60 cents. *Xinning Magazine*, no. 8 (1935): pp. 70–71.

36. Zheng and Cheng, *Taishan qiaoxiang yu Xinning tielu*, pp. 84–85.

37. Chen would not have been able to predict the Communist victory or the Cold War's splitting of the world into "red" and "free" with the subsequent exaggeration of Hong Kong's role as a gateway for political reasons.

38. For an example of this kind of rhetoric, see *Taishan Overseas Chinese Magazine*, no. 1 (1932), p. 6.

Chapter 7

1. The first aerial attack by Japanese over Taishan City occurred on September 30, 1937. Residents panicked and fled into the countryside. On December 28, 1937, two Japanese warships invaded and occupied Shangchuan Island off the coast of Taishan. In October of the following year, Japanese troops landed at Daya Bay and within eight days had taken Guangzhou. A flood of refugees swept into Hong Kong. On August 15, 1940, Japanese troops also invaded Xiachuan Island. Japanese made repeated incursions onto the Taishanese mainland from these southern bases. On March 3, 1941, three warships suddenly attacked from off the coast of Guanghai. Seven hundred men landed and attacked through the Sanjia seaport, then passed through Xialang Village and went on to capture Doushan District. Under the cover of air support, a separate force entered Chonglou and followed Tainan Road to Taishan City. Late that afternoon, the county seat of Taishan fell into enemy hands. Huang Jianyun, *Taishan gujin gailan*, vol. 1, pp. 20–22.

2. *Xinning Magazine*, no. 27 (1940), pp. 57–58.

3. Huang Jianyun, *Taishan gujin gailan*, vol. 1, p. 22.

4. Interview with Mai Yizhao.

5. Li Yiji, *Haiyan xiangtu shi*, p. 214.

6. *Yuesheng Monthly*, December 25, 1947, p. 20. Huang Jianyun estimates that before the war, Taishan's population stood at 1,117,865 and fell to 777,306. According to his count, only 1,171 died of war injuries, 144,052 starved to death, and 195,336 left the county. *Shencun Clan Magazine*, February 1, 1947, p. 21.

7. *Xinning Magazine*, no. 4 (1947), p. 87.

8. Ibid., no. 3 (1948), p. 86.

9. Lau, "Educational Development in Taishan County," p. 69.

10. *Yuesheng Monthly*, April 15, 1947, p. 1.

11. See *Xinning Magazine*, no. 5 (1946), p. 40.

12. Kevin Scott Wong, personal communication with author, June 24, 1996.

13. United States Department of Justice, *Annual Report 1950*, table 9A.

14. Huang Jianyun, *Taishan gujin gailan*, vol. 1, p. 181.

15. *Taishan Industrial and Commercial Magazine*, no. 8 (1948), pp. 2, 4.

16. Lin Jiajin et al., "Jindai Guangdong qiaohui yanjiu," p. 57.

17. See William Petersen, "Success Story, Japanese American Style," *New York Times Magazine*, January 9, 1966. Although Petersen initially held up only Japanese Americans for praise as a persecuted minority that attained success without government assistance. "Success Story of One Minority Group in U.S." (*U.S. News and World Report*, December 26, 1966) described the similar achievements of Chinese.

18. See Sucheng Chan, *Asian Americans*, for an account of the changes in attitude and world view that led to these dramatic changes in immigration law.

19. Chen Yintao, "Guangdong sheng Taishan," pp. 98–99.

20. Ibid., p. 99.

21. Liao Liqiong, "Gaige kaifang yilai Guangdong Taishan," p. 125.

22. Chen Yintao, "Guangdong sheng Taishan," p. 99.

23. Liang Yan, "Guangdong sheng Taishan qiaoxiang," p. 165.

24. K. Y. Chan, "The Role of Migration," p. 42.

25. Johnson, "Family Strategies," p. 130.

26. Chen Yintao, "Guangdong sheng Taishan," pp. 66, 117; and Wu Xingci and Li Zhen, "*Gum San Haak* in the 1980s," p. 25.

Bibliography

Anderson, Benedict. *Imagined Communities*. London: Verso, 1991.

Angel Island Immigration Station: Interviews with Chris Chow, Mr. Yuen, Ira and Ed Lee. San Francisco: Combined Asian American Resources Oral History Project and the Regents of the University of California, 1977.

Anzualdua, Gloria. *Borderlands/La Frontera: The New Mestiza*. San Francisco: Aunt Lute Book Company, 1987.

Appadurai, Arjun. "Disjuncture and Difference in the Global Cultural Economy." In *Theory, Culture and Society* 7 (1990): 295–310.

The Argonaut (newspaper), December 29, 1877.

Armentrout-Ma, Eve. *Revolutionaries, Monarchists, and Chinatowns: Chinese Politics in the Americas and the 1911 Revolution*. Honolulu: University of Hawaii Press, 1990.

Basch, Linda, Nina Glick Schiller, and Cristina Blanc-Szanton, eds. *Nations Unbound: Transnational Projects, Postcolonial Predicaments and Deterritorialized Nation-States*. New York: Gordon and Breach, 1994.

Berner, Richard C. *Seattle 1900–1920: From Boomtown, Urban Turbulence, to Restoration*. Seattle: Charles Press, 1991.

Burke, Padraic. *A History of the Port of Seattle*. Seattle: Frayn Printing Company, 1976.

Brettell, Caroline B. *Men Who Migrate, Women Who Wait: Population and History in a Portuguese Parish*. Princeton, N.J.: Princeton University Press, 1986.

Chan, Charles. "Chronology of Treaties and Major Federal Laws Affecting Chinese Immigration to the United States." In *The Life, Influence, and the Role of the*

Chinese in the United States, 1776–1960. San Francisco: Chinese Historical Society of America, 1976.

Chan, David R. "The Tragedy and Trauma of the Chinese Exclusion Laws." In *The Life, Influence, and the Role of the Chinese in the United States, 1776–1960.* San Francisco: Chinese Historical Society of America, 1975.

Chan, K. Y. "The Role of Migration in China's Regional Development—A Local Study of Southern China." Master's thesis, Department of Geography and Geology, University of Hong Kong, 1990.

Chan, Sucheng. *Asian Americans: An Interpretive History.* New York: Twayne, 1990.

———. "The Economic Life of the Chinese in California, 1850–1920." In *Early Chinese Immigrant Societies: Case Studies from North America and British Southeast Asia,* edited by Lee Lai To. Singapore: Heinemann Asia, 1988.

———. "The Exclusion of Chinese Women, 1870–1943." In *Entry Denied,* edited by Sucheng Chan. Philadelphia: Temple University Press, 1991.

———. *This Bittersweet Soil: The Chinese in California Agriculture, 1860–1910.* Berkeley: University of California Press, 1986.

———, ed. *Entry Denied: Exclusion and the Chinese Community in America, 1882–1943.* Philadelphia: Temple University Press, 1991.

Chen Bang 陳邦. "Aiguo huashang Chen Yixi yu Xinning tielu" 愛國華商陳宜禧與新寧鐵路· [Patriotic overseas merchant, Chen Yixi, and the Xinning Railroad]. In *Taishan wenshi* 台山文史, no. 9 (1987): 46–58.

Chen Hansheng 陳翰笙, ed. *Chuguo huagong shiliao huibian* 出國華工史料匯編 [Collected historical materials on the emigration of Chinese labor]. Beijing: Zhonghua shuju, 1984.

Chen, Helen. "Chinese Immigration into the United States: An Analysis of Changes in Immigration Policies." Ph.D. dissertation, Brandeis University, 1980.

Chen Lanbin 陳蘭彬, "ShiMei jilue" 使美記略 [A brief account of my mission to America]. In *Xiaofang huzhai yudi congchao* 小方壺齋輿地叢鈔 [Collected essays on Chinese and Western geography and politics], edited by Wang Xiqi 王錫祺. N.p., 1877. Folio 12.

Chen Qian 陳前. "Taishan xianqiao" 台山先僑 [Taishan's first overseas Chinese]. In *Taishan fengcai* 台山風采 [The elegance of Taishan]. Taishan: Taishan renmin yinshuachang, 1985.

Chen T'a. *Emigrant Communities in South China: A Study of Overseas Migration and Its Influence on Standards of Living and Social Change.* Shanghai: Kelly and Walsh, 1939.

Chen, Wen-hsien. "Chinese Under Both Exclusion and Immigration Laws." Ph.D. dissertation, University of Chicago, 1940.

Chen Yintao 陳印陶 and Zhang Rong 張蓉. "Guangdong sheng Taishan, Xunde nuxing renkou guoji qianyi ji qi yinxiang de bijiao yanjiu" 廣東省台山, 順德女性人口國際遷移及其影響的比較研究 [Comparative research into the international migration of women from the two counties of Taishan and Shunde, Guangdong Province, and their effects]. In *Guangdong renkou wenti yanjiu* 廣東人口問題研究 [Research on population questions in Guangdong] (Jan. 1989): 90–121.

Chen Yixi. Personal letters. Guangzhou: Guangzhou Municipal Museum, unpublished materials, 1924–26.

Chen Yong. "The Internal Origins of Chinese Emigration to California Reconsidered." In *Western Historical Quarterly* 28 (Winter 1997): 521–46.

Cheng, Lucie. "Collaborating with Chinese Scholars in Social Science Research: Problems and Prospects." In *Methodological Issues in Chinese Studies*, edited by Amy Auerbach Wilson, Sidney Leonard Greenblatt, and Richard W. Wilson. New York: Praeger, 1983.

———. "Free, Indentured, Enslaved: Chinese Prostitutes in 19th-Century America." In *Labor Immigration Under Capitalism: Asian Workers in the United States Before World War II*. Edited by Lucie Cheng and Edna Bonacich. Berkeley: University of California Press, 1984.

———, and Edna Bonacich, eds. *Labor Immigration Under Capitalism: Asian Workers in the United States Before World War II*. Berkeley, California: University of California Press, 1984.

———, and Liu Yuzun, with Zheng Dehua. "Chinese Emigration, the Sunning Railway and the Development of Toisan." In *Amerasia* 9, no. 1 (1982): 59–74.

Cheng Tzu-ts'an 鄭紫燦. *Xianggang Zhonghua shangye jiaotong renmin zhinanlu* 香港中華商業交通人民指南錄 [The Anglo-Chinese commercial directory of Hong Kong]. Hong Kong: n.p., 1915.

Chin, Art. *Golden Tassels: A History of the Chinese in Washington, 1857–1977*. Seattle, Wash.: n.p., 1977.

The Chinese Commercial Directory. Hong Kong: The Chinese Commercial Directory Company, 1930.

Chinese Exclusion Case Files. Record Group 85. Immigration and Naturalization Service Records. National Archives, Pacific-Sierra Regional Branch.

Chinese Ministry of Information. *China Handbook, 1937–45*. New York: Macmillan, 1947.

Chinn, Thomas W. *Bridging the Pacific: San Francisco's Chinatown and Its People*. San Francisco: Chinese Historical Society of America, 1989.

———, with Him Mark Lai and Philip P. Choy, eds. *A History of the Chinese in California: A Syllabus*. San Francisco: Chinese Historical Society of America, 1969.

Chirot, Daniel, and Anthony Reid, eds. *Essential Outsiders: Chinese and Jews in the Modern Transformation of Southeast Asia and Central Europe.* Seattle: University of Washington Press, 1997.

Chixi xianzhi. 赤溪縣志 (Chixi County gazetteer). 1920.

Chiu, Franklin Y. T. "Lineage and Rural Industry in South China: The Case of Taishan." Master's thesis, University of Hong Kong, 1995.

Chiu, Ping. *Chinese Labor in California, 1850–1880: An Economic Study.* Madison: State Historical Society of Wisconsin, 1963.

Choy, Philip, Lorraine Dong, and Marlon Hom, eds. *The Coming Man.* Seattle: University of Washington Press, 1996.

Cinel, Dino. *The National Integration of Italian Return Migration, 1870–1929.* Cambridge: Cambridge University Press, 1991.

Cohen, Myron. "Being Chinese." In *Daedalus* 120, no. 2 (Spring 1991): 113–34.

————. "Developmental Process in the Chinese Domestic Group." In *The Family: Its Function and Destiny,* edited by Ruth Nanda Anshen. New York: Harper, 1959.

————. "The Hakka or 'Guest People': Dialect as a Sociocultural Variable in Southeast China." In *Guest People: Hakka Identity in China and Abroad,* edited by Nicole Constable. Seattle: University of Washington Press, 1996.

————. *House Divided, House United.* New York: Columbia University Press, 1976.

Cohen, Robin. *Global Diasporas: An Introduction.* Seattle: University of Washington Press, 1997.

Constable, Nicole, ed. *Guest People: Hakka Identity in China and Abroad.* Seattle: University of Washington Press, 1996.

Coolidge, Mary Roberts. *Chinese Immigration.* New York: Henry Holt, 1909.

Crissman, Lawrence W. "The Segmentary Structure of Urban Overseas Chinese Communities." In *Man* 2, no. 2 (1967): 185–204.

Cronon, William. *Nature's Metropolis: Chicago and the Great West.* New York: W. W. Norton, 1991.

Cushman, Jennifer Wayne. *Fields from the Sea.* Ithaca, N.Y.: Southeast Asia Program, Cornell University, 1993.

Davis, Winfield J. *History of Political Conventions in California, 1849–1892.* Sacramento: California State Library, 1893.

Denby, Charles. *China and Her People.* Boston: L. C. Page, 1906.

Duanfen Monthly 端芬雜志. 1920, 1923, 1936, 1949.

Elvin, Mark, and G. William Skinner, eds. *The City in Late Imperial China.* Stanford, Calif.: Stanford University Press, 1977.

Endacott, G. B. *A History of Hong Kong.* Rev. ed. Hong Kong: Oxford University Press, 1973.

Far East Chinese-English Dictionary. Taipei: Yuandong tushu gongsi, 1992.

Fei Xiaotong. *Peasant Life in China: A Field Study of Country Life in the Yangtze Valley.* London: Routledge and Kegan Paul, 1939.

———. *Xiangtu Zhongguo* 鄉 土 中 國 [Rural China]. Shanghai: Shanghai guanchashe, 1947.

Feldwick, W., ed. *Present Day Impressions of the Far East and Prominent and Progressive Chinese at Home and Abroad: The History, People, Commerce, Industries, and Resources of China, Hong Kong, Indo China, Malaya, and Netherlands India.* London: Globe Encyclopedia, 1917.

Fitzgerald, Stephen. *China and the Overseas Chinese: A Study of Peking's Changing Policy, 1949–1970.* Cambridge: Cambridge University Press, 1972.

Fok, K. C. "Wanqing qijian Xianggang dui neidi jingji fazhan zhi yingxiang" 晚 清 期 間 香 港 對 內 地 經 濟 發 展 之 影 響 [Hong Kong's impact on the interior's economic development during the late Ch'ing period]. In *Xueshu yanjiu* 學 術 研 究 [Scholarly research], no. 2 (1988): 70–74.

———. *Lectures on Hong Kong History.* Hong Kong: Commercial Press, 1990.

Fong, Timothy. *The First Suburban Chinatown: The Remaking of Monterey Park, California.* Philadelphia: Temple University Press, 1994.

Four Counties Magazine 四 邑 雜 志 (1916).

Freedman, Maurice. "The Chinese in Southeast Asia." In *The Study of Chinese Society: Essays by Maurice Freedman.* Stanford, Calif.: Stanford University Press, 1979.

———. "Chinese Kinship and Marriage in Singapore." In *The Study of Chinese Society: Essays by Maurice Freedman.* Stanford, Calif.: Stanford University Press, 1979.

———. "Emigration from the New Territories." In *The Study of Chinese Society: Essays by Maurice Freedman.* Stanford, Calif.: Stanford University Press, 1979.

———. *Lineage Organization in Southeastern China.* New York: Athlone, 1965.

———. *The Study of Chinese Society: Essays by Maurice Freedman.* Stanford, Calif.: Stanford University Press, 1979.

———, ed. *Family and Kinship in Chinese Society.* Stanford, Calif: Stanford University Press, 1970.

Fritz, Christian G. "Due Process, Treaty Rights, and Chinese Exclusion, 1882–1891." In *Entry Denied: Exclusion and the Chinese Community in America, 1882–1943*, edited by Sucheng Chan. Philadelphia: Temple University Press, 1991.

Fushan Monthly 浮 山 月 刊. 1935–37, 1940, 1946–49.

Ge Gongzhen 戈 公 振. *Zhongguo baoxue shi* 中 國 報 學 史 [History of newspaper publishing in China]. Shanghai: Shangwu yinshu guan, 1928.

Gellner, Ernest. "The Coming of Nationalism and Its Interpretation: The Myths of Nation and Class." In *Mapping the Nation*, edited by Gopal Balakrishnan. London: Verso, 1996.

Gibson, Otis. *The Chinese in America.* Cincinnati, Ohio: Hitchcock and Walden, 1877.

Gilroy, Paul. *The Black Atlantic.* Cambridge, Mass.: Harvard University Press, 1993.

Glenn, Evelyn Nakano. "Split Household, Small Producer and Dual Wage Earner: An Analysis of Chinese-American Family Strategies." In *Journal of Marriage and the Family* (February 1983): 35–46.

Godley, Michael R. *The Mandarin-Capitalists from Nanyang: Overseas Chinese Enterprise in the Modernization of China, 1893–1911.* Cambridge: Cambridge University Press, 1981.

Goodman, Bryna. *Native Place, City, and Nation: Regional Networks and Identities in Shanghai, 1853–1937.* Berkeley: University of California Press, 1995.

Guanghai Monthly 廣海月刊. 1927.

Gupta, Akhil, and James Ferguson. "Beyond 'Culture': Space, Identity, and the Politics of Difference." In *Cultural Anthropology* 7, no. 1 (February 1992): 6–23.

Gyory, Andrew. *Closing the Gate: Race, Politics, and the Chinese Exclusion Act.* Chapel Hill: University of North Carolina Press, 1998.

Haiyan Magazine 海宴雜志. 1936.

Hammond, Jonathan. "Xiqi Village, Guangdong: Compact with Ecological Planning." In *The Village as Place,* edited by Ronald Knapp. Honolulu: University of Hawaii Press, 1992.

Handlin, Oscar. *Boston's Immigrants: A Study in Acculturation.* Cambridge, Mass.: Harvard University Press, 1941.

———. *The Uprooted.* 2d ed. Boston: Little, Brown, 1973.

Hayner, Norman S., and Charles N. Reynolds. "Chinese Family Life in America." In *American Sociological Review* 2, no. 5 (October 1937): 630–37.

Heidhues, Mary Somers. *Southeast Asia's Chinese Minorities.* Melbourne: Longman Australia, 1974.

Helmreich, Stefan. "Kinship, Nation, and Paul Gilroy's Concept of Diaspora." In *Diaspora* 2, no. 2 (1992): 243–49.

Hiroaki, Kani. *Kindai Chugoku no kuri to choka* [Coolies and slave girls of modern China]. Tokyo: Iwanami Shoten, 1979.

"History of Chinese Detained on Angel Island." Berkeley, Calif.: Chinese Culture Foundation of San Francisco and University of California at Berkeley, Asian American Studies Library, 1976.

Ho P'ing-ti. *Studies on the Population of China, 1368–1953.* Cambridge, Mass.: Harvard University Press, 1959.

Hom, Marlon. *Songs of Gold Mountain: Cantonese Rhymes from San Francisco Chinatown.* Berkeley: University of California Press, 1987.

Honig, Emily. *Sisters and Strangers: Women in the Shanghai Cotton Mills, 1919–1949*. Stanford, Calif.: Stanford University Press, 1986.

Hoy, William. *The Chinese Six Companies*. San Francisco: Consolidated Chinese Benevolent Association, 1942.

Hsieh, Winston. "The Ideas and Ideals of a Warlord: Ch'en Chiung-ming (1878–1933)." In *Papers on China*, no. 16 (1962): 198–251.

Hsu, Madeline. "Living Abroad and Faring Well: Migration and Transnationalism in Taishan County, Guangdong 1904–1939." Ph.D. dissertation, Yale University, 1996.

_____. "What Is Special About Taishan?: Migration and Dependency." Paper presented at the Duke-Harvard Workshop on International Migration, Durham, North Carolina, May 28, 1999.

———. "Trading with Gold Mountain: *Jinshanzhuang* and Networks of Kinship and Native Place, 1848–1949." Presented at the annual meeting of the Association for Asian Studies, Boston, March 13, 1999.

Huaqiao lunwenji 華僑論文集 [Collected essays on Overseas Chinese]. Guangzhou: Guangdong huaqiao lishi xuehui, 1982.

Huaqiao shi lunwen ziliao suoyin 華僑史論文資料索引 [Index of articles and materials on Overseas Chinese]. Guangzhou: Dongnanya lishi yanjiusuo and Zhongshan daxue tushuguan, 1982.

Huaqiao yanjiu 華僑研究 [Research on overseas Chinese]. Guangzhou: Guangdong gaodeng jiaoyu chubanshe, 1988.

Huang Chaohuai 黃朝槐. *Ningyang zacun* 寧陽雜存 [Miscellaneous essays from Ningyang]. Taishan: n.p., 1900.

Huang Clan Monthly 黃氏月刊. 1926–27.

Huang Jianyun 黃劍云, ed. *Taishan gujin gailan shang xia ce* 台山古今概覽上下冊 [An overview of the past and present in Taishan, vols. 1 and 2]. Guangzhou: Guangzhou renmin chubanshe, 1992.

Huang Meixian. Interview, January 19, 1995.

Huang Zhongji 黃仲楫. "Taishan qiaokan shihua" 台山僑刊史話 [History of overseas Chinese magazines in Taishan]. *Xinning Magazine*, no. 2 (1983): 45.

Huang Zhongyan 黃重言. "Qiaoxiang shehui de lishi he qiaoxiang diaocha" 僑鄉社會的歷史和僑鄉調查 [History and survey of emigrant societies]. In *Qiaoshi xuebao* 僑史學報 [Overseas Chinese studies newspaper], no. 1/2 (1989): 23–29.

Huenemann, Ralph. *The Dragon and the Iron Horse: The Economics of Railroads in China, 1876–1937*. Cambridge, Mass.: Harvard University Press, 1984.

Hung Ssu-ssu, ed. *Xinhai geming yu huaqiao* 辛亥革命與華僑 [Overseas Chinese and the 1911 Revolution]. Beijing: Renmin chubanshe, 1982.

"Interviews with Detainees at Angel Island Project." San Francisco: History of Chinese Detained on Island Project, 1976.

Irick, Robert. *Ch'ing Policy Toward the Coolie Trade, 1847–78.* Taipei: Chinese Materials Center, 1982.

Jiang Yongkang 江永康. Interview, May 13, 1994.

Jin Huaibi. *Taishan de gushi* 台山的故事 [The Story of Taishan]. Hong Kong: Zhonghua shuju, 1974.

Johnson, Graham. "Family Strategies and Economic Transformation in Rural China: Some Evidence from the Pearl River Delta." In *Chinese Families in the Post-Mao Era*, edited by Deborah Davis and Stevan Harrell. Berkeley, Calif.: University of California Press, 1993.

Kanghe Monthly 康合月刊. 1930.

Kulp, David Harrison II. *Country Life in South China: The Sociology of Familism.* Vol. 1: *Phenix Village, Kwantung.* New York: Teachers College, Columbia University, 1925.

Kung, S. W. *Chinese in American Life.* Seattle: University of Washington Press, 1962.

Kwong, Peter. *The New Chinatown.* New York: Noonday Press, 1987.

Lai, Him Mark 麥禮謙. *Cong huaqiao dao huaren—ershi shiji Meiguo huaren shehui fazhan shi* 從華僑到華人──二十世紀美國華人社會發展史. [From overseas Chinese to Chinese American—History of the development of Chinese American society in the twentieth century]. Hong Kong: Sanlian shudian, 1992.

———. "Historical Development of the Chinese Consolidated Benevolent Association / *Huiguan* System." In *Chinese America: History and Perspectives* (1987): 13–52.

———. *A History Reclaimed: An Annotated Bibliography of Chinese Language Materials on the Chinese of America.* Los Angeles: Asian American Studies Center at the University of California, Los Angeles, 1986.

———. "Kuomintang in Chinese American Communities." In *Entry Denied*, edited by Sucheng Chan. Philadelphia: Temple University Press, 1991.

———, Genny Lim, and Judy Yung, eds. *Island: Poetry and History of Chinese Immigrants on Angel Island, 1910–1940.* San Francisco: History of Chinese Detained on Island Project, 1986.

Lau, Wing Fong 劉榮方. "Educational Development in Taishan County, Guangdong Since the Late Qing Period" 近百年來廣東省台山縣教育之發展. Master's thesis, School of Education, Chinese University at Hong Kong, 1986.

Lee, En-han. *China's Quest for Railway Autonomy, 1904–1911: A Study of the Chinese Railway-Rights Recovery Movement.* Singapore: Singapore University Press, 1977.

Lee, Erika. "At America's Gates: Chinese Immigration During the Exclusion Era, 1882–1943." Ph.D. dissertation, U.C. Berkeley, 1998.

Lee, James. "Migration and Expansion in Chinese History." In *Human Migrations: Patterns and Policies*, edited by William McNeill. Bloomington: Indiana University Press, 1979.

Lee, Leo, and Andrew Nathan. "The Beginnings of Mass Culture: Journalism and Fiction in the Late Ch'ing and Beyond." In *Popular Culture in Late Imperial China*, edited by David Johnson, Evelyn Rawski, and Andrew Nathan. Berkeley: University of California Press, 1985.

Lee, Robert. "The Origins of Chinese Immigration to the U.S., 1848–1882." In *The Life, Influence, and the Role of the Chinese in the United States, 1776–1960*. San Francisco: Chinese Historical Society of America, 1976.

Lee, Rose Hum. *The Chinese in the United States of America*. Hong Kong: Hong Kong University Press, 1960.

Leong Gor Yun. *Chinatown Inside Out*. New York: Barrows Mussey, 1936.

Leong, Sow-theng. *Migration and Ethnicity in Chinese History: Hakkas, Pengmin, and Their Neighbors*. Edited by Tim Wright. Stanford, Calif.: Stanford University Press, 1997.

Li Gui 李圭. *Huanyou diqiu xinlu* 還遊地球新錄 [New accounts of travels around the globe]. N.p., 1877.

Li Yiji 李奕楫. *Haiyan xiangtu shi* 海宴鄉土史‧ [Local history of Haiyan]. Hong Kong: Yongde yinwu, 1960.

Liang Yan 梁燕. "Guangdong sheng Taishan qiaoxiang guoji yimin jiating shouru tedian fenxi" 廣東省台山僑鄉國際移民家庭收入特點分析 [Analysis of the special characteristics of international migration and family income from Taishan County, Guangdong Province]. In *Renkou yanjiu luncong* 人口研究論叢 [Collected essays on population research] (1988): 165–75.

Liao Liqiong 廖莉瓊. "Gaige kaifang yilai Guangdong Taishan, Denghai qiaoxiang renkou guoji qianyi gaikuang" 改革開放一來廣東台山, 澄海僑鄉人口國際遷移概況 [Overview of the international migration of population from emigrant communities in Taishan and Denghai in Guangdong since 1978]. In *Renkou yanjiu luncong* 人口研究論叢 [Collected essays on population research] (1988): 123–137.

Lin Clan Magazine 林族雜志 N.d.

Lin Jiajin et al. 林家勁等. "Jindai Guangdong qiaohui yanjiu" 近代廣東僑匯研究 [Research on remittances in modern Guangdong]. In *Dongnanya xuekan* 東南亞學刊 [Scholarly journal of Southeast Asia], no. 4 (1992): 46–59.

Lin Jinzhi 林金枝. "Haiwai huaren zai Zhongguo dalu touzi de xianzhuang yu qianjing" 海外華人在中國大陸投資的現狀與前景 [The present state and future prospects of overseas Chinese investment in the Chinese mainland]. In *Huaqiao lishi luncong* 華僑歷史論叢 [Collected essays on overseas Chinese history] 5 (May 1989): 341–54.

———. *Huaqiao huaren yu Zhongguo geming he jianshe* 華僑華人與中國革命和建設 [Overseas Chinese, Chinese and Chinese revolution and construction]. Fuzhou: Fujian renmin chubanshe, 1993.

———. "Jiefangqian huaqiao zai Guangdong touzi de zhuangkuang ji qi zuoyong" 解放前華僑在廣東投資的狀況及其作用 [The circumstances and uses of overseas Chinese investment in Guangdong before Liberation]. In *Xueshu yanjiu* 學術研究 [Scholarly research], no. 5 (1981): 45–51.

———. *Jindai huaqiao touzi guonei qiye gailun* 近代華僑投資國內企業概論 [Overview of modern overseas Chinese business investments in China]. Xiamen: Xiamen daxue chubanshe, 1988.

———. *Jindai huaqiao touzi guonei qiyeshi yanjiu* 近代華僑投資國內企業史研究 [Research on the modern history of overseas Chinese investment in Chinese enterprise]. Fujian: Fujian renmin dazong chubanshe, 1983.

———. *Jindai huaqiao touzi guonei qiye shi ziliao xuanji: Fujian zhuan* 近代華僑投資國內企業史資料選集: 福建傳 [Selected materials on modern overseas Chinese business investments in China: Fujian section]. Fuzhou: Fujian renmin chubanshe, 1985.

———. *Jindai huaqiao touzi guonei qiye shi ziliao xuanji: Guangdong zhuan* 近代華僑投資國內企業史資料選集: 廣東傳 [Selected materials on modern overseas Chinese business investments in China]. Fuzhou: Fujian Renmin chubanshe, 1989.

Lin Yizhong 林翼中, *Guangdong jiuji shiye huiguo huaqiao jishi muci* 廣東救濟失業回國華僑紀實目次 [Table of contents of the record of efforts to save unemployed overseas Chinese in Guangdong]. Guangdong: Guangdong mingzheng ting, 1934.

Ling, Pyau. "Causes of Chinese Emigration." In *American Academy of Political and Social Science* 39 (1912): 74–82.

Liu Boji 劉伯驥. *Meiguo huaqiao shi* 美國華僑史· [A history of the Chinese in the United States of America, 1848–1911]. Taipei: Commission of Overseas Chinese Affairs, 1976.

Liu Chiang. "Chinese Versus American Ideas Concerning the Family." In *Journal of Applied Sociology* 10 (1925–26): 243–49.

Liu, Haiming. "The Trans-Pacific Family: A Case Study of Sam Chang's Family History." In *Amerasia* 18, no. 2 (1992): 1–34.

Liu, Fu-ju. "A Comparative Demographic Study of Native-Born and Foreign-

Born Chinese Populations in the United States." Ph.D. dissertation, University of Michigan, 1953.

Liu Yuzun 劉玉遵 and Cheng Luoxi 成露西 "Xinhai geming yundong zhong de Taishan xian yu huaqiao" 辛亥革命運動中的台山縣與華僑 [Taishan county and overseas Chinese during the 1911 revolution]. In *Xinhai geming yu huaqiao* 辛亥革命與華僑 [Overseas Chinese and the 1911 Revolution], edited by Hung Ssu-ssu. Beijing: Renmin chubanshe, 1982.

Liu Zuoren 劉佐人. "Jinshanzhuang de yanjiuo" 金山莊的研究 [Research on *jinshanzhuang*]. In *The China Economist*, no. 101 (February 10, 1959): 20–23.

The Living Tree: The Changing Meaning of Being Chinese Today. Daedalus 120, no. 2 (Spring 1991).

Lo, C. P. *Hong Kong*. London: Bedhaven, 1992.

Lo, Karl, and Him Mark Lai. *Chinese Newspapers Published in North America, 1854–1975*. Washington, D.C.: Center for Chinese Research Materials, 1976.

———. "The Chinese Vernacular Presses in North America 1900–1950: Their Role in Social Cohesion." In *Annals of the Chinese Historical Society of the Pacific Northwest* (1984): 170–78.

Longgang Magazine 龍岡雜志 1937–38.

Lyman, Stanford M. *Chinese Americans*. New York: Random House, 1974.

———. "Marriage and the Family Among Chinese Immigrants to America, 1850–1960." In *The Asian in North America*. Santa Barbara, Calif: ABC-Clio, 1977.

Maalki, Liisa. "National Geographic: The Rooting of Peoples and the Territorialization of National Identity Among Scholars and Refugees." In *Cultural Anthropology* 7, no. 1 (Feb. 1991): 24–44.

Mai Yizhao. Interview, Taishan City, Taishan, March 6, 1993.

Malone, Michael P. *James J. Hill: Empire Builder of the Northwest*. Norman: University of Oklahoma Press, 1996.

Mann, Susan. "The Ningpo *Pang* and Financial Power at Shanghai." In *The Chinese City Between Two Worlds,* edited by Mark Elvin and G. William Skinner. Stanford, Calif.: Stanford University Press, 1974.

Mazlish, Bruce. "An Introduction." In *Conceptualizing Global History*, edited by Mazlish and Ralph Buultjens. Boulder, Colo.: Westview, 1993.

Mazumdar, Sucheta. "Asian American Studies and Asian Studies: Rethinking Roots." In *Asian Americans: Comparative and Global Perspectives*, edited by Shirley Hune, et al. Pullman: Washington State University Press, 1991.

———. *Sugar and Society in China: Peasants, Technology, and the World Market*. Cambridge, Mass.: Harvard University Asia Center, 1998.

McClain, Charles. *In Search of Equality: The Chinese Struggle Against Discrimination in Nineteenth-Century America*. Berkeley: University of California Press, 1994.

————, and Laurene Wu McClain. "The Chinese Contribution to the Development of American Law." In *Entry Denied: Exclusion and the Chinese Community in America, 1882–1943*, edited by Sucheng Chan. Philadelphia: Temple University Press, 1991.

McCunn, Ruthanne Lum. *Chinese American Portraits*. Vancouver, B.C.: Raincoast Books, 1988.

Mei, June. "Economic Origins of Emigration: Guangdong to California, 1850–1882." In *Modern China* 5, no. 4 (October 1979): 463–501.

Mei Shiming 梅仕明. Interview, Yougan Village, Duanfen District, May 11, 1994.

Mei Yimin 梅逸民. "Taishan yinjin qiaozhi qiaoli gaishu" 台山引進僑智僑力概述 [Overview of the import of overseas Chinese knowledge and strength into Taishan]. In *Taishan wenshi* 台山文史 [Taishan literature and history], no. 10 (March 1988): 17–23.

Miller, Kerby. *Emigrants and Exiles: Ireland and the Irish Exodus to North America*. New York: Oxford University Press, 1985.

Miller, Stuart Creighton. *The Unwelcome Immigrant: The American Image of the Chinese, 1785–1882*. Berkeley: University of California Press, 1969.

Mo Xiuping 莫秀萍. "Aiguo huaqiao Chen Yixi zhuanlue" 愛國華僑陳宜禧傳略 [Biography of loyalist overseas Chinese, Chen Yixi]. In *Huaqiao lunwen ji* 華僑論文集 [Collection of essays on overseas Chinese] 3 (1986): 269–77.

Morawska, Ewa. *For Bread with Butter: The Life-Worlds of East Central Europeans in Johnstown, Pennsylvania, 1890–1940*. Cambridge: Cambridge University Press, 1985.

Murray, Dian. "Migration, Protection, and Racketeering: The Spread of the Tiandihui Within China." In *Secret Societies Reconsidered*, edited by David Ownby et al. New York: M. E. Sharpe, 1993.

————, with Qin Baoqi. *The Origins of the Tiandihui: Chinese Triads in Legend and History*. Stanford, Calif.: Stanford University Press, 1994.

"The Nam Pak Hong (Nanbei hang 南北行) Commercial Association of Hong Kong." In *Journal of the Hong Kong Branch of the Royal Asiatic Society* 19 (1979): 216–26.

Nanshe Monthly 南社月刊. 1920.

Naquin, Susan, and Evelyn S. Rawski. *Chinese Society in the Eighteenth Century*. New Haven, Conn.: Yale University Press, 1987.

Nee, Victor, and Brett de Bary Nee. *Longtime Californ': A Documentary Study of an American Chinatown*. Stanford, Calif.: Stanford University Press, 1986 [1973].

New Shuinan Monthly 新水南月刊. 1931.

Ng Chin-keong. *Trade and Society: The Amoy Network on the China Coast, 1683–1735*. Singapore: Singapore University Press, 1983.

Ng, Judy. Interview, March 1, 1995.

Ngai, Mae M. "Legacies of Exclusion: Illegal Chinese Immigration During the Cold War Years." *Journal of American Ethnic History* 18, no. 1 (Fall 1998): 3–35.

North China Herald. March 16, 1906.

Ong, Aihwa. *Flexible Citizenship: The Cultural Logics of Transnationality.* Durham, N.C.: Duke University Press, 1999.

———, and Donald Nonini, ed. *Ungrounded Empires: The Cultural Politics of Chinese Transnationalism.* New York: Routledge, 1997.

Osborne, Anne. "The Local Politics of Land Reclamation in the Lower Yangzi Highlands." In *Late Imperial China* 15, no. 1 (June 1994): 1–46.

Pan, Lynn. *Sons of the Yellow Emperor: A History of the Chinese Diaspora.* Boston: Little, Brown, 1990.

———, gen. ed. *The Encyclopedia of the Chinese Overseas.* Cambridge, Mass.: Harvard University Press, 1999.

Pan Zhiqiu 潘志裘. *Ningyang cundu* 寧陽存牘 [Ningyang deposited letters]. Taishan: n.p., 1898.

Park, Robert. "Human Migration and the Marginal Man." In *American Journal of Sociology* 33 (May 1928): 881–93.

Perry, Elizabeth. *Shanghai on Strike: The Politics of Chinese Labor.* Stanford, Calif.: Stanford University Press, 1993.

Purcell, Victor. *The Chinese in Southeast Asia.* London: Oxford University Press, 1951.

Reid, Anthony. "Flows and Seepages in the Long-Term Chinese Interaction with Southeast Asia." In *Sojourners and Settlers: Histories of Southeast Asia and the Chinese,* edited by Anthony Reid. St. Leonards, NSW: Allen and Unwin, 1996.

———. *Southeast Asia in the Age of Commerce, 1450–1680.* Vol. 1: *The Lands Below the Winds,* and Vol. 2: *Expansion and Crisis.* New Haven, Conn.: Yale University Press, 1988 and 1993.

———, ed. *Sojourners and Settlers: Histories of Southeast Asia and the Chinese.* St. Leonards, NSW: Allen and Unwin, 1996.

Remer, C. F. *Foreign Investments in China.* New York: Macmillan, 1933.

Rosaldo, Renato. "Ideology, Place, and People Without Culture." In *Cultural Anthropology* 3, no. 1 (February 1988): 77–87.

Rouse, Roger. "Mexican Migration and the Social Space of Postmodernism." In *Diaspora* 1, no.1 (Spring 1991): 8–23.

Rowe, William. *Hankow: Commerce and Society in a Chinese City, 1796–1889.* Stanford, Calif.: Stanford University Press, 1984.

Safran, William. "Diasporas in Modern Societies: Myths of Homeland and Return." In *Diaspora* 1, no. 1 (Spring 1991): 83–99.

Salyer, Lucy E. "'Laws Harsh as Tigers': Enforcement of the Chinese Exclusion Laws, 1891–1914." In *Entry Denied: Exclusion and the Chinese Community in America, 1882–1943*, edited by Sucheng Chan. Philadelphia: Temple University Press, 1991.

Sandmeyer, Elmer Clarence. *The Anti-Chinese Movement in California*. Urbana: University of Illinois Press, 1991 [1973].

Saxton, Alexander. *The Indispensable Enemy: Labor and the Anti-Chinese Movement in California*. Berkeley: University of California Press, 1971.

Schiller, Nina Glick, Linda Basch, and Cristina Blanc-Szanton, eds. *Towards a Transnational Perspective on Migration: Race, Class, Ethnicity, and Nationalism Reconsidered*. New York: New York Academy of Sciences, 1992.

Schwartz, Shephard. "Mate-Selection Among New York City's Chinese Males, 1931–38." In *American Journal of Sociology* 61 (July 1950–May 1951): 562–68.

Seagrave, Sterling. *Lords of the Rim: The Invisible Empire of the Overseas Chinese*. New York: G. P. Putnam's Sons, 1995.

See, Lisa. *On Gold Mountain*. New York: St. Martin's, 1995.

Shafu Monthly 沙甫月刊. 1927.

Shen Village Clan Magazine 莘村族刊. February 1, 1947.

Shengyi Monthly 聖頤月刊. 1935.

Sinn, Elizabeth. *Power and Charity: The Early History of the Tung Wah Hospital, Hong Kong*. Hong Kong: Oxford University Press, 1989.

Siu, Paul C. P. *The Chinese Laundryman: A Study of Social Isolation*. New York: New York University Press, 1987.

Six Villages Taihe Hospital Report 六村太和醫院. 1941–45.

Skinner, G. William. "The Chinese Minority." In *Indonesia*, edited by Ruth McVey. New Haven, Conn.: Hraf, 1963.

———. *Chinese Society in Thailand: An Analytical History*. Binghampton, N.Y.: Cornell University Press, 1957.

———. "Introduction: Urban Social Structure in Ch'ing China." In *The City in Late Imperial China*, edited by Mark Elvin and G. William Skinner. Stanford, Calif.: Stanford University Press, 1977.

———. *Leadership and Power in the Chinese Community of Thailand*. Ithaca, N.Y.: Cornell University Press, 1958.

———. "Mobility Strategies in Late Imperial China: A Regional Systems Analysis." In *Regional Analysis*, Vol. I: *Economic Systems*, edited by Carol A. Smith. New York: Academic Press, 1976.

Smith, Carl. *A Sense of History: Studies in the Social and Urban History of Hong Kong*. Hong Kong: Hong Kong Educational Publishing Co., 1995.

Snow, Phillip. *The Star Raft: China's Encounters with Africa.* Ithaca, N.Y.: Cornell University Press, 1988.

Southern California Chinese American Oral History Project. Los Angeles: UCLA Asian American Studies Center and the Chinese Historical Society of Southern California, 1982.

Strand, David. *Rickshaw Beijing.* Berkeley: University of California Press, 1989.

Su Yan 蘇 燕. "Guangdong Taishan xian guoji yimin jiating shouru fenxi" 廣 東 台 山 縣 國 際 移 民 家 庭 收 入 分 析 [Analysis of international migrants' household earnings in Taishan County, Guangdong]. In *Nanfang renkou* 南 方 人 口 [Southern population], no. 4 (1988): 130–42.

Sung, Betty Lee. *The Adjustment Experience of Chinese Immigrant Children in New York City.* New York: Center for Migration Studies, 1987.

————. *Mountain of Gold: The Story of the Chinese in America.* New York: Macmillan, 1967.

Suryadinata, Leo, ed. *Ethnic Chinese as Southeast Asians.* Singapore: Institute of Southeast Asian Studies, 1997.

Taeuber, Irene. "The Families of Chinese Farmers." In *Family and Kinship in Chinese Society,* edited by Maurice Freedman. Stanford, Calif.: Stanford University Press, 1970.

Taishan bainian shiji lue, 1498–1987 台 山 百 年 事 紀 略 [Outline of events in Taishan in centuries, 1498–1987]. Jiangmen, Guangdong: Guangdong Jiangmen shi difangzhi xuehui, 1988.

Taishan County Museum. Coaching books display. Taishan City, Taishan County: unpublished materials, n.d.

Taishan dilizhi 台 山 地 理 志 [Geographical gazetteer of Taishan]. Taishan: Zhonggong Taishan xian weiyichuanbu, Zhonggong Taishan xian weidangshi yanjiu bangongshi, and Taishan xian dang'anguan, 1984.

Taishan Education Bi-Monthly 台 山 教 育 半 月 刊. 1929.

Taishan fangyan 台 山 方 言 [Taishan dialect]. Guangzhou: Zhongshan daxue chubanshe, 1990.

Taishan fengcai 台 山 風 采 [The elegance of Taishan]. Taishan: Taishan renmin yinshuachang, 1985.

Taishan Overseas Chinese Magazine 台 山 華 僑 雜 志. 1932–34, 1938, 1940, 1946.

Taishan Teacher's College Seasonal 台 師 季 刊. 1933.

Taishan wenshi 台 山 文 史 [Literature and history of Taishan]. Taishan: Taishan xian zhengxie wenshi weiyuan hui, 1984–93.

Taishan xian huaqiao zhi 台 山 縣 華 僑 志 [Gazetteer of overseas Chinese from Taishan]. Taishan: *Taishan xian qiaowu ban'gongshi,* 1992.

Tan Xin 譚心. *Siyi fengguang* 四邑風光 [Scenery of the Four Counties]. Hong Kong: Wanye chubanshe, 1974.

Tangmei Seasonal 唐美季刊. 1935.

Thistlethwaite, Frank. "Migration from Europe Overseas in the Nineteenth and Twentieth Centuries." In *Population Movements in Modern European History*, edited by Herbert Moller. New York: Macmillan, 1964.

Thomas, William I., and Florian Znaniecki. *The Polish Peasant in Europe and America*. Edited and abridged by Eli Zaretsky. Urbana: University of Illinois Press, 1984.

Tololyan, Khachig. "The Nation-State and Its Others: In Lieu of a Preface." In *Diaspora* 1, no. 1 (1991): 3–7.

———. "Rethinking Diaspora(s): Stateless Power in the Transnational Moment." *Diaspora* 5, no. 1 (1996): 3–36.

Tom, Roger. Interview, March 7, 1995.

Tsai, Henry Shih-shan. *China and the Overseas Chinese in the U.S., 1868–1911*. Fayetteville: University of Arkansas Press, 1983.

Tsai, Jung-fang. *Hong Kong in Chinese History: Community and Social Unrest in the British Colony, 1842–1913*. New York: Columbia University Press, 1993.

U.S. Department of Commerce and Labor. Bureau of Immigration. *Annual Reports.* Washington, D.C.: U.S. Government Printing Office, 1904–5, 1907, 1909–12, 1926.

U.S. Department of Justice, Bureau of Immigration and Naturalization, *Annual Reports.* Washington, D.C.: U.S. Government Printing Office, 1947–48, 1950.

U.S. Department of Labor. Bureau of Immigration. *Annual Report 1928*. Washington, D.C.: U.S. Government Printing Office, 1928.

U.S. Treasury Department, Bureau of Immigration. *Annual Reports*. Washington, D.C.: U.S. Government Printing Office, 1902, 1903.

Wah Ying Cheong 華英昌. Account books. Hong Kong: Special Collections, University of Hong Kong, unpublished materials, 1899–1937.

Wakeman, Frederic. *Strangers at the Gate*. Berkeley: University of California Press, 1966.

Waltner, Ann. *Getting an Heir*. Honolulu: University of Hawaii Press, 1990.

Wang Gungwu. *China and the Overseas Chinese*. Singapore: Times Academic Press, 1991.

———. *The Chinese Minority in Southeast Asia*. Singapore: Chapman, 1978.

———. *Community and Nation: Essays on Southeast Asia and the Chinese*. Singapore: Heinemann, 1981.

———. "Migration and Its Enemies." In *Conceptualizing Global History*, edited by Bruce Mazlish and Ralph Buultjens. Boulder, Colo.: Westview, 1993.

———. "The Origins of Hua-Ch'iao." In *Community and Nation: China, Southeast Asia, and Australia.* St. Leonards, NSW: Allen and Unwin, 1992.

———. "Sojourning: The Chinese Experience in Southeast Asia." In *Sojourners and Settlers: Histories of Southeast Asia and the Chinese,* edited by Anthony Reid. St. Leonards, NSW: : Allen and Unwin, 1996..

———. "Upgrading the Migrant: Neither Huaqiao nor Huaren." In *Chinese America: History and Perspectives* (1996): 1–18.

———, and Jennifer Cushman, eds. *Changing Identities of the Southeast Asian Chinese Since World War II.* Hong Kong: Hong Kong University Press, 1988.

Wang Sing-wu. *The Organization of Chinese Emigration.* San Francisco: Chinese Materials Center, 1978.

Wang Xiqi 王錫祺, ed. *Xiaofang huzhai yudi congchao* 小方壺齋輿地叢鈔 [Collection of essays on Chinese and Western geography and politics]. N.p., 1877.

Wartime Shen Village 戰時莘村. 1937, 1939, 1940.

Watson, James. *Emigration and the Chinese Lineage: The Mans in Hong Kong and London.* Berkeley: University of California Press, 1975.

Wickberg, Edgar. "The Chinese in Philippine Economy and Society, 1850–1898." Ph.D. dissertation, Cornell University, 1961.

———. *The Chinese in Philippine Life, 1850–1898.* New Haven, Conn.: Yale University Press, 1965.

———. "The Chinese Mestizo in Philippine History." *Journal of Southeast Asian History* 5, no. 1 (March 1964): 62–100.

Wong, Johnny. Interviews, March 6 and 8, and May 3, 1994.

Wong, Kevin Scott. Personal communication, June 24, 1996.

———, and Sucheng Chan, eds. *Claiming America: Constructing Chinese American Identities During the Exclusion Era.* Philadelphia: Temple University Press, 1998.

Wong Louie Sue [pseud.]. Interview, September 30, 1993.

Wong, S. N., and S. K. Woo. *Siyi* 四邑 [Four counties]. Taipei: Haiwai wenku chubanshe, 1957.

Wong, Sandra M. J. "'For the Sake of Kinship': The Overseas Chinese Family." Ph.D. dissertation, Department of Anthropology, Stanford University, 1987.

Wong Siu-lun. *Emigrant Entrepreneurs: Shanghai Industrialists in Hong Kong.* Hong Kong: Oxford University Press, 1988.

Woon, Yuen-fong. *Social Organization in South China, 1911–1949.* Ann Arbor, Mich.: Center for Chinese Studies, 1984.

Wright, Arnold, and H. A. Cartwright. *Twentieth-Century Impressions of Hongkong, Shanghai, and Other Treaty Ports of China: Their History, People, Commerce, Industries, and Resources.* London: Lloyd's Greater Britain Publishing, 1908.

Wu, Chun-hsi. *Dollars, Dependents and Dogma: Overseas Chinese Remittances to Communist China.* Palo Alto, Calif.: Hoover Institution, 1966.

Wu Xingci and Li Zhen. "*Gum San Haak* in the 1980s: A Study on Chinese Emigrants Who Return to Taishan County for Marriage." In *Amerasia* 14, no. 2 (1988): 21–35.

Wu Yimin. Interview, February 17, 1995.

Wyman, Mark. *Round-Trip to America: The Immigrants Return to Europe, 1880–1930.* Ithaca, N.Y.: Cornell University Press, 1993.

Xicun Monthly 西村月刊. 1930.

Xiao Bolian 蕭伯濂. Interview, May 30, 1993.

Xiao Dexing letters. New York: Museum of the Chinese in the Americas, 1909–1937.

Xiao Fangye 蕭芳葉. Interview, May 12, 1993.

Xiao Jinliu 蕭金榴. Interview, July 15, 1993.

Xinning xiangtu dili 新寧鄉土地理 [Local geography of Xinning]. Taishan: n.p., 1900.

Xinning xianzhi 新寧縣志 [Xinning County gazetteer]. Taipei: n.p., 1965 [1893].

Xinning Magazine 新寧雜志. 1909–17, 1919, 1921–23, 1927–28, 1930–1937, 1939.

Yang Guobiao 楊國標, Liu Hanbiao 劉漢標, and Yang Anyao 楊安堯. *Meiguo huaqiao shi* 美國華僑史 [History of American overseas Chinese]. Guangzhou: Guangdong gaodeng jiaoyu chubanshe, 1989.

Yans-Mclaughlin, Virginia. *Family and Community: Italian Immigrants in Buffalo, 1880–1930.* Ithaca, N.Y.: Cornell University Press, 1971.

———, ed. *Immigration Reconsidered: History, Sociology, and Politics.* New York: Oxford University Press, 1990.

Yao Zengying 姚曾蔭. *Guangdong sheng de huaqiao huikuan* 廣東省的華僑匯款 [Overseas Chinese remittances of Guangdong Province]. Shanghai: Commercial Press for the Academia Sinica, 1943.

Yen Ching-hwang. *Coolies and Mandarins: China's Protection of Overseas Chinese During the Late Ch'ing Period, 1851–1911.* Singapore: Singapore University Press, 1985.

Yingchuan Monthly 潁川月刊. 1926.

Yu, Henry. "The 'Oriental Problem' in America, 1920–1960: Linking the Identities of Chinese American and Japanese American Intellectuals." In *Claiming America: Constructing Chinese American Identities During the Exclusion Era*, edited by K. Scott Wong and Sucheng Chan. Philadephia: Temple University Press, 1998.

Yu, Renqiu. "Chinese American Contributions to the Educational Development of Toisan 1910–1940." *Amerasia* 10, no. 1 (1983): 47–72.

———. *To Save China, to Save Ourselves.* Philadelphia: Temple University Press, 1992.

Yuesheng Monthly 粵聲月刊. 1947.

Yung, Judy. *Unbound Feet.* Berkeley: University of California Press, 1995.

Zheng Dehua 鄭德華. "*Qingchu Guangdong yanhai qiantu ji qi shehui yinxiang*" 清初廣東沿海遷徒及其社會影響 [Migration along the coast of Guangdong during the early Qing and its social effects]. In *Jiuzhou xuekan* 九州學刊 [Jiuzhou monthly] 2, no. 4 (1988): 47–71.

———. "Shijiu shiji mo Taishan qiaoxiang de xingcheng ji qi pouxi" 十九世紀末台山僑鄉的形成及其剖析 [Development and analysis of emigrant communities in Taishan at the end of the nineteenth century]. In *Guangzhou huaqiao yanjiu* 廣州華僑研究 [Guangzhou overseas Chinese research], no. 4 (1986: 63–71.

———, and Cheng Luoxi. *Taishan qiaoxiang yu Xinning tielu* 台山僑鄉與新寧鐵路. [Taishanese overseas Chinese and the Xinning Railroad]. Guangzhou: Sanlian shudian, 1989.

———, and Wu Xingzi 吳行賜. "Yipi you jiazhi de huaqiaoshi ziliao—Taishan jiefangqian chuban de zazhi, zukan pinglun" 一批有價值的華僑史資料——台山解放前出版的雜志, 族刊評論 [A group of valuable materials about overseas Chinese history—a discussion of magazines and clan magazines published in Taishan before Liberation]. In *Huaquiao lunwen ji* 華僑論文集 [Collection of essays about overseas Chinese] 1 (1982): 454–88.

Zhu Shijia 朱士嘉, ed. *Meiguo pohai huagong shiliao* 美國迫害華工史料 [Historical materials on the persecution of Chinese laborers]. Beijing: Zhonghua shuju, 1958.

Zinn, Howard. *A People's History of the United States.* New York: HarperPerennial, 1980.

Zo, Kil Young. "Emigrant Communities in China, Sze-Yap." In *Asian Profile* 5, no. 4 (August 1977): 313–23.

Zuoxin Seasonal 作新季刊. 1929.

Character List

The Chinese characters are alphabetized according to the pinyin romanizations of their *putonghua* pronunciations. Terms in brackets are those commonly used in Cantonese or dialect.

Anhe li 安和里

Anliang ju 安良局

Bai'anlong Yinhao 百安隆銀號

Baisha 白沙

Baochang yinhao 寶昌銀號

Beidou 北陡

benxian xinwen 本縣新聞

bo sheng [pok sen] 搏盛

bushou yanggu, bujie 不收洋股,
yangkuan, bugu 不借洋款,
yanggong, yi mian 不雇洋工,
chuanli waiyi 以免權利
外益

Cang'an li 倉安里

Cao Yazhi 曹亞志

Changsheng jinpu 昌盛金鋪

Chaozhou 潮州

Chen 陳

Chen Chengjiu 陳誠就

Chenhua cun 陳花村

Chen Huangyang 陳黃陽

Chen Jitang 陳濟棠

Chen Jiongming 陳炯明

Chen Kongzhao 陳孔照

Chen Mingrui 陳明瑞

Chen Qinqing 陳錦慶

Chen Yixi 陳宜禧
　[Chin Gee Hee]

Chen Yuanxi 陳元熙

Chen Xidao 陳禧道

Chen Xiangyuan 陳相元

Cheng Chang 成昌

Cheng Fulong 程福瀧

Chenghua 成化

253

Chengwu xiaoxue   成務小學

Chijin   遲金

Chixi   赤溪

Chonglou   沖蔞

Chonglou shizhan   沖蔞驛站

Chen Apei   陳阿培

chuyang zhi ren   出洋之人

Cen Chunxuan   岑春暄

Dajiang   大江

Dalongdong   大隆洞

Damei cun   大美村

daquan   打拳

Datang xiang   大塘鄉盤
   Panlong cun   龍村

Danjia shan   蛋家山

Dongguan   東筦

Dongkeng yuekan   東坑月刊

Dongyang lunchuan   東洋輪船
   gongsi   公司

Doushan   斗山

Duhu   都斛

Duhu jie   都斛街

duli wu wenyan   都里無聞言

Duanfen   端芬

Duanfen zhongxue   端芬中學

Enping [Yanping]   恩平

fazheng   法政

fan   反

fanlian   凡鈴

Fan Zhi   范志

Fucao   甫草

Fulin cun   福林村

Fushan yuebao   浮山月報

Fushi   浮石

Fu Yuan   富源

Gan cun he   甘村河

Gangzhou   岡州
   [Kong Chow]

geke fuji   各客附奇

geke xiewei bu   各客寫位部

ge xiongdi qinpeng   各兄弟親朋

gongdu   公牘

Gonglu qiche gongsi   公路汽車
   公司

gongsi fang   公司房

gongye   工業

Gongyi   公益

guxiang   故鄉

Gu Yaxing   顧亞興

Guan   關

Guan Yu   關羽

Guangde hang   廣德行
   [Quong Tuck]

Guangdongsheng   廣東省教育
   jiaoyu gaikuang   概況

Guangfeng tai   廣豐泰

Guangfu Chang   廣福昌
   [Quong Fat Cheung]

Guanghai   廣海

Guangsheng yingyuan   光聲影院

Guangzhao huiguan   廣肇會館

guiqiao   歸僑

Guomindang   國民黨
   [Kuomintang]

Guo Qizhao   廓其照

haiwai Ningren   海外寧人

haiwai yiqiao   海外邑僑

haiwai yiren 海外邑人
Haiyan 海宴
Heshan 鶴山
Heshenglong hao 和生隆號
Hongfa gongsi 鴻發公司
Hongling shan 紅嶺山
Hong Xiuquan 洪秀全
Huachang hao 華昌號
  [Wah Chong]
Huashang Gongyi 華商公益
  gongsi 公司
Hua'an li 華安里
huamei 華美
Hua'nanchang shi 花南昌市
huaqiao [wah-kiu] 華僑
Huaxin can'er hang 華信參耳行
Huaying Chang 華英昌
  [Wah Ying Cheong]
Huang 黃
Huang Chuanmou 黃傳某
Huang Jin 黃金
Huang Jingqiu 黃鏡秋
Huang Mouqiang 黃某強
Huang Mouzhuan 黃某傳
Huang Shi'an 黃式庵
Huang Shi'en 黃世恩
Huang Wenzong 黃文宗
Huang Zaihua 黃栽華
Huang Zichu 黃子初
hui [wui] 會
huidiaoju 匯兌局
huiguan 會館
Huiyang 慧陽
huoqi 活期

jiguan 籍貫

jimin zi 籍民仔
jia 家
Jiaqing 嘉慶
Jiaying zhou 嘉應州
Jiangmen 江門
jiaoyu 教育
Jiaoyu hui 教育會
Jinshan [Gumsaan] 金山
jinshanke 金山客
  [gumsaan hock]
jinshanpo 金山婆
jinshanshao 金山少
jinshanzhuang 金山莊
  [gumsaan jong]
jinshi 進士
Jinshu xingche gongsi 金屬行車
  公司
Jiuba hang 九八行
  [Kau Pat Hang]
jiujiyuan 救濟院
jiu zhi 舊紙
Juzheng zhongxue 居正中學

kaikuo jiaotong, 開括交通,
  chuangjian tielu 創建鐵路
Kaiping [Hoiping] 開平
Kang Youwei 康有為
Kuang Mingpu 鄺明溥
Kuang Zhuoqing 鄺桌卿

Laitian 來添
Lanjuan 蘭娟
Langmei cun liucun 朗美村六村
Laojia 老家
laoren 老人
Lei Wei 雷慰

Lei Yintang　　　　雷蔭棠
Lei Yuchuan　　　　雷雨泉
Li　　　　　　　　李
li　　　　　　　　厘
Li Chudu　　　　　李初都
Li Daochao　　　　李道朝
Li Jinzhao　　　　　李金釗
Lishenghe　　　　　利生和
　[Lee Sang Wo]
Li Sunzhi　　　　　李遜之
Li Yalian　　　　　李亞廉
Li Yanwen　　　　　李衍文
Liangxing　　　　　良星
Liao Yaquan　　　　廖亞全
lienu　　　　　　　列女
Lin Jinyan　　　　　林覲延
Lin Yizhong　　　　林翼中
Linghai yinhang　　嶺海銀行有
　youxian gongsi　　限公司
Liu　　　　　　　劉
Liu Bei　　　　　　劉備
Liu cun　　　　　　六村
Liu Jia　　　　　　劉甲
Liu Kong'an　　　　劉孔安
Liu Richu　　　　　劉日初
Liu Xiaoyun　　　　劉小雲
Liu Yamao　　　　　劉亞茂
Liu Zanchen　　　　劉贊臣
lao mien [lo min]　老面
Longwen　　　　　隆文
Longxi　　　　　　龍溪
Luhai tongludian　陸海通旅店
luju haiwai yiren　旅居海外
　　　　　　　　邑人
lunshuo　　　　　　論説
Luo Yuanying　　　羅沅英

Ma Guangzhan　　　馬光湛
Ma Huidong　　　　馬輝東
Ma Liqing　　　　　馬醴卿
Mamen cun　　　　馬門村
Ma Zhuo　　　　　馬濯
Mai Dun'gu　　　　麥敦固
manxin huanxi, yiwei　滿心歡喜,
　xuhou you ren　　以為繼后
　　　　　　　　有人
Maoli lunchuan gongsi　茂利輪船
　　　　　　　　公司
Mei　　　　　　　梅
Mei Guanyao　　　梅觀耀
Mei Ren　　　　　　梅仁
Mei Rongmou　　　梅榮某
Mei Shiming　　　　梅仕明
Meiwan xiang　　　美灣鄉
Mei Yaoxuan　　　梅耀萱
Mei Jianxing　　　　梅健行
minxin ju　　　　　民信局

Nafu　　　　　　　那扶
Namou cun　　　　那某村
nanbei hang [nam　南北行
　pak hong]
Nancun　　　　　　南村
Nanhai [Namhoi]　南海
nanqiao　　　　　　難僑
Nansheng cun　　　南盛村
Nanxiong zhou　　南雄州
neibu gehao laiwang　內埠各號來
　shu　　　　　　往書
Ning　　　　　　　寧
Ningbo baihua bao　寧波白話報
Ningyang huiguan　寧陽會館
　[Ning Yeung]

Niulu cun	牛路村	Shaonian Zhongguo	少年中國
Niuwan he	牛灣河	chenbao	晨報
		Shen cun	莘村
Panyu [Punyu]	潘禺	Shalan	沙欄
Pan Huichou	潘輝疇	Shenjing	深井
paolou	炮樓	Shengwang	勝旺
pixinju	批信局	shengyi zhi	生意紙
piju	批局	Shengyuan yinhao	生源銀號
		Shibao	時報
Qi Hu	啓湖	Shijie ribao	世界日報
Qianlong	乾隆	Shuibu	水步
qiaobao	僑胞	shuike	水客
qiaohui	僑匯	Shuixu	水墟
qiaojuan	僑眷	Shunde [Shuntak]	順德
qiaokan	僑刊	Sijiu	四九
qiaozhi	僑志	Siyi [Sze Yup]	四邑
qiaozi	僑資	Siyi huiguan [Sze Yup	四邑會館
qiaoxiang	僑鄉	Wuigwun]	
Qinji gongsi	欽記公司	Sun Zhongshan [Sun	孫中山
		Yatsen]	
Renhe [Yan Wo]	人和		
Rixin bao	日新報	tai	台
Ruan Dixian	阮帝顯	Taicheng [Toiseng]	台城
		Tainan lu	台南路
Sanba	三八	Taishan [Toisan]	台山
Sanbu	三埠	Taishan gonglu ju	台山公路局
Sandianhui	三點會	Taishan ribao	台山日報
Sanhe he	三合河	Taishan xianli tongsu	台山縣立通
Sanhehui	三合會	tushuguan	俗圖書館
Sanjia haikou	三夾海口	Tan'an Village	坦安村
Sanxi cun	三溪村	Tan Guangmou	譚光某
Sanyi [Sam Yup]	三邑	Tan jiang	潭江
sangzi	桑梓	Tan Weichen	譚偉臣
Shanju xincun	山咀新村	Tan Wenbing	譚文炳
Shangchuan	上川	Tan Wenyue	譚文約
Shangge cun	上閣村	Tan Xiaofang	覃孝方

Tan Yuzhi	譚毓芝	Xicun	西村
Tan Ziju	譚子駒	Xiguo xu	西廓墟
Tangkou cun	塘口村	Ximen cheng	西門城
Tao Lu	陶魯	Xi'ning shi	西寧市
Tao Zhengzhong	陶正中	xiyi guan	洗衣館
Tiantou	田頭	Xize xiang	西澤鄉
Tiendihui	天地會	Xiachuan	下川
Tienshou tang yaohang	天壽堂藥行	Xiakeng xiang	霞坑鄉
		Xialang	霞朗
Tong'an cun	同安村	xiancheng wei qi	咸稱為奇
Tonggu	銅鼓	Xianli shifan xuexiao	縣立師范學校
Tongsheng dianhua gongsi	同聲電話公司		
		xiaotiqing	小提琴
Tongwen gongsi	同文公司	Xie Baijin	謝百進
tusheng zaizhi	土生仔紙	Xiehe yaohang	協和藥行
tushi zaizhi	土世仔紙	Xin Zhongguo bao	新中國報
tusheng zi	土生仔	Xinchang shi	新昌市
tusheng sun	土生孫	xincun	新村
		Xinhui [Sunwui]	新會
wan	玩	xinju	信局
Wansheng Hao	萬盛號	Xinning [Sunning]	新寧
Wei Laoying	衛老英	Xinning gongbao	新寧公報
Wencun	汶村	Xinning gongli zhongxuetang	新寧公立中學堂
Wenjiang yuebao	文疆月報		
Wenxing ribao	文興日報	Xinning ren	新寧人
Wu	伍	Xu Chongzhi	許崇智
Wuhe qu	五和區	Xu Dacun	許大純
Wu Huci	伍乎秩	xunchengma	巡城馬
Wu Hui	伍輝		
Wu Limen	伍禮門	Yanghe [Young Wo]	陽和
Wu Mingxin	伍明忻	Yangjiang	陽江
Wu Renzhun	伍認準	yanglou	洋樓
Wu Shihui	伍時會	Yang Xiuching	楊秀清
Wu Yusheng	伍于勝	Ye Mingchen	葉銘琛
Wuzhou huidiao youxian gongsi	五洲匯兌有限公司	Yichang	怡昌
		Yishangguan	衣裳館

Yongdecheng hao 永德成號

Yongle jie [Wing Lok Street] 永樂街

Yongming dianli gongsi 永明電力公司

Yongtai hao 永泰號

Yougan cun 柚柑村

You Zuoheng 游祚恆

Yu [Yee] 余

Yu Kunji 余昆季

Yu Lianhe 余連和

Yu Shi 余石

Yu Youkui 余友夔

Yu Zhongshan 余仲珊

yuanji 原籍

Yuan Yiyan 袁奕彥

zazu 雜俎

Zeng 曾

Zhan Tianyou [Jeme T'ien-yow] 詹天佑

Zhang 張

Zhang Fei 張飛

Zhangguang Yuan [Cheung Kwong Yuen] 張廣源

Zhang Mingqi 張鳴岐

Zhang Shipeng 張石朋

Zhang Yaliang 張亞良

Zhang Yu'nan 張煜南

Zhao 趙

Zhao Gongchen 趙拱宸

Zhao Jianping 趙劍平

Zhao Xuanmin 趙宣民

Zhao Yu 趙煜

Zhao Yun 趙雲

Zhen 甄

Zhen Cheng 甄成

zhengpi huiGang 整批匯港

Zhenji taoqi dian 貞吉瓷器店

Zhongguo weixin bao 中國維新報

Zhongshan [Chungshan] 中山

Zhongwai yaowen 中外要聞

Zhongxi ribao [Chung Sai Yat Po] 中西日報

Zhongxing gongsi 中興公司

Zhudong xiang 朱洞鄉

Zhuhai 珠海

Ziyou xinbao 自由新報

zizhi 自治

Index

adoption, 121–23
advertising in *qiaokan,* 134, 138–41, 152
agriculture, and Taishan, 21–23
Ah Louis, 51–52
Anderson, Benedict, 219n6
Anliang Bureau. *See* Education Committee
announcements in *qiaokan,* 134–35, 138–41, 198n85
anti-Chinese sentiment. *See also* Exclusion
   era; U.S. immigration policy
   in California, 59, 62, 63–64
   Chen Yixi and, 159–60, 164–65
   legal exclusion and, 61–66
   violence and, 59
antimiscegenation laws (U.S.), 101–102
Arthur, Chester A., 64
Australia, 29, 193n49

bachelor communities, 3. *See also* families of
   sojourners; Taishanese Americans
   brides and, 3, 102–103, 120, 181, 184
   as fluid, 4–5
   sources of gender imbalance and, 92–99
   split households and, 99–100
banditry, 43, 50–52, 170, 172
Bank of Canton, 39

Bank of China, 39
Baochang Money Shop (Taishan firm), 36
Basch, Linda, 7–8
bendi ("natives"), 22. *See also* Hakka-*bendi*
   war
Bigler, John, 61–62
Blanc-Szanton, Cristina, 7–8
border crossing, 72, 75–78
brides, 3, 102–103, 120, 181, 184
Burke, Thomas, 159, 160f, 172
Burlingame Treaty, 24, 64
business partnerships, and immigration, 73–74

Cable Act of 1922 (U.S.), 96
California, anti-Chinese sentiment in, 59, 62, 63–64
California, as destination. *See* Gold
   Mountain dream
Canton Restaurant, Jackson Street, San
   Francisco, 58
Cao Yazhi, 23f
census statistics, 16–17, 30. *See also* number
   of Chinese immigrants in U.S.
certificates of residence, 72f
Chan, David R., 74
Chan, Sucheng, 94, 204n14